Multimedia e

WITHDRAWN

i

OTHER TITLES BY THE SAME AUTHOR

BP 418   Word 95 assistant

BP 421   Windows 95 assistant

BP 422   Essentials of computer security

BP 425   Microsoft Internet Explorer assistant

BP 427   Netscape Internet Navigator assistant

BP 434   PC hardware assistant

BP 437   Word 97 assistant

BP 439   Troubleshooting your PC

Multimedia explained

by

Ian Sinclair

BERNARD BABANI (publishing) LTD

THE GRAMPIANS

SHEPHERDS BUSH ROAD

LONDON W6 7NF

ENGLAND

© 1998 BERNARD BABANI (publishing) LTD

First Published –February 1998

British Library Cataloguing in Publication Data:

A catalogue record for this book is available from the British Library

ISBN 0 85934 447 9

Cover Design by Gregor Arthur
Cover Illustration by Adam Willis
Printed and Bound in Great Britain by Cox & Wyman Ltd., Reading

ABOUT THIS BOOK

Multimedia means the use of sound added to the normal visual output of a computer, along with the storage of data on a compact disc used in a computer drive. This is by now a normal configuration for computers intended for family uses, and can be specified even if this is not the primary purpose for the computer.

It is difficult to describe the enhancement that multimedia can make if you have experienced nothing like it. For example, an encyclopaedia entry dealing with the life of a composer would allow you to read text, see a drawing, and hear music, with all the data supplied from a CD. The faster CD players that are now in use will also permit good quality animation, something that was not easy for earlier designs.

In addition, all kinds of things become possible, such as placing a document on the screen and having a program read it in a reasonably human-sounding voice, or (using a microphone) placing your voice comments into a file that is mainly of text. This opens up ways in which business applications of the PC machine can become more attention-grabbing, particularly for presentation purposes, and also the use of mixed media to reduce fatigue and the errors caused by fatigue.

The true multimedia machine would be able to control video recorders (preferably video disc recorders), tape recorders (either audio or video) and CD units to allow full interaction of sound and moving pictures with the computer, allowing you, the user, to decide what you want to see and hear and in what form. When you buy what is currently described as a multimedia pack you have full control over sound, but the video portion uses still or animated images that are held on the same CD rather than by controlling a separate video system, though add-on cards for a conventional video recorder or camcorder are widely available. This book concentrates on the most popular choice at present, that of the single CD containing text, still images and sound. The use of MIDI is not dealt with in detail because it is explained thoroughly in other Babani books.

This book aims to introduce the whole topic to a PC user who is a newcomer to the ideas of multimedia, starting with the CD ROM itself, its use in storing programs and text, graphics use, and finally sound. Multimedia is already the main growth area of PC computing, and its importance will grow as the already large selection of CD discs becomes greater. Look in here to find what multimedia can do for your computer applications and what combination of hardware and software you will need. In addition, both the background of CD and sound is explained as well as the purely practical aspects of installing the equipment and using the software.

Adding a multimedia package to the PC machine is by no means as simple as adding a disc drive, and the software complications and limitations are not always well explained in the manuals and leaflets that accompany the equipment — in some cases the leaflets may describe software that is not the same as has been supplied, because of rapid changes in versions. It is not possible in the space of one book to cover all the combinations of sound cards and CD-ROM drives that exist, but because the similarities between models are strong, detailed descriptions of Sound Blaster 16 and the Panasonic CR562B have been given, along with notes on installing and using the software. Even if your own equipment differs in detail, these descriptions will be more useful than generalisations such as 'follow the manufacturers instructions', and the explanations will assist you when the instructions for your own equipment fail to guide you.

A few assumptions must be made. Your PC computer must be capable of running multimedia, and the minimum standard is now taken to be a 150 MHz Pentium machine with enough memory and disc space to run Microsoft Windows 95. You should know how to use the MS-DOS operating system, and how to use Windows, and to know that some programs can be run only using Windows (*'running under Windows'*). If your machine can make use of a high-resolution display (SVGA) for Windows you should take advantage of this if you want to use applications which show high-definition pictures.

Ian Sinclair

Autumn 1997

ABOUT THE AUTHOR

Ian Sinclair was born in 1932 in Tayport, Fife, and graduated from the University of St. Andrews in 1956. In that year, he joined the English Electric Valve Co. in Chelmsford, Essex, to work on the design of specialised cathode-ray tubes, and later on small transmitting valves and TV transmitting tubes.

In 1966, he became an assistant lecturer at Hornchurch Technical College, and in 1967 joined the staff of Braintree College of F.E. as a lecturer. His first book, "Understanding Electronic Components" was published in 1972, and he has been writing ever since, particularly for the novice in Electronics or Computing. The interest in computing arose after seeing a Tandy TRS80 in San Francisco in 1977, and of his 180 published books, about half have been on computing topics, starting with a guide to Microsoft Basic on the TRS80 in 1979.

He left teaching in 1984 to concentrate entirely on writing, and has also gained experience in computer typesetting, particularly for mathematical texts. He has recently visited Seattle to see Microsoft at work, and to remind them that he has been using Microsoft products longer than most Microsoft employees can remember.

ACKNOWLEDGEMENTS

I would like to thank the friendly and helpful staff of Text 100 Ltd. for providing the MS-DOS and Windows 95 software on which this book has been based, and Word 97 on which it was composed and typeset.

TRADEMARKS

Microsoft, MS-DOS, Windows, Windows 95 and NT are either registered trademarks or trademarks of Microsoft Corporation.

All other brand and product names used in this book are recognised as trademarks, or registered trademarks, of their respective companies.

Contents

1 **What is multimedia?**..1
  Beginnings 1
  What does it do?...3
  What do you need?...6
  Restrictions 8
2 **Programs and text** 11
  Software 11
  DMA use 12
  CD-ROM setup..14
  Program collections..15
  Copying text 19
  Other text sources 22
3 **Images and image files**...23
  Bitmaps and vector files..23
  Bitmap images 26
  Images from multimedia packages 28
4 **Editing graphics** 33
  Editing bitmaps..33
  Using Paint Shop Pro 42
  Vector editing...49
5 **Sound and numbers**...55
  What is sound?...55
  Amplitude and frequency..55
  Stereo sound 57
  Waves and numbers 58
  Conversion..60
6 **The sound card**...63
  Mixers 63
  Other mixing...68
  Playing other sound files...71
  Associating WAV files 73
  Soundo'LE..75
  Object embedding...76

Playing MIDI files...78
Text to Speech 80
Texto'LE 85
Microphone recording 87
7 Adding Hardware...93
The sound card..93
Installing a sound card..94
Unwanted noise...99
CD-ROM Drives and specifications............................100
Installing a CD-ROM drive 101
Installation work 102
Software 105
Appendix A..107
The Public Domain Software Library (PDSL) 107
Appendix B..109
Specialised Suppliers..109
Appendix C..111
Printing out a README file 111
Appendix D..113
Glossary of Terms...113
INDEX 137

1 What is multimedia?

Beginnings

The first PC computers in the early 1980s came with monitor screens so that computers could show text and some crude pictures on a TV type of screen, and a later innovation was a built-in loudspeaker so that sound also could be obtained. This laid the basis for the main features of a *multimedia* computer, the ability to work with text, pictures and sound, but that was, for some time, where it stopped, certainly as far as the PC type of machine was concerned. The PC was, after a brief period of hesitation in 1981, intended primarily for serious business uses, not for games, so that program software made little use of the extra facility of sound.

Other machines at that time, however, like the Atari and the Amiga, developed these abilities and for a while had sound and graphics capabilities well beyond those of the PC of the time. As a result, software writers wrote games for such machines, and wrote serious business software for the PC, and this has resulted in the predominance of the PC machines today — they are the machines for which most of the really useful software has been written. In addition, because the basic design of the machine has changed very little (as far as running programs is concerned), software for the PC has always had a long life — there is no need to change all of your software when a new PC machine is installed. By contrast, some other machines have changed considerably and these new machines have required new software.

In those days, the main restriction when a computer worked with images and sound was the storage space on a floppy disc. Characters of text are stored as numbers, using the well-established ASCII code. Pictures also can be coded as numbers that represent the colour and position of each

Multimedia explained

portion of the image, and the problem of coding sound into numbers (digital sound) and storing it had already been solved by the time that small computers were beginning to flex their muscles. The coding system that was devised by Philips and Sony was incorporated into the familiar audio CD, and from the moment that CDs and CD players started to appear, the speed of change to the new (digital) sound system was breathtaking. In addition, the CD system incorporated a large number of computing methods into the sound reproduction system.

In the 90s, the word *multimedia* started to appear. The original meaning was that the computer should act as the brains for a set of equipment that would include both video and sound recorders, so that the user had total control over what was seen and heard. Potentially, each multimedia user could be his/her own video producer, determining what images and sounds would appear in the course of a show. The applications for presentational work and for entertainment are exciting, but achieving it all fully is not quite so easy and needs more equipment and more skill than most people possess. This, however, is still the full definition of multimedia.

The more restricted definition, and the one that applies in this book, is the use of CDs to store text, images (still or moving) and stereo sound so that the computer can control the output to the screen and the loudspeakers. The whole thing is made possible because of the vast amount of data that can be stored on a CD. Used in this way, the CD is called CD-ROM, with ROM having its usual meaning of read-only memory, because you cannot record for yourself on this type of CD, though read-write CD is possible. The Sony Minidisc system may have some effect on this situation fairly soon.

Putting it into figures, the average CD will store some 650 Mbyte of information. By contrast, a 3.5" floppy will store

1.4 Mbyte, you might have some 16 Mbyte of RAM memory in the computer and perhaps a hard drive of some 2 Gbyte (of which, typically, only 1 Gbyte will be free by the time all your programs are in place). Though there are now file compression methods that allow you to record, on to your hard drive, video from a camcorder or from a video cassette unit, this development is one that only a minority can afford both in terms of the time needed to master the techniques and the money needed for the equipment.

A CD-ROM drive is therefore the centre of any multimedia work on the PC (and on the Apple Mac, the other machine for which CD-ROM is produced), and the use of CDs and other devices has now been standardised for the PC. A standard known as MPC ensures that a CD labelled with this name will be usable on any PC that has been equipped for multimedia using the equipment described in this book, allowing you full access to the large and rapidly-growing set of CDs that are available in MPC form.

What does it do?

The best way to get an inkling of what multimedia can do for you is to experience it for yourself. A description in words is always second-best, because it uses only one of your senses and it cannot simulate the experience — it's like the difference between reading a play and seeing it performed. Until you know what to expect, however, you may be reluctant to part with the cash, though prices are attractively low at the time of writing.

Imagine that you want some information on three topics — the life of the composer Saint-Saëns, the LNER Gresley Pacific steam locomotives, and Burmese cats. You could look up each of these topics in a conventional encyclopaedia, but you would have to find the right entries (not so easy for the steam loco), pick the (large) volumes, get to the pages and read the text. This would probably require a visit to a public library, and a few hours spent looking at books.

You would, if you picked a good encyclopaedia, get the facts and figures. You would know when Saint-Saëns was born and some of the titles of his music. You would find out the wheel formation for the Pacific type of locomotive, perhaps also the firebox area and boiler pressure for the Gresley designs. You would learn the colour varieties for Burmese cats, their life span and their illnesses. You would, unless you noted it down, forget most of this information fairly quickly. You arm would ache with the weight of the volumes and if you used them in a library you could not take them away to browse over them at home. You would also find that looking up any cross-references was immensely time-consuming and tiring.

Now contrast this with the use of a multimedia encyclopaedia. You put the CD into the player on your PC machine, and start the program running. Select *Saint-Saëns*, and you will see some text that you can read. Click the mouse and you will see the face of the man, and some scores from his music. Click again, and a fragment of the third movement of the Organ Symphony sounds out from the loudspeakers (in stereo, of course). Tapping the mouse key allows you to switch your attention between text, images and sound, building up a body of information that is more substantial, more rounded, and infinitely easier to remember.

Now change your selection to steam locomotives and click to get the information on the Gresley Pacifics. The facts and figures are there, but so also is an image. Perhaps you want to know what's going on inside these cylinders, or how the Walschaerts valve gear works — click again to see a slow-motion animation. Another click and you can hear the note of the locomotive hauling a long passenger train up a gradient, some time in 1949 You might also see a picture of one of the few that have been preserved, with details of when and where to see it in steam.

Burmese cats? Click for the topic, and see pictures of all the subtle colour varieties, along with text on the history of the breed and what to look for. Click again, and hear the characteristic sound or see the antics (switching on a light or opening a door) that these cats (who think they are dogs) get up to.

- One very valuable feature is that the use of a multimedia encyclopædia allows easy cross-referencing, something that is a very hard work when the encyclopædia is in book form. On the MPC version you simply look for the cross-references (also called *hyperlinks*, and usually in a different colour), click the mouse on them, and watch the new information appear. If you are equipped for the Internet you may even be able to update and supplement information by clicking on the appropriate button in the text.

- In addition, you can extract text and pictures for your own use, either printing it on paper or saving it on your hard drive.

The multimedia encyclopædia puts a vast amount of information into a small space, and it allows you to get information that is more like a slice of reality, not just a dry written description. We have lived with text references for so long that we have become used to their restrictions, so that using a multimedia reference is like stepping out from a dark cave into the full colour and sound of the world beyond. Any printed encyclopædia can offer colour pictures, but sound and animation add very much more.

Now imagine that you have some text of your own that you have written, using a word-processor, for a speech. You look at the text on the screen, select a portion of it, or all of it, and click with the mouse. You can now hear the words spoken, perhaps with a slightly strange Dalek accent, but clearly, giving you some idea of what your speech will sound like when spoken by some-one else. You can even choose from a selection of different voices, and correct the pronunciation of words that are not well enunciated. As an illustration of the opposite process, you can also annotate your typed text with voice messages, reminders to yourself that you don't want to see in print but which will be available when you click on the appropriate piece of text.

Obviously, the use of multimedia is not confined to programs that are intended primarily for business and education. Games can benefit by becoming more realistic and considerably less of the "zap the alien" type (otherwise known as optical haemorrhoids, or a pain in the eyes). A golf game, for example, can include scenes of real fairways and show the progress of a real game. Flying the F-15 can become very much more realistic when it is interspersed with video frames taken in the actual aircraft. Adventure games gain from sound and pictures taken in the locations that are being used. One of the main gainers in this respect is any form of strategy game, because the CD can store so much more information, making computer chess very much more challenging than it was before multimedia came along.

What do you need?

The basic requirements for multimedia work, apart from a fast computer system, are a fast CD-ROM drive and a sound card, along with suitable loudspeakers. A microphone is an optional, but sometimes worthwhile, extra; and you can add headphones if you don't want the sound to waken the children, the neighbours, or the dead.

All this equipment is, of course, already incorporated into a new PC that is described as a multimedia model, and the software that is necessary to operate these additions will also be present and correctly set up. If your computer has been a basic model, or one intended primarily for business use or Internet communications, it will lack the sound system, though it is by now unusual for any computer to be sold without a fast CD-ROM drive.

You might be tempted to buy either the sound card (and accessories) or the CD-ROM player separately, but you need to be careful about this. Sometimes a sound card and a CD-ROM player are matched to each other, with the sound card providing the socket (interface) to which the CD-ROM player connects. Modern systems use a CD-ROM drive that connects to the hard disc drive cables, and a sound card that operates independently, but you can fit this type of system only if your computer is modern enough to use such equipment. See Chapter 7 for the details of a DIY installation.

You can get more than half-way to multimedia using a CD-ROM drive by itself, so that you can see text and still or moving pictures, omitting only the sound, but you will be cutting yourself off from one dimension of the display; almost like a return to the days of silent films before 1928. This does not invalidate the encyclopædia use, and in some circumstances you might almost welcome a lack of sound. If you have a sound-card, however, you have the choice — switch on for sound or leave it off. With no sound card you might be left wondering what spoken Swahili sounds like, or what contribution the basset-horn makes to the orchestra.

The clinching factors are cost and compatibility. A full package of CD-ROM, sound card and all accessories (loudspeakers and amplifier, often microphone also), software for using the sound card and the CD-ROM player, and some CDs such as an encyclopædia and other works; all of this will cost much less than you would have to pay if you bought all of the items, or even a judicious selection of items, separately. The cost is even less if you specify all this equipment on a new computer.

Multimedia explained

In addition, you can be certain that the parts will all work well together, something that might be much less easy to ensure if you bought them separately at different times. If you have tried in the past to assemble hi-fi units from different suppliers you will understand what I mean. Hi-fi units are by now reasonably easy to match up, but it has taken a long time to get to that happy state.

Restrictions

Not all PC machines can run multimedia packages. In particular, the older machines described as PC/XT, using the 8088 or 8086 processor, are **totally incapable** of using the MPC hardware and software. Even the later machines that use the 80286 processor are not suitable, because the 80286 chip is not in the same class as the more modern ones, and even the 80386 type of PC is also too slow for modern multimedia software, though it can run the multimedia software that was available around 1993.

The **absolute** minimum for modern software, in terms of processor, is the 80486, and even a machine using this chip will not be really suitable unless the chip is run at a high speed. In this respect, speed means that the quoted clock rate should be 66 or 100 MHz, preferably the faster of these two. If you are the fortunate owner of a PC that uses the Pentium processor, run at any speed from 120 MHz upwards, your machine is well suited for MPC. The ideal, currently, is one of the machines described as MMX (Pentium 166MMX, for example) or Pentium-2, running Windows 95 or Windows 98, with at least 16 Mbyte of RAM and a hard drive of 2 Gbyte or more.

A fast machine is one essential, but the amount of RAM memory that is fitted in the machine also needs to be adequate. Adequate can be interpreted in various ways, but 16 Mbyte is usually taken to be the critical quantity nowadays for a machine that uses Windows 95 and its successor, Windows 98. Many modern machines now come with 32 Mbyte as standard, and some are offering 64 Mbyte.

You also need adequate capacity on the hard drive. The hard drive itself is essential for any modern computer, but not very long ago manufacturers thought that a hard drive of some 500 Mbyte was good enough. It isn't now, because the use of Windows and a few matching programs such as Word for Windows will occupy several hundred Mbytes of space just for installation, before you start to generate any text or picture data.

You need a large amount of hard drive storage space, correctly set up, to run the Windows system efficiently. Your machine should be set up with a **permanent** Windows swapfile on the hard drive — and if you haven't heard that phrase before you need to dust down the Windows manual and take a look.

In brief, a swapfile allows Windows to tuck a working program onto the hard drive when something else is in use, using the hard drive as if it were additional RAM — this is often referred to as *virtual memory*. Unless you have a large amount of RAM (64 Mbyte, for example) the use of such a swapfile is an essential part of the Windows system. Making a **permanent** swapfile speeds up swapping actions, because the file does not have to be created from scratch each time a swapfile is needed.

- You might think that the 650 Mbyte or so that a CD-ROM adds to your system would allow you to work with more modest hard-drive space. Don't you believe it! Every CD-ROM package you install will place, typically, 3–10 Mbyte of data on the hard drive, so that the program that controls the CD-ROM can run quickly and so that items that you yourself put in (such as bookmarks in an encyclopaedia) can be stored. In addition, if you want to add to your data by downloading from the Internet, you will need to use the hard drive to store this supplementary information.

- There are also some poorly-designed programs around that require you to transfer all the data from the CD-ROM to the hard drive, calling for some 100 Mbyte or more to be stored on the hard drive.

The speed of the CD-ROM drive is a very important factor. CD-ROM drive speeds are quoted in terms of the speed of the CD players that are used for audio systems. If this is taken as 1×, then a CD-ROM drive of modest speed would be quoted as 8×, meaning that it can be read at up to eight times the rate of an ordinary audio CD.

A high CD drive speed is very desirable on several counts, but the main advantage is that it allows realistic animation. Using a slow drive, animation is jerky, and even still pictures take some time to appear. Even still pictures can take some time to appear. A fast drive, 8× or more, is much more satisfactory, and speeds of 24× are now supplied with new computers. The faster drives make more noise — you can hear the whine of the drive motor change to a higher pitch when the computer is fetching information.

- Beware of bargain offers of very old drives described as single-speed or single-session. Even drives of 4× speed are not exactly bargains if you cannot run your software at a satisfactory speed.

Given, then, that you have all the hardware that you need to use multimedia, what exactly can you do with all of this equipment? That's our starting point for the next chapter.

2 Programs and text

Software

CD-ROM is now to a very considerable extent used to distribute programs, particularly program collections and some of the very large programs that would otherwise have called for a large number of conventional 3.5" discs. Both DOS and Windows programs are available on CD-ROM, but the larger programs are almost always of the Windows type; though collections of smaller programs are likely to be either of the DOS or Windows varieties or a mixture of both.

Reference and educational programs are usually designed to run under Windows; but some of the games and other leisure programs are likely to be intended to run directly under DOS. The large multimedia CDs contain sound files, but these discs can still be used for text and images, with no error messages, if you have no sound card. The sound commands and options will simply be ignored.

- Remember that you can run DOS programs from Windows 95 (and Windows 98) — you do not need to leave Windows completely (using the *Shut Down* options) to use MS-DOS programs, unless your DOS program is an unusually awkward one. Some games that are intended to run under DOS seem to cause problems with modern machines that use Windows.

- Make sure that any new software that you buy on CD is suitable for the PC and also for the version of Windows that you are using. Software for other machines (mainly the Apple Mac) is also distributed on CD-ROM, and any multimedia CD should carry the MPC mark to indicate that it employs the standard system that your hardware is designed to use. A few multimedia programs will run only under Windows 3.1, and not under Windows 95 or Windows 98. Be

11

very careful about software on CD-ROM that you buy
abroad — some examples will not run on Windows 95.

Because you buy a large program on CD-ROM, do not
imagine that this totally relieves the strain on your hard drive
space. CD-ROM, even if you are using a ×24 drive speed, is
slow in comparison to a conventional hard drive — it takes
much longer to find data on the CD than on the hard drive,
though the rate of loading data, once found, is fast. For that
reason, large programs on CD usually consist of a part that is
most often executed, and which will be copied to the hard
drive, and another part that is needed less often, such as data
for a database, which can stay on the CD-ROM. Such
programs contain a SETUP or INSTALL file on the CD.

DMA use

The configuration of your machine can be very important.
Modern versions of Windows allow a system called DMA
(direct memory access) to be used for the CD-ROM drive,
allowing information to be transferred into the memory at a
very high speed, without making much use of the main
processor, which is free to get on with other work. If you
have a version of Windows 95 that is identified as 4.00.950B
(or later), or you are using Windows 98, it is possible to turn
on this DMA feature and use the extra speed.

If you bought your computer in mid-1997 or later, it is likely
that it uses the later version of Windows 95. To check this,
open Windows Explorer, and click on *My Computer*. Now
click on *File* and *Properties*. The message should show the
Windows version as 4.00.950B. As confirmation, click on
the hard drive and then use File — Properties again. This
should show a message such as *Local disc (FAT 32)*, and the
FAT 32 label indicates also that this is the later version of
Windows 95.

• This check is not needed if you use Windows 98

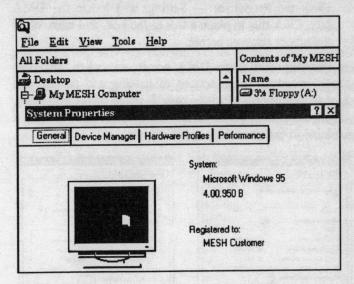

On a computer that uses this version of Windows 95, you can speed up access to the hard drive and to the CD-ROM drive by enabling the DMA. This is done as follows:

1   Start Control Panel, and click in succession *System*, *Device Manager* and *Disk Drives*.

2   The *Disk Drives* section should show both the floppy and the hard drive, with the hard drive usually identified as IDE, possibly with the label *Type 46*.

3   Click this line, and then click on the *Properties* button. Click *Settings*, and look for a box labelled DMA.

4   If this is not ticked, click on it. When you leave the Settings panel you will be asked to reboot the computer.

5   When your computer is running again, go back to the Device Manager and this time find your CD-ROM name.

Multimedia explained

6   Click the Properties — Settings and locate the DMA
    box. Click this to place a tick in the box, and carry on to
    the reboot stage as before.

By ensuring that these DMA boxes are ticked, you can
greatly speed up these actions of loading and saving, and
since these are critical to the overall speed of the computer,
you should gain in better performance. These options are not
available in earlier versions of Windows.

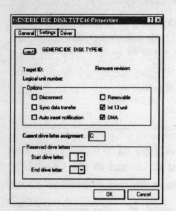 

CD-ROM setup

When you use a CD-ROM program that requires a setup
action, as most do, you must place the CD in the drive and
run the SETUP program. This is done using Windows 95,
and you may be reminded by a note on the cover of the CD
of the method that you are expected to use.

The most usual method is to click the *Start* button, and select
Run. In the space (marked *Open*) that appears, type the drive
letter, backslash, and the name of the installation program,
which can be *Install* or *Setup*. Assuming that the letter
assigned to the CD-ROM drive is D, the line will therefore
appear as:

D:\SETUP, or

D:\INSTALL,
and you can click on the OK box to start the installation.

- The letter D will be used for the CD-ROM drive unless you have more than one hard drive, which is unusual on modern machines. The CD-ROM drive *Properties* panel (obtained using Control Panel — System) will show what drive letter is used, if you are uncertain.

The alternative, which is slightly more automated, makes use of the Control Panel of Windows 95. Make sure that the CD-ROM disc is in its drive. Click the *Start* button (or use the flag key) and this time click on *Settings*. You will see another list with the words Control Panel, Printer and Taskbar. Click on *Control Panel*. When the Control Panel appears, **double-click** on *Add/Remove Programs*, and then on *Install/Uninstall*. Follow the instructions, and the installation program for the CD-ROM will be found and used automatically with no need to type anything.

The installation program will transfer program files to the hard drive, typically requiring some 3–5 Mbyte of hard disc space. The program is then run from the hard drive, calling on the CD for data as and when required. This is a compromise that makes the program run considerably faster than would be possible if everything had to be read from the CD, but it allows for the use of very much more data than you could normally be expected to fit on a normal hard drive for a single program.

Program collections

There are several CDs of program collections, of which a typical one is the huge set of shareware and public-domain programs called *Libris Britannia*, distributed by PDSL (see Appendix A) and several others. The important factor about any such collection is the ease with which you can get any program or program set on to your hard drive, and in this respect Libris Britannia is excellent. Though the majority of the programs are intended to be run under MS-DOS, there are a healthy number of Windows programs, some of which are for Windows 95.

- The Libris Britannia is also know by its origin, the Walnut Creek CD-ROM, originating in Walnut Creek, California. PDSL also distributes other collections, such as the *Taskbuster* set of utilities.

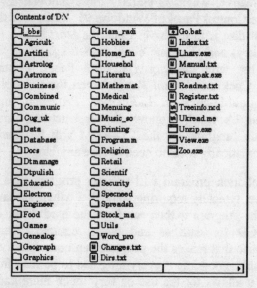

The illustration shows a display from Windows Explorer when the CD-ROM drive has been activated (in this case by clicking on the D icon in the left-hand panel of Explorer) with the Libris Britannia disc in place. This illustration shows the right-hand Explorer panel displaying the large set of folders into which the disc is organised. These are only the main folders — this display does not show the sub-folders, though some of the utility programs appear at the end of the list.

The Libris Britannia contains also some utility programs, of which one, VIEW.EXE is an excellent system for listing the programs and copying them to the hard drive, creating hard drive folders as required.

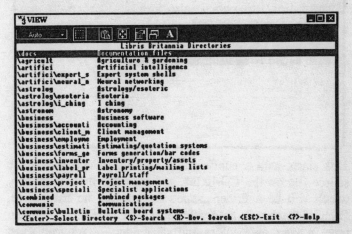

The example below shows the start of a VIEW display, with the first twenty-two folders listed together with a brief summary of the programs. This display shows the sub-folders for each main folder. The colours have been reversed to make reading easier — since VIEW operates under MS-DOS it normally displays white lettering on a black background.

When you place the cursor on to a topic in the VIEW list, you can press the ENTER key to get the cursor on to one of the individual programs that will then appear. You can then press the ENTER key to install the program from the CD-ROM

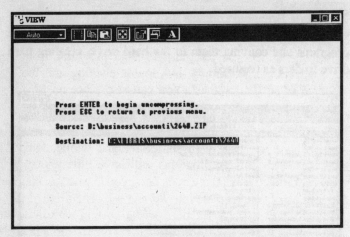

This starts with a confirmation message which shows the source file on the CD-ROM, and indicates the destination, which will be a folder created for you on the hard drive. Each of these will be a sub-folder of C:\LIBRIS. You can type in your own folder and sub-folder — you can even direct the files to a floppy if you are sure that there will be space on the floppy.

The program then very rapidly unpacks the compressed files, providing a message for each. If, as often happens, a duplicated file is found you have to confirm that it can be over-written. This is a point you need to watch if you extract several different sets of files to the same folder because files with names such as READ.ME are bound to conflict with each other.

You can then check that the files have been extracted. When VIEW has finished, you are returned to MS-DOS in the folder that you chose for extraction, and you can leave MS-DOS and use Windows Explorer to check the contents. You should then read and/or print out any READ.ME type of files so that you know how to use the program and what its limitations are. See Appendix C for how to deal with

README files. You can move the files to a more suitable folder if you decide to use the program.

- Remember that you can run MS-DOS programs from Windows 95/98 simply by double-clicking on the name in an Explorer list. You can also place an MS-DOS program into your Taskbar list of Windows 95 so that it can be started by a single click.

As is always the case with shareware and public domain programs, many of the programs will have little appeal to you, but among them there will be several, perhaps many, that will be of considerable interest and use. The price of the CD represents a small fraction of the cost of only a few programs in conventional format, and if you are looking for utilities in particular, there is a very rich harvest to be gained.

Copying text

All multimedia discs will contain some text and some, such as an Encyclopædia, will contain a very large amount of text. Reference works will usually provide for text to be copied so that you can make use of it, subject to copyright and acknowledgement. The copy action is usually virtually identical to the Copy and Paste action of a word-processor, or it can be more specific to the package.

- If the extract contains *hyperlinks* (coloured text that can be clicked to move to a different part of the text) then this action will not be available when the text is pasted into another document.

A typical example of the use of a Copy and Paste action starts by selecting text in the usual way by dragging the mouse cursor over it (with the left-hand mouse button held down), and you can copy this text to the Windows Clipboard by clicking on the *Copy* option of the Edit menu item. There is often a *Select All* option which allows you to select the whole of a piece of text without the need to drag the mouse. The illustration has been taken from the Grolier Encyclopædia.

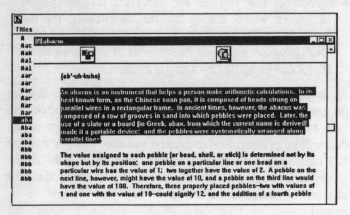

The text can then be pasted into any text editor, word processor, database, spreadsheet — anything that will accept text and which runs under Windows. The example shows a small portion of text copied from an information list into Windows Notepad. This can be saved from Notepad as a TXT file (as illustrated), and from there it can be read into any other package that accepts ASCII text, which means any word processor or desk-top publisher package.

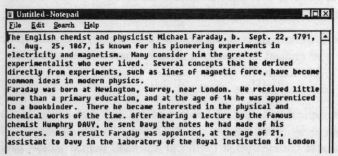

The Grolier Encyclopædia which is bundled with many multimedia computers contains a very large amount of textual material, and you can opt to use either the *File* or the

Edit menus for transferring text. With text displayed, if you click on the *File* menu you can then select *Save*. This will produce the Save menu which allows you to specify all of the text in the current list, a selection of text (which you have marked by dragging the mouse) or a single window of text (as much as is visible on the screen). When you make this choice and click on the OK button, you are offered a *Save As* window. You can opt for saving as a TXT file if the window you are saving contains text only — other options allow the copying of graphics as well as text.

The Edit menu contains the usual Cut, Copy and Paste commands, and when you select a piece of text the *Copy* command will become available (Cut and Paste can be used only for your own annotations). This, as usual, copies to the Clipboard so that you can paste in elsewhere. All copied text contains a copyright notice.

- You can quote from Grolier text, citing the source, but you must **not** copy text and claim it as your own. This is the usual copyright stipulation for material on CD-ROM.

You can also print text from the Grolier, using either the *Print* option from *the File* menu, or by clicking on the printer symbol on the top line. As before you will be presented with options, this time of *All text*, *Selection of text* or *Pages*. The full number of pages of the text will be displayed so that you can make a selection if you want to.

A very different method of copying is illustrated by the Hutchinson Encyclopædia. The text cannot be selected using the mouse, and you have to start a copying action by clicking on the Print icon. When you have done this, you will see a menu that allows printing of text, a picture or a table, or copying of text or a picture. When the text copying option is used, the whole text of an article will be copied and can be pasted into any suitable application.

Multimedia explained

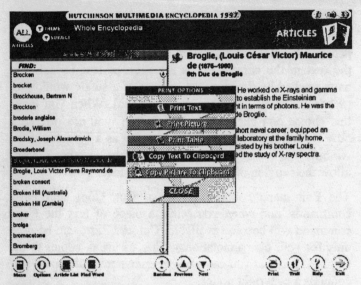

Other text sources

You can buy CDs that consist of text only, such as articles copied from the Internet, catalogues of items such as electronic components, or advice on practical matters such as using your PC. These CDs would be of very little use unless you could copy the text, and this is normally done by using selection by dragging as illustrated for the Grolier Encyclopædia.

3 Images and image files

Bitmaps and vector files

Unlike text, which uses the universal ASCII coding, there is no agreed single standard way of coding or storing an image. To start with, there are two completely different basic ways of coding images, one of which is the use of a *bitmap*. The other method is variously described as a *vector* file or *object-oriented* file.

A bitmap file consists of a set of numbers each of which describes the position of a dot in an image and the colour of that dot. The size of a bitmap file depends on the total number of dots or pixels on the screen, and how many colours are to be used. For example, a standard VGA screen uses 640 x 480 dots, a total of 307,200 dots. Now if you are working with a purely black and white picture, only one digital bit is needed to store this information for each dot, 0 for black, 1 for white, and the positions of the dots can be taken as the order in which they are scanned. Since there are 8 bits to a byte of memory, we can store a monochrome image like this in 307200/8 bytes, which is 38,400 bytes. This is still 37.5 Kbyte, emphasising the point that a bitmap needs a lot of storage space.

Bitmaps become much larger if you want a range of colours. The standard VGA 16 colours range needs 4 bits so that only two dots can be coded in a single byte. This requires 307200/2 = 153,600 bytes to store a picture, and the requirements are greater for 256 colours (8 bits for each dot), 32,000 colours (15 bits per dot) and 16,000,000 colours (24 bits per dot). For a lot of images, using more than 256 colours is a waste of disc space and the higher values, referred to as *High Colour* or *Photo-real* images are useful only if you have access to a high-resolution colour printer and need to work with photographic images.

Multimedia explained

- The Windows Clipboard will work with bitmap images, and when these are transferred to Windows Paint they can be saved in BMP (bitmap) format. The older Windows Paintbrush utility could save in the more economical PCX format, and other packages can use the tightly compressed JPEG system.

The bitmap sizes referred to above are for the standard VGA 640 × 480 screen. If you wanted to print a bitmap with a laser printer on A4 paper, using the 300 dots per inch of the laser printer you would need to use much larger bitmaps, which is why it is often necessary to have a large amount of memory in a laser printer.

The main advantage of bitmap files is that they can be easily edited, erasing some parts and adding others. This includes adding text and changing colours. The Windows MS Paint package is a typical bitmap editing program, and the well-known Paint Shop Pro (currently Version 4.0) is one that offers a much larger range of options. Later versions of Windows 95 included the PhotoEditor package that is intended for editing images of photographic quality.

The trouble with a bitmap is that it is device-dependent. A bitmap for a VGA screen of 640 × 480 will look smaller when it is displayed on a 800 × 600 screen, or when it is printed on paper with a 300 dot per inch laser printer (when it will be 2.13" x 1.6" in size). There is no simple way of altering the sizes of such images while preserving the sharpness of the picture and the way that many graphics programs use for making larger images is simply to use larger dots, making the image look very coarse.

- Most multimedia packages now in use are geared to a resolution of 800 × 600 with 256-colours, and the images will not look particularly attractive if you use a smaller number of colours. These images will not look very good when printed on a monochrome printer, but a colour inkjet printer will produce reasonable results.

The other option for images is the *vector* or *object-oriented* format. In this type of image, dots are not coded, and the image is constructed and analysed as a set of straight or curved lines. A line can be represented by a mathematical equation whose numbers can be stored as a set of binary codes, so that this form of coding is potentially more economical in disc space. The drawbacks are that it requires software that will perform the calculations on the stored number in order to reproduce the picture, and that these calculations will take time.

CAD programs are universally of this type, as are most of the programs for business images (graphs, etc.). The nearest we have to a standard format is the Windows Metafile (WMF) that is used for a lot of clipart images. For CAD work a form of file called DXF (data exchange format) can be used by most packages to transfer images. Vector files are used also by some general-purpose drawing packages, particularly Serif DrawPlus, which is available on CD-ROM and is very often available as a free offer with computer magazines.

A vector image file is the same size no matter how large or small the image is, and a picture that uses this system can be scaled up or down with no loss of detail. This means that the image looks as clear as the medium permits, almost irrespective of scale, so that an image printed at 300 dots per inch by a laser or inkjet printer will look very much better than the same image on a screen (usually 75 dots per inch).

- Older computers deal with vector files very slowly unless they are fitted with a maths co-processor chip. The later 486DX and Pentium machines have built-in co-processors, but of these only the Pentium machines will deal with large vector files at a speed suitable for extensive use of such files.

Multimedia explained

The editing of WMF and other vector files is not difficult, but it requires the use of drawing programs that are, with a few exceptions, more expensive. One notable exception was a package called SmartSketch, but this no longer seems to be available. SmartSketch offered facilities that have not been available on other low-cost packages, such as the ability to erase a portion of a shape, or to smooth out a jagged line.

Another exception is Serif DrawPlus, which is often featured in magazine CD bundles, and is a very able drawing package, either for new drawings or for editing existing drawings. Vector editing allows for picking out a part of a drawing for alteration, something that cannot be done with bitmap images.

Bitmap images

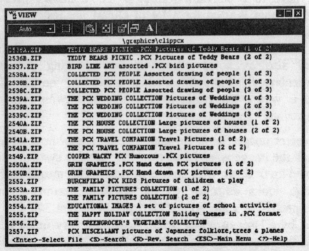

When you buy any graphics package on CD-ROM it will usually contain a large set of pre-drawn images, called *clipart*, that you can use for yourself either as they are or as a basis for your own images. The Libris Britannia CD that was referred to earlier contains also a large number of bitmap images. The VIEW utility for Libris Britannia allows you to find what is available, and the illustration shows this program running and the cursor placed on the CLIPPCX folder which contains the PCX files, one of the most popular of bitmap formats. This system for accessing picture files is fairly typical of CD-ROMs that contain such files.

• Note also that there is clipart in DR-Halo, Gem and Mac formats. Many graphics utilities will convert freely between different formats, but the DR-Halo and Gem formats are by now very old and you cannot expect to find them available on modern software.

Each file in this set is in fact a collection of compressed files of images, and using the cursor and the ENTER key once again will de-compress to get the individual PCX files. You cannot check how many files are contained here other than by copying them to a hard drive file.

The range of images is enormous, and many are in large formats, so that the ability to re-scale images is very useful, and any software that can re-scale without too much loss of resolution should be part of your armoury. The shareware utility *Paint Shop Pro* is highly recommended for use with bitmap images, and has been used on many of the images in this book — see later in this Chapter for a brief description.

Images of animals, as illustrated, are particularly popular, but the range of artwork in PCX format is huge, and you will find that a lot of the other collections, particularly the assorted set, are simply the same images in another format

Multimedia explained

(often TIF). One point to watch for is that most collections are still in compressed form when they are stored on your hard drive. For example, the 2729 Libris Britannia set are in the format called ZIP, and to extract the individual files you can use the utility called PKUNZIP.EXE which must be run using MS-DOS. This is included on the Libris Britannia CD, and the easiest way of using it is to copy it to the folder on the hard drive that contains the zipped files and use it in the form:

    PKUNZIP *.ZIP

which will unpack all the files in the folder. As each file is unpacked, a message such as :

    EXPLODING CLOCK1S.PCX

will appear.

An alternative form of unpacking is the WINZIP utility that, as the name suggests, works from within Windows. WINZIP makes it unnecessary to switch to MS-DOS, and is very fast in action. You need to select the folder in which the ZIP files are contained, and also select a folder in which the unzipped files will be placed.

Images from multimedia packages

Images that occur in other multimedia packages can usually be copied either to a file or to the Windows clipboard, using commands that are built into the program.

For example, the illustration shows an image of a Bugatti Type 41, obtained from the Classic Cars section of the New Grolier Encyclopædia. Clicking on the *Edit* menu and then on the *Copy* command in that menu will copy the image into the Windows clipboard, using the same size as it appears on the screen. If you want to copy a larger version of the image, maximise the size of the picture and then press the Print Screen key. Either way, you can then retrieve the image in Windows Paint as follows:

1. Switch to MS Paint, or open it if it is not already running. Maximise the display.

2. Click on Edit — Paste. The image will appear on screen and in colour.

3. You can now edit the picture, removing the framing, and altering the image as you want. In this example, the image has been changed to black and white, and the defects of bitmap images are clearly shown by the coarse appearance of this image, which looks clear at its original size.

Select caption icon or icon for related articles

- Don't forget copyright — I have acknowledged the image as coming from the New Grolier, and unless you have **totally** altered it you should do the same if you publish your image.

- Note also that these images are usually large in terms of bits. This image was around 15 Kbyte in PCX form, but is closer to 59 Kbyte in pure bit-map form, as a BMP file.

Multimedia explained

You may find problems with some captured colour images, as this illustration has also demonstrated. The original uses a 16-colour scheme, but changing this into black and white considerably degrades the image. If, however, you want to print the image using a laser or other monochrome printer you will have to put up with this degradation unless you specify a grey scale illustration. Using Paint Shop Pro, you can convert a colour image into grey-scale or monochrome as you please, and the illustration below shows a grey-scale used, though the quality is degraded by the printing process.

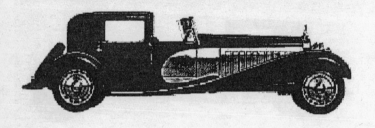

It is better, however, to check any colour WP file that has been obtained by way of the Clipboard before you alter the contents of the Clipboard by using another Cut or Copy command. The menu of the New Grolier has in the past also allowed for saving some mixed text and pictures in a format designated as ART; so that the files have the ART extension. This is not a format that is well supported nowadays, and if you have obtained an older copy of the New Grolier you should not be tempted to save in this format.

- Some Grolier pictures can be printed, using the *Print* command from the *File* menu. A copyright notice is also printed under each picture. The same pictures can be saved as BMP files by using the File menu or clicking on the disc symbol.

The Hutchinson Encyclopædia provides a gallery of still pictures when you click on the camera icon in the main menu page. The example here, which has been converted to black and white, shows a portion of the display with the table of entries on the left and each image appearing on the right when selected. The image in this illustration is of Alexander the Great, and the full-colour version is impressive, like most of the images in this Encyclopædia.

To print this image, you can click on the printer icon (not shown in this illustration) at the foot of the screen. You then have the options of printing the picture, the table of entries, or the text that accompanies the picture. In this case, for example, the text would deal with the life of Alexander the Great.

- Most of these images will look very poor if you are using a 16-colour graphics driver. If possible, switch to 800 × 600 resolution and 256 colours.

Multimedia explained

NOTE: If you import bitmap files into a Microsoft Word 97 document you may find that after you have saved the document, reloading it produces placeholders in place of some or all of the pictures. These placeholders are frames with a red cross in them, and are of exactly the same size as the original picture. As a permanent cure, you can install software called Service Release 1 (SR1), of about 7 Mbyte, and run this software to fix the problem. At the time of writing, no revised version of Word 97 that incorporated these changes was available.

Incorporating SR1 into Word 97 will not fix documents that were created earlier, and for such documents (also applicable if you have not used SR1), Microsoft suggest the following, one of which may be applicable to your problem:

1. Make sure that the option *Allow Fast Saves* is turned off.

2. Delete the placeholder, and use Insert — Picture to replace the image.

3. Double-click the "picture" to open the Picture Editor. Click Edit — Select All, and then Edit — Copy. Click File — Close and return, and when you return to Word, click Edit — Paste.

4. For a linked picture, click the picture and then press the F9 key.

You may find that only the second method has any effect, and without the SR1 patch, the problem may reappear when you save and then reload the file.

4 Editing graphics

Editing bitmaps

Bitmaps are, as noted earlier, stored as rather large files, and unless you have a large amount of spare capacity on the hard drive you would normally want to store your image files in one of the many compressed formats. A compressed file makes use of the fact that many entries in a bitmap are likely to contain very little information or to contain repeated information. You might, for example, have a run of 2000 red dots, so that this information consists of the data for one red dot repeated 2000 times. On a bitmap each dot has to be coded, but there is no reason why a file should not consist of the data for one followed by the number of times the data has to be repeated.

- Descriptions of graphics packages in this chapter are for rough guidance only; they are not detailed.

There is, however, no single standard method for compressing image files, but there are several methods that are used more than others. Some compression systems are virtually one-application systems, used only with some particular drawing program. Others, such as PCX and TIF, are used very widely and have become standards. The important point is that unless you have some form of file conversion program you are limited to the file formats your image software supports, and if your image software is confined to Windows MS Paint you have the choice of reading Windows bitmaps or PCX only, and of saving in bitmap form only. There is nothing wrong with this except that you cannot read a file in TIF or GIF format, for example.

- The older Windows Paintbrush that was distributed with Windows 3.1 could read and write files in the PCX format, and if you can get hold of a copy it is in

33

my opinion a much better bitmap editor. Apart from the PCX aspect, the older Paintbrush program allows you to move the cursor one pixel at a time by using the cursor keys, which is much easier than trying to use the mouse for small changes.

- Several graphics packages now offer the JPEG compression, producing files with the JPG extension letters. These files can for many purposes be used like any other graphics file, but you should not retrieve a JPEG file, edit it, and then re-save it, because the image will be degraded by being compressed again.

Since MS Paint is part of Windows it makes sense to make use of it as far as possible, particularly since it is so easy to place an image into it by using the Clipboard. MS Paint allows you to **read** in PCX format as well as the BMP format, so that you can read images that were saved using the older Windows Paintbrush. An image can be put into MS Paint from the Clipboard, or by reading a BMP or PCX file. The illustration shows the toolbar of MS Paint, with its functions labelled.

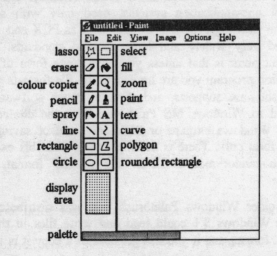

If the image is smaller than the full-screen size of MS Paint, you can simply use the Edit — Paste option of MS Paint to paste in the image. If you find that only part of the picture is displayed, because the picture is a large bitmap, then you will have to alter the size setting of MS Paint. You do not, however, need to re-paste the picture.

- An alternative is to use the low-cost shareware utility Paint-Shop Pro, from PDSL, which will always paste in the complete picture. This, however, does not allow the bit-editing and other image shape alteration methods of Paintbrush. It is remarkably difficult to find a bitmap editor that does all of the most desirable actions, and you may have to keep three editors running just for convenience.

Once an image has been placed into MS Paint, unwanted parts of the image can be removed with the Eraser tool, selecting the ordinary (monochrome) eraser on the right-hand side of the strip. The size of this eraser depends on the setting of line width, so for removal of large areas you should select the widest line size from the set at the bottom left hand corner of the screen, and then select the eraser. When you move the mouse the eraser appears as a large square. In this illustration, the eraser is working on an image of a page in Word.

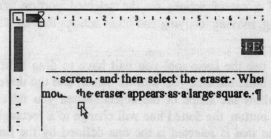

Moving the eraser in perfectly horizontal or vertical lines is difficult because it requires precise movements of the mouse. On the older Windows Paintbrush, precise horizontal or vertical movement was possible if the cursor was positioned on one side, the mouse button pressed, and the appropriate cursor key used to move the eraser rather than moving the mouse. This is one very good reason for preferring the older version, and it is worth buying an old copy of Windows 3.1 just to get this utility. The following illustrations will show MS Paint rather than the older Windows Paintbrush utility. Remember, however, that apart from the use of the cursor keys and the ability to save in PCX format, MS Paint is functionally similar to Windows Paintbrush.

- MS Paint scores over Windows Paintbrush in allowing magnified views that appear on a pixel grid, allowing very precise editing on small portions of the image. Tools like selection and copying can also be used in these views, but some action, like the eraser can be very erratic — Eraser will, for example, sometimes leave a trail of dots behind it.

The most important feature to learn is the selection process. There are two selection tools, a rectangular box and a lasso (shown on the toolbox as a star shape). Clicking on the rectangular box will allow you to drag a rectangle around any part of your image, and when you release the mouse button a dotted rectangle can be seen. You can then carry out any of a set of actions on the selected portion, such as deleting, moving, copying and other actions that are detailed later.

If you use the lasso tool you will have to drag a freehand loop around the area you want to select, and the dotted line will follow the shape of the object. When you release the mouse button, the dotted line will change to a rectangle, but the area that is selected is the one defined by the line you drew, not by the rectangle. This allows you to select shapes and portions of shapes that cannot be surrounded by a rectangular box.

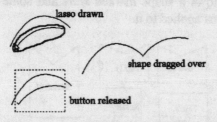

lasso drawn

shape dragged over

button released

Selection followed by using the Delete key can be used to remove a large part of an image. Any small part of a captured image, text, and background shading, can be removed using the Eraser. Selecting Undo from the Edit menu will restore the erasure if needed. The colour eraser to the left of the ordinary eraser will alter the colour of areas it is dragged over. On a monochrome screen it has the same action as the ordinary eraser.

Note that if the ordinary eraser size is too large, you can use the Pencil tool and paint in background (instead of foreground) colour. This is particularly useful if you want to work with large Zoom settings, see later. You select white for the pencil colour by clicking on the colour in the set of colour panels at the bottom left-hand corner of the Paint window (use the View menu to ensure that the *Color Box* is enabled).

• The portion of the Paint window that is labelled *display area* is used to display options such as line thickness, fill colours, or selection icons. The appearance of this area will change according to what tool has been selected, and it will be blank if it is not needed.

The *Image* menu commands (called *Pick* on Windows Paintbrush) are available only when an image is selected. These consist of *Flip* (horizontal or vertical), *Rotate* (in units of 90°), *Stretch* (horizontal or vertical), *Skew* (by a specified angle), *Inverse colours*, *Attributes* and *Clear Image*. The illustration shows a shape marked *start* and some of these transformations applied to it.

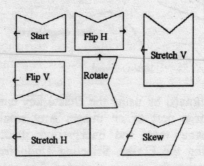

The first four of these effects are combined into Flip/Rotate and Stretch/Skew commands, so that clicking produces a panel that allows you to select one command and specify amounts. Note that you can stretch an image by selecting it and dragging one of the buttons that appear in the middle of each side of a selection box.

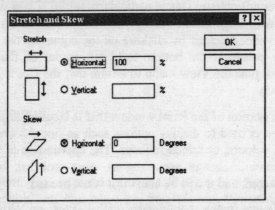

The other commands are simpler. The Inverse option reverses the colours of a selected image (reversing black and white, or foreground and background). The Attribute menu item allows you to select the size of the bitmap, either as inches, centimetres or pels (pixels), and as Colour or Black and White. You can convert a colour image into black and white using this action, something that was not possible using the older Windows Paintbrush.

Using View — Zoom allows you to specify a magnification figure (as a percentage), and you can also use this menu to turn on a Grid and a Thumbnail. The grid shows the pixel size, and is most effective when you are working with 800% Zoom. You can use the tools such as eraser, pencil (illustrated) and brush on this zoomed version, allowing you to make detailed changes to an image. This action is called bit-editing, and it is the main advantage of using bit-map file types (whether compressed or not) as compared to vector files.

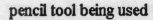

pencil tool being used

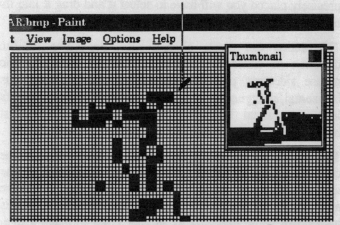

- The older Windows Paintbrush permitted only limiting use of tools in a Zoomed view, and only one choice of Zoom size.

- You can perform an instant Zoom by clicking on the Magnifier tool and clicking this over part of your drawing, indicated by a selection rectangle that appears in place of the cursor.

Multimedia explained

Drawing, for straight-line patterns, makes use of the side-tools set of the plain rectangle and the straight line. You need to start by selecting a line width from a set of five, and the smallest line-width (one pixel) is usually preferable for this type of effort. Holding down the Shift key while drawing a straight line will force the line to be perfectly horizontal or perfectly vertical, or a rectangle to be a perfect square.

A circle is produced by selecting the circle tool and choosing a starting point for the circle. The circle is then created by pressing down the mouse button and dragging the rim of the circle out, releasing the mouse button when the circle has reached the size required. Note that no part of the circle will be on the starting point — if you want the circle to be precisely placed you will have to select it and drag it into its final position.

This action can create ellipses also, depending on the direction in which the mouse is dragged. Dragging the mouse sideways produces an ellipse with its long axis horizontal, dragging up or down produces an ellipse with its long axis vertical. To create a true circle the Shift key must be held down as the mouse is dragged.

The rounded rectangle is drawn in the same way as the ordinary rectangle, but the polygon tool, represented by the icon of a skewed L shape, works rather differently. To make a polygon a starting point is selected and the mouse button is held down while dragging to another point to make a line. You can then select another point, and when the button is released, this point and the previous point will be joined by a straight line. Clicking somewhere else will create a line from the previous point to this next one, and this can be continued for any number of sides until the first point is selected again to make a closed pattern. There is no provision for creating polygon shapes with exactly equal sides.

Each of the closed shapes can be drawn in outline or in filled form, with the filling using the paint chosen from the palette. When the shaded option is used, the shading does not appear until the last point has been selected. Some very complicated patterns can be created.

In addition, any unshaded closed shape can be shaded by using the paint-roller tool, first selecting the type of paint from the palette at the bottom of the Paint window. The bottom left-hand portion of the paint-roller icon is the point at which the colour (or shade) filling will start and this must be inside the area that is to be filled. An area to be filled must be completely enclosed, otherwise colour will leak uncontrollably. If in doubt, check that a shape is complete, using a Zoom.

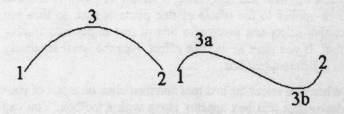

The curve drawing tool (Bézier tool) is a very useful method of creating curved shapes which are open and non circular. A starting point is selected and the mouse button pressed and dragged to produce a straight line, releasing the mouse button at the end of the line. If the mouse is then moved to take the cursor outside the straight line, pressing the button and dragging the mouse will convert the line into a curve which can be rubber banded about the screen to produce shapes that can be hyperbolic, parabolic, or even pass as part of a wave. You can repeat this process to bend the line somewhere else, or click on the end of the line to stop the action. In each of these examples, the line has started at

41

point 1, ended at point 2 and been pulled from point 3. In the case of the double-curve, pulling has been used at points 3a and 3b.

The paintbrush tool allows for freehand drawing, the least useful option, using the mouse to guide the pencil around the screen. The shape of the brush, by default a small square dot, can be changed by double-clicking on the brush shape or by using the Options menu.

The spray or airbrush is rather easier to use than the brush. Each click of the mouse button will place a blob of the current palette pattern on the screen at the cursor position, so that outlines can be traced by placing and pressing. As an alternative, keep the mouse button depressed and drag the mouse to get more continuous patterns. The density of the spray depends on how fast the mouse is dragged.

Paint can also add text, using a variety of fonts. A selected font applies to the whole of one piece of text, so that you cannot select one piece of a line of text to put into another font. If you want to use this effect, type the word separately in a different text box.

When you select the text tool and then click on a part of your drawing, a text box appears along with a toolbox. You can select the font and size of text in the toolbox, and you can drag the text box to change the width and height of the text space (not the size of the text). If you do not see the text you have types, drag the text box out to a large size. The default font is Arial, and Paint reverts each time you start it afresh.

Using Paint Shop Pro

Paint Shop Pro, (PSP) is shareware which is included in Libris Britannia, and widely distributed by way of discs given away with computing magazines. Paint Shop Pro is now available in Version 4, but the old versions, particularly Version 2.0, are very useful and might be as much as you will need, particularly as the later version offer photographic editing actions that are also available in Microsoft Photo Editor which is now part of Windows 95. Registration for Paint Shop Pro in the UK is obtained from Digital Workshop, First Floor, 8 West Bar, Banbury, Oxon. OX16 9RR

PSP is a most valuable tool for image manipulation, and it really comes into its own with images from multimedia sources. Paint Shop Pro does **not** carry out bit-editing, but it will read, convert and write a wide selection of file formats (and sub-formats), which include:

BMP Windows RGB, RLE or OS/2
CLP Windows Clipboard
CUT DR Halo
DIB Windows RGB, RLE or OS/2
EPS Colour or monochrome, preview or no preview
GIF Version 87a or 89a, interlaced or non-interlaced
IFF Amiga Compressed or non-compressed
IMG Gempaint
JIF JPEG - JFIF
JPG JPEG - JFIF
LBM Deluxe Paint, compressed or uncompressed
MAC Macpaint, header or no header
MSP Microsoft Paint of Windows 2.0
PCX ZSoft, versions 0, 2 or 5
PIC PC Paint
RAS Sun Raster images
RLE Compuserve or Windows
TGA Truevision Targa, 8 or 16 bit, compressed or not
TIF TIFF uncompressed, LZW or Packbits compressed
WPG WordPerfect, version 5.0 or 5.1

- Batch conversion is also available from the File menu. This allows you to specify input and output folders and the output format and then convert all the files of that format that exist in a folder.

- Later versions have some limited drawing tools

Multimedia explained

The File menu also contains *Preferences*, in which you can set options for input, output and other aspects of graphics files. These are best left at their default setting until you are really familiar with graphics editing.

The Preferences allow you to stipulate when a new windows will be used. This is done automatically when an image is pasted (so that you can never paste two images into the same space — use the *Paste From* facility of MS Paint *Edit* to do this). The options that are presented allow you to opt to use a new window for each possible change that Paint Shop Pro will make. Finally, the Undo preference allows you to select None, memory or disc, and the None option will disable the Undo facility.

Capture (from the Capture menu) can be of a selected area, the full screen, a window or a client area, and you can, unusually, opt to capture the cursor shape. You can opt for capturing other Windows screens, either capturing the screen as it exists immediately after selecting the process, or of activating the capture by clicking the F11 (or other selected) key

The Edit menu contains Undo, Cut Copy, Paste and Empty Clipboard. The *Copy* command is used only when you want to copy some item on an existing image into a separate window, from which it can be saved for further processing. The *Empty Clipboard* option will release some memory if the clipboard contains a large image that is not needed again.

The View menu allows for rapid selection of Normal view, Full Screen, and Zoom settings that allow up to a sixteen-fold increase or decrease in viewed size. These settings do not affect the image as stored, but they allow you to copy a portion of an image at a different scale. The *Full Screen* view shows the image with no tools visible, and only the title bar of Paint Shop Pro. Also in this menu you can opt to show or hide the Toolboxes (tools for selection and copying) and the *Histogram* which shows the image in graphical form. The Histogram is normally hidden, because it slows down the actions and is not of interest except in a minority of actions once you learn how to use it.

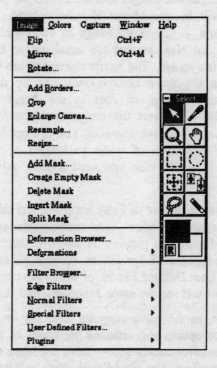

The illustration above shows the important *Image* menu and the Toolbox. The Toolbox is floating, and it can be removed from the screen or moved to any place by dragging it. The image menu is available when an image is present, either by being pasted in, captured, or loaded from a file. The Flip, Mirror and Rotate actions are very much the same as those of Paintbrush. The Crop command is available only when an area has been defined, see later.

Add Borders can be used at any stage when an image is present. You can specify a colour for the border and select which sides shall have the border. You then specify the width of border and click on the OK button.

Resample is rather more restricted, and can be used only on greyscale images and images that use 24 bits per pixel — the command will be greyed out if not available. When the option is used, it allows an image to be re-sized without altering the dot size, so that the usual coarse and jagged appearance is avoided. The *Resize* command can be used to alter size in the more conventional way by deleting or increasing the number of dots in the image. You are recommended to convert the image to 24-bit format, see later, before carrying out a re-size. You can opt to keep the aspect ratio (the ratio of width to height) of the image unchanged, in which case you need specify only the new width.

The Filters are a feature of Paint Shop Pro and other photo-editor packages that allow very considerable amounts of image modification to pictures in 24-bit or higher colour. They are grouped as Edge Filters, Normal Filters, Special Filters, and User Defined Filters, of which the latter are your own creations and require some experience and skill.

Edge Filters, as the name suggests, alter the image edges. The Enhance option will enhance the edges of the image, leaving the interior unchanged — there is a More option that increases the effect. The *Find Edges* action will trace around all the edges, or you can opt to find only the horizontal edges or only the vertical edges. The *Trace Contour* action will trace around all the edges in the drawing. Remember that these effects require a 24-bit image, so that if you are working on a monochrome or grey-scale image, or even a 4-bit colour image, the Colour menu must be used to alter the bits per pixel figure before these effects are used.

The Normal Filters set have actions described as *Blur*, *Sharpen* and *Soften*, each with the More option. The Special Filters all carry out actions that change the image in ways that can look quite drastic. *Add Noise* will fuzz an image with black dots (a speckled image), and you can choose the type of speckling you add. By contrast, the *Despeckle* option will try to clean up an image if it contains such noise (as many scanned images do). *Dilate* enhances the brighter colours in an image and *Erode* enhances the darker colours.

Emboss makes the image look more three-dimensional by adding shading. *Median* will average out all the colours, brightness values and contrast of an image. *Mosaic* makes the image look cubist, and the effect can be seen on televised images when a face must not be recognised — the size of the mosaic squares can be selected when this filter is used. *Posterize* reduces the number of bits used for colour so that the colour range of the image is decreased (such reductions can also be carried out by the Colours menu.

The Colours menu allows a large range of actions that concern brightness and contrast as well as colour, and some of these are of considerable value in making colour images suitable for monochrome printing. The Brightness/Contrast options allow you to alter these two factors, using a form of scroll-bar control for each, and with a very useful Preview option so that you can see before you carry out the actions what the effect on an image will be.

Gamma correction uses the same form of scroll-bar control, and allows the gamma factor of images to be adjusted — this may be needed to ensure that a set of different images will not look too differing in gamma value when printed. The gamma factor for an image is a technical term used mainly in TV work, where the cathode-ray tube produces a brightness that is not proportional to the value of the electrical signal input, but is closer to being proportional to the square of the signal input; a gamma of 2.0

In other words, the brightness is proportional to the signal size raised to the power gamma, where gamma is a number less than 5.0. Many computer monitors have a gamma value

47

of around 2.2. The practical effect on colour is that if a picture contains blue, green and red signals that are in the ratio of 3:2:1 then the picture tube will show intensities of 9:4:1 if the gamma value is 2. This is corrected for, but if your obtain a colour picture from a colour scanner, the gamma value will be quite different and will need to be compensated.

• Gamma correction is very useful if you find that a captured image looks too dark in places, with detail hidden. Raising the gamma value will often make such a picture much more acceptable.

The *Grey Scale* option allows a colour picture to be converted to a picture that contains as many shades of grey as the picture contained colours — this means that the number of colour bits per pixel is unchanged. The Highlight/Shadow option uses the scroll-bar controls again to allow you to set what amount of shading will the considered as highlight or shadow, and a Preview is available. For example, increasing the shadow figure to 30% will darken the image because a shading of 30% of white will now be taken as being shadow.

Negative Image will invert dark and bright (and reverse colour values) — it is more useful on a greyscale image. The Red/Blue/Green controls, using scrollbars, allow you to specify for yourself what the balance of these primary (light) colours will be in the image. This can be extremely useful to correct colour bias in, for example, a colour printer. The *Solarise* option alters the image to one that is partially inverted — the name comes from the effect of sunlight on undeveloped film which causes a partial reversal of this type.

The second section of the Colours menu allows you to load in a colour palette that you have prepared and to apply it to an image — you can also edit a palette and save it for future use. These options are available only for 16-colour or 256-colour images. The last section allows you to count the number of colours actually used in an image, and to increase or decrease colour depth, meaning the number of bits used for colour in each pixel. You can specify ways of representing colours when you reduce, particularly to monochrome.

- Remember that some changes are irreversible — if you reduce a 256-colour picture to monochrome (1-bit) you cannot see the colours again if you later expand it back to 256-colours.

Vector editing

The least costly path to creating and editing vector files is Serif DrawPlus, and the description following applies to Version 2.0, as distributed in 1997.

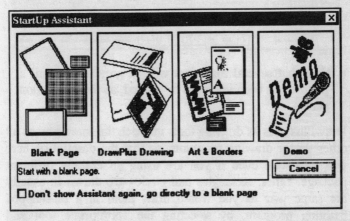

When DrawPlus starts, the Startup Assistant page (illustrated) offers the choice of a blank page, a ready-made drawing, the Art and Borders menu, or the Demonstration. You can also opt to tick a box to ensure that this page does not appear again unless you enable it.

The main screen of DrawPlus is a drawing space which by default will contain a set of grid points. There are toolbars on the left hand side and the top of the screen, and a status

Multimedia explained

bar at the bottom of the screen. The Toolbars can be used for almost all the drawing actions of DrawPlus, so that many of the menu items, other than those in the File menu, will not be needed if you prefer to use the Tools.

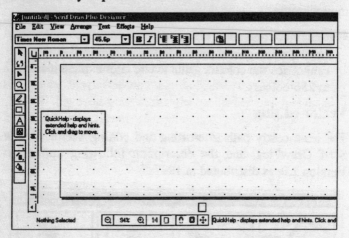

- Note that several toolboxes will be greyed out until a picture has been imported or created, as the illustration shows

DrawPlus uses its drawing tools in much the same way as all other vector drawing programs, so that the description here will be useful even if you are using an entirely different package. Lines, rectangles and circles are drawn in exactly the same way as you would draw them in a bit-mapped painting program, by selecting the appropriate tool and dragging out the shape.

Several tools are represented with a single icon, and clicking on the small arrowhead of such an icon will display a large box of tools or colours that you can use. For example, the tool illustrated as a square opens out to offer a large selection (25) of closed shapes, and the line tool opens out to offer freehand, straight or curved (Bézier) lines.

- Curves are not easy to create or edit, and you will need considerable practise with this aspect of DrawPlus. Once you have mastered tools such as the Node Editor, however, you will find that DrawPlus can produce virtually any shape that you want.

When you draw a shape, however, it appears with several 'handles' showing, and the shape can be changed at any time by dragging these handles (illustrated). When the handles are visible, the shape is selected, and can be moved, altered or deleted without affecting any other shapes, even if other lines overlap. This is something that sharply distinguishes a vector drawing from a bit-map. There are three handles on a straight line, eight on a rectangle or circle.

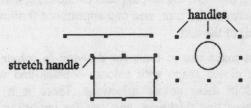

Clicking and dragging a handle will change the shape of an object, altering the length of a line, altering the width or height of a rectangles, or changing an ellipse into a circle. If an object is drawn with the Ctrl key held down the effect is to make a straight line horizontal, vertical or diagonal (depending on the direction of drawing), to make a rectangle into a square, and to make an ellipse into a circle. DrawPlus also uses a 'stretch handle' which can be dragged to move the whole object.

Another action that is very much a feature of a vector program is the Node Editor, whose icon is an arrowhead. When this is selected, a handle can be dragged to alter the shape of a selected object completely. For example, a square can be changed to a Maltese-cross shape or a circle into a sector. There is also a warp tool which can apply other forms of distortion to any selected shape.

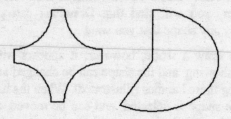

The remaining tools on the left-hand toolbar are more conventional. The *Text* tool can be clicked to produce a box into which you type your text. When you click the *OK* button on this box, the text appears on the page, and you can then determine the font, size and appearance (hollow, filled, coloured) of the text.

You can make use of tools for drawing in colour and for filling a closed shape with colour — black and white are included in these colour selections. There is a tool for determining line thickness, and one for importing existing drawings to add to your page (not replacing the existing draing). A *Rotate* tool allows you to rotate a drawing through any angle you want, and you can hold the Shift key down while using this tool if you want to rotate in 15° steps.

The top toolbar contains text tools for bold and italic text, along with left, centre and right alignment of text. These are followed by the usual Cut, Copy and Paste tools, and an Undo. The other tools in this set are for *Flip* (horizontal or vertical), bring in front or send to back (when objects overlap), *Group* (to place several objects into one selection), *Combine* (to make a stencil effect) and *Convert to Curves* (to change large-size text into a set of curves that can be edited like a drawing).

When you save a DrawPlus drawing, it can be saved in the normal DrawPlus format as a DPP file, or you can opt to use the Windows Metafile (WMF) format. WMF files can be imported into any word processor or DTP program, and can be read (though not necessarily written) by most other vector drawing programs. This makes DrawPlus particularly useful for editing WMF files and for creating your own drawings either from scratch or by basing the drawing on an imported WMF file.

Multimedia explained

5 Sound and numbers

What is sound?

Sound is a repeating pattern of changes of pressure in the air. These reach our ears and affect the eardrums, pushing them in and out and so creating signals in the nerves that lead to the brain. Because the pattern of a sound signal is a repeating one, we refer to it as a sound **wave**, and the similarity between sound waves and other waves is very strong — the illustration shows a graph of air pressure plotted against time to show the sinewave shape.

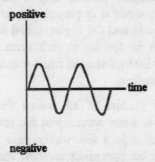

A microphone will convert these sound waves into electrical waves of the same shape. The simplest type of wave is the smooth up-and-down type, which technically is called a sine wave. It's the shape of wave that you create when you whistle, but the waves that musical instruments generate are much more complicated, of a more jagged shape, and the exact shape depends a lot on the type of instrument and how it is being played. That's one of the reasons a note played on a flute does not sound like the same note played on a clarinet, for example, or the same note played on a piano.

Amplitude and frequency

The amplitude of a wave means the height of its wave, and the peak amplitude is the maximum height the wave attains. For a water wave, you would measure this peak amplitude from the level of still water to the crest of a wave, and the same meaning is used for a sound wave and for its electrical form.

Since you can't normally see this, how does it affect you? The answer is loudness. The greater the amplitude of a sound wave, the louder it sounds to your ear — assuming that you can hear it at all. The ear is most sensitive to sounds in the range that we make for ourselves when we speak, and it's less sensitive to sounds outside this range. To put it another way, the voice and the ear were designed as a matching pair, and any other source of sound seems to have been an afterthought. This is why a recording of music sounds so feeble when it is played at a low volume — the low-pitched sounds and the high-pitched sounds simply are not loud enough for the ear to pick them up properly, and sound is equally badly distorted when it is too loud, as a visit to a disco will confirm.

There's another feature of all waves that affects sound. When you look at water waves, you see some that are slow-changing, so that only a few waves pass you in a minute. Others seem to be spreading rapidly, many more in the minute. The number of sound waves that passes a point in each second is called the **frequency** of the sound. The second is chosen as the measure of time because a minute is much too long. Sound waves are packed quite closely together, with several hundred typically passing your ear per second. This frequency of waves corresponds to what we call the *pitch* of a sound. A low pitch corresponds to a low frequency, and a high pitch to a high frequency.

The lowest notes of a church organ might have a frequency of about 30 waves per second, and the highest notes of a piccolo about 4000 waves per second. A frequency of one wave per second is called one hertz (after Heinrich Hertz, who discovered radio waves) so that the range of these musical sounds is from 30 hertz, written as 30 Hz, to

4000 Hz. To avoid writing a lot of zeros, 4000 Hz is usually written as 4 kHz, where the k means kilo, a thousand.

Your ear, if it's in perfect condition and never exposed to disco sound, can detect sounds in the range of about 30 Hz to 18 kHz. As you get older, though, the ear becomes less sensitive to the higher notes, and you end up with the top end of the range at about 7 kHz or less. You might think that since the highest note that a musical instrument can make is at about 4 kHz, this doesn't matter. Unfortunately, it does. A simple smooth sinewave at 4 kHz consists only of waves at this frequency, but a wave of any other shape is more complicated, and complicated wave-shapes also contain higher frequencies, called harmonics. It's the harmonics that make a sound richer, so that you can tell one instrument from another.

Stereo sound

There is a very noticeable difference between listening to music from a mono radio and listening to the same performance live. Quite apart from the sound quality, you are always aware that the sound from a mono radio comes from one small loudspeaker, whereas the live sound comes from a variety of instruments that are spread out in front of you.

You can't, however, overcome the difference by listening to the sound from two loudspeakers placed some distance apart and playing the same sound through each. The effect of using two loudspeakers like this is simply that you hear the sound coming from either one or the other, with no illusion of space. The essential feature of sound that creates the illusion of a wide-spaced source is that the loudspeakers should each play slightly different sounds. Even if you imagine that the musicians at each end of a stage are playing the same notes on the same instruments, it is quite impossible that the sound-waves which they are creating are identical in every way. Because of these slight differences, we can locate the positions of sound sources.

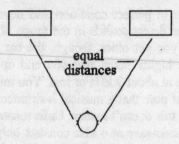

equal
distances

This is possible only if the loudspeakers are correctly placed. Ideally, the loudspeakers and your head should be arranged in a triangle, with the distances from your head to either speaker equal. If you have one speaker much closer than the other, you will hear mainly that speaker and the stereo effect is lost, as it is if one speaker is turned away or if there is some object between your head and one speaker.

Your sound card will either have an amplifier built into it, or will permit an external amplifier to be connected. If you use a high-powered external amplifier you can generate sounds that will strip the paint from the walls if you want it to. If the amplifier is built into the sound card it will usually be of a more modest output, because the power to operate it has to be taken from the computer.

One very common option is to use **active** loudspeakers, which means that the loudspeakers themselves contain amplifiers. This allows the power to be taken from the mains rather than from the computer, and it also allows you to use higher power. Another possibility is to record the sound on a stereo cassette so that you can hear it in all its glory later.

Waves and numbers

A microphone converts a sound wave into an electrical wave, a pattern that will repeat and which we call a waveform. The important point here is that the shape and frequency of the electrical wave is identical to the shape and frequency of the sound wave and the shape and frequency of the sound wave in turn is entirely responsible for the type of sound that we hear. In the past, we have recorded sound by trying to reproduce the shape of the sound wave in the form of a wave pattern on a plastic disc, as changes in magnetism on a strip of magnetic tape, or as changes in a pattern of light and dark on a cinema film.

All of these older ways of recording and reproducing sound are called analogue methods and they suffer from the same difficulties — it's just too easy to distort the shape of the wave, and too difficult to ensure that the full range of frequencies is recorded, free of the other disturbances that we call noise.

The alternative, that has only been possible for a comparatively few years, is to record and reproduce sound using *digital* signals, meaning that each wave is coded as a set of numbers. Because we can reduce errors in digital recording to zero, or as near as makes no difference, there are great advantages in using digital recording methods. No advantages are ever obtained without paying some sort of price, however, and the price to be paid consists of the problems of converting between wave shape (analogue) and number (digital) signal systems, and the increased rate of processing of data.

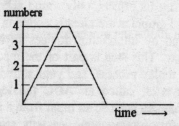

To start with, the electrical counterpart of the sound wave must be converted into digital form. What we have to do is to represent each part of the wave by a number that measures the size of the wave at that point. For example, we might end up with a set of number such as 0,1,2,3,4,4,3,2,1,0 to represent a wave with a roughly triangular shape.

This is a very crude shape, and the more numbers we can use for each wave, the closer the wave comes to its original pattern. To produce good coding of a sound wave we need to sample at a very high rate. For CD, the rate of sampling is around 44,000 samples per second, so that each second of sound is represented by 44,000 numbers. We can use lower rates for speech, and for sounds that do not need to be of high quality.

The numbers that are used are in binary code, using digits 0 and 1 only, as are used for all other computing work. It is generally agreed that modern digital audio systems should use a sixteen-bit number to represent each wave amplitude, so that the wave amplitude can be any of up to 65536 values. For each sample that we take of a wave, then, we have to record 16 digital signals, 0 or 1, and all 16 will be needed in order to reconstitute the original wave. For that reason, it is better to buy a 16-bit sound card rather than an 8-bit one, because its capability will be better matched to that of a CD.

Conversion

The conversion of analogue signals into digital form is the essential first step in any digital recording system for sound. Of all the multimedia effects, only sound needs this coding, because text and graphics are already coded in the computer, or can be coded by interfacing devices such as scanners, video boards, etc. This step is part of the recording process rather than the replay process, and your sound card contains a suitable converter, called an ADC (analogue to digital converter) so that you can use an input from a microphone or from other sources (gramophone, cassette recorder, etc.) to generate a sound file of numbers.

The CD player must contain circuits that convert digital numbers into an electrical wave, a digital to analogue conversion (DAC). This is also a difficult process, the reverse of the original conversion, and most of the improvements in CD players since their introduction in the early 1980s have concerned this conversion. Your sound card also contains the DAC section that will convert from a stream of numbers into an electrical wave that can be passed to the loudspeakers to form a sound wave.

The main snag with all multimedia sound is the size of files it uses. As an example, one minute of recorded sound on CD means that 60 x 44,100 samples are used. That's 2,646,000 samples, and with each sample consisting of 16 bits, that makes 5,292,000 bytes of numbers, some 5 Mbyte for just one minute of sound. This is a considerable under-estimate, because each byte is recorded along with error-correcting bits and made into a 14-bit number rather than just an 8-bit one. Storage of this size is available on the sizes of hard drives we use at present, but it takes a lot of memory, so that CD-sound quality is best reserved for CDs only; the sounds that we add into multimedia documents of our own, recorded on hard or floppy discs, cannot be allowed to take up this space.

Some relief is obtained by reducing the sampling rate. We don't, for example, need to sample 44 thousand times per second just for speech, and even computer music need not be of such a high quality. More importantly, we can use methods that have been known for a long time to reduce the size of numbers, using fewer digital bits in each number and also working on the numbers to reduce their range. All of this is very complicated, but the complications are hidden from you and carried out within the sound card. What it boils down to is that one minute of speech can be stored in about 600 Kbyte, a considerable improvement on the 5 Mbyte or more that would be needed at full CD quality.

Multimedia explained

These compression methods are, incidentally, also used on DAT and Sony Mini-disc systems.

Of course, if the sound is contained on a multimedia CD it will not take up space on your hard drive, so that the storage problem concerns you only if you record sounds for yourself or store files of sounds from other sources.

6 The sound card

Mixers

Your sound card, whatever the manufacturer, is provided with several inputs, so that the selection of an input or of more than one input is the first priority in using the sound system. Some of these inputs are provided as sockets (jack sockets) at the back of the computer, but the input from the CD-ROM drive is connected internally. In addition, these inputs are controlled by software, so that unless you have set up the software you are liable to hear nothing from the loudspeakers.

If you want to try out the CD player using the loudspeakers you must first of all enable the CD input to the sound card, and set the software volume control. You can listen to CD sound through earphones without using the resources of the sound card (other than as an interface for the data cable of the CD-ROM drive). Any output to the loudspeakers requires you to set controls, and the most important of these are provided in the form of a *mixer* panel.

The hardware version of a mixer is a box to which signal inputs and one output can be connected. By altering the mixer settings, you can control sounds from several sources and, if required, mix them together. Several inputs can each be set to whatever volume level you want, and a master volume control will then act to control the volume of the mixed sound. You can specify a microphone input to recording digital sound on disc, or inputs that will be used to provide sound directly from the CD player to the loudspeaker or to feed any other devices (such as a cassette recorder). There are controls also for muting inputs that you are not using, and sometimes for controlling treble and bass response.

Once again, the utilities that come with the Sound Blaster card are typical of those that are packaged with other sound

Multimedia explained

cards. The Sound Blaster provision consists of mixers that operate under MS-DOS and others that are specifically for Windows. Only the Windows software will be described here because you will be using Windows for all your multimedia work. Though the software that is described is specific to the Sound Blaster card, similar software will accompany any other sound card, so that the illustrations that follow should be useful to anyone who is working with sound for the first time.

The simplest mixer for Windows is obtained by double-clicking on the loudspeaker icon on the status bar of Windows 95. These icons are at the right hand side of the bottom line, and next to the time display. When you place the pointer over the loudspeaker icon, you will see the word *Volume* appear as a reminder. The Windows Mixer panel appears as soon as you double-click.

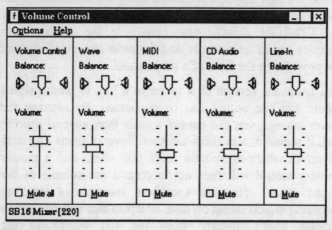

The screen display of the mixer is illustrated here showing five setting columns inputs listed as Volume, Wave, MIDI, CD Audio, and Line-in. The Volume Control set is a Master volume control that affects the output to the loudspeakers from all inputs.

- You do not need to use a Mixer in order to get sound from a **multimedia** CD, only when you use the DOS or Windows sound utilities or sound from a **music** CD. The defaults of the sound card will ensure that the loudspeakers play the sounds from a multimedia CD, but a music CD requires you to use the Mixer software.

The master volume setting can be left at about ¾ of its maximum until you have had some experience with the amount of sound — remember that there will also be a hardware volume control on one of the loudspeakers. To use the CD drive for music CDs, ensure that the volume control marked *CD Audio* is set to around half-way, and that the *Mute* box for this set is **not** ticked. You can tick the Mute boxes for Wave, MIDI and Line in if you are not currently using these inputs.

In addition to the control of volume through this Mixer and from the hardware, you can go directly to the master volume control from the Windows 95 Taskbar. Click the loudspeaker icon once, and you will see the small volume control panel appear. This is a floating panel that can be moved around on your screen so that it does not obstruct your view.

To play a music CD directly through the speakers, set the volume control on the mixer and on the hardware. Make sure that Windows 95 is set so that it will start playing when a CD is inserted. Try inserting a music CD, not forgetting to make sure that your loudspeakers are switched on. If you hear the music start, then *Autoplay* is enabled, and you do not need to alter the setting unless you particularly do not want this.

Multimedia explained

- Note that if the CD contains computer data as well as music, as some CDs do, the Autoplay action may not operate and you will have to start using the CD Player software as detailed below.

If there is no automatic play action when you insert a music CD, you need to use the CD Player software to play this and all other music CDs. Another option is to set Autoplay for all future music CDs, and this is done from Explorer.

To set AutoPlay, open Windows Explorer and then click View — Options — File Types. Find the *Type* called *AudioCD* and click the *Edit* button. The word *Play* should appear in the *Actions* list. Click on this word and then click the *Set Default* button.

If the word *Play* is not on the *Actions* list, click the *Edit* button on the panel that appears, and click in the *Actions* panel. Type the word *Play*, and then move to the *Application used to perform this action* panel. Use the Browse key to find the program CDPLAYER.EXE (usually in the C:\WINDOWS folder), and click. When this panel is complete, click on *Play* and *Set Default* as noted above.

- You can remove the AutoPlay action from the same menu by clicking on *Play* and then on the *Remove* button.

- You can also temporarily disable the AutoPlay action if you hold down the Shift key when you load in an audio CD.

If you want to play your CDs from the CD Player panel, you can run this from the Start button of Windows 95, going through the sequence Start — Programs — Accessories — Multimedia — CD Player. When this accessory starts it provides information on the audio CD that has been inserted, with a large (but not bright) display of time, and strips for *Artist*, *Title*, and *Track*. If no disc has been inserted the *Artist*

text will read: *Data or no disc loaded*, meaning that you
have either inserted no disc or that you have used a CD-
ROM with no music content. If no disc has been inserted,
the *Title* bar will read: *Please insert an audio compact disc*.

The icons next to the time display are the usual (video
recorder style) ones for play, pause, stop, previous track,
skip backwards, skip forwards, next track, and eject actions.

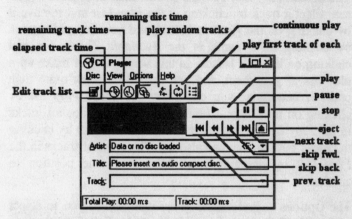

The icons above the timer panel are for *Edit play list*, *Show
elapsed track time*, *Show remaining track time*, *Show
remaining disc time*, *Play tracks at random*, *Continuous
play*, and *Play start of each track* respectively. These items
are also available from the *Disc*, *View* and *Options* menus.

Currently, music CDs do not contain track data, but you can
enter such data into a file on the hard drive that will be
loaded when your CD is identified. This is done through the
Play list when an audio disc has been loaded. When you
click on the icon or the menu item, you will see a panel that
contains lines marked *Drive*, *Artist* and *Title*, and you can
enter your own text into the *Artist* and *Title* lines. Below
these is space for the *Play List* and *Available Tracks*, used
for display only. You can enter information for each track on
the bottom line which will initially be marked as *Track 01*.

When you have typed data, click the Set *Name* key to add the information to the *Play List* and *Available Tracks* list.

• This data is stored on your hard drive, because you cannot write data to a music CD. The file on your hard drive can identify the CD that you have used, so that the list will appear each time this CD is inserted.

The default *Play List* consists of all tracks in sequence. You can select a track by clicking in the *Play List* and remove it by clicking on the *Remove* button, and you can add a track by clicking on a name in the *Available Tracks* list and clicking on the *Add* button. In this way, you can make up a play list of your own, and you can add a track more than once. If necessary, you can delete the entire *Play* list by clicking on the *Clear All* button. You can replace all tracks in the *Play List* (using the *Available Tracks* list) by clicking the *Reset* button. You can also alter the order of tracks in the *Play List* by dragging track titles from one position to another.

The Options —Preferences menu item allows you to select each of the following: *Stop CD Player on Exit, Save Settings on Exit* and *Show Tool Tips*. You can also change the default time of 15 seconds gap between tracks.

Once you have your music CD playing you can set volume with the master volume control, and also set treble and bass if these are provided on the hardware. If you have separate left and right volume controls on active speakers you should set them to about three-quarters of full volume, and do all your adjustments with the mixer Master volume control.

Other mixing

If your sound card is a SoundBlaster (or a clone) you will probably have the *Creative Mixer* program, or something similar, on your hard drive, in a Sound Blaster folder. This is a more complex mixer, with provision for other inputs, and is launched using Start — Programs — Accessories — Multimedia — Sound Blaster — Creative Mixer. The appearance is illustrated here.

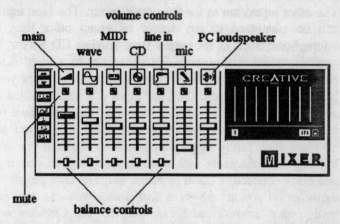

The Mixer panel contains one master volume control, and, as noted earlier, if this is at its minimum setting you will hear nothing from the loudspeakers. The small dots are mute switches, and clicking one of these will switch sound off or on, depending on the existing setting. You need also to look at the settings of the other volume controls. These are usually set to midway for all inputs, but if you see any set to zero, check that these are for inputs that you do not use. If the panel (as in the example) shows only icons for the inputs, placing the pointer on the button under the icon will produce an explanation for each icon.

The main differences in facilities are the provision of a microphone input and the ability to control the built-in loudspeaker of the PC. The microphone input can be used only if your sound card provided for a hardware microphone jack input (as most do), and this is particularly important if you intend to make use of programs for adding sound files to documents (as are provided with SoundBlaster boards) or if you want to use modern dictation software. Note that the

Multimedia explained

Line Input is not sensitive enough to be used with a microphone. The Master output should be muted before you connect the microphone.

The other inputs are as for the simple mixer. The Line input can be connected to any source of sound other than a microphone, such as the output from another CD player, a cassette recorder, a preamplifier connected to a vinyl disc player, a radio, or whatever source of audio signals you have. Note that because the Line input is a socket called a stereo jack (sometimes called a stereo jill) you may have to make or buy adapter cables if you want to connect to anything else. Tandy shops are particularly useful if you are looking for connectors with a stereo jack-plug on one end and other connectors (such as phono plugs or DIN plugs) at the other; if you are nowhere near a shop you can rely on mail order sources such as Maplin or Cricklewood Electronics.

- The Wave input is used with the WAV files of sound effects, and should be enabled if you make use of these effects.

If you make use of the Mic input, always start with the gain right down, because if the sound from the loudspeakers can be picked up by the microphone the result will be a loud squealing — this effect is called acoustic feedback and is the bane of amateur users of microphones. The microphone input is best avoided if the microphone is located anywhere near the loudspeakers; in any case you are unlikely to need to use the microphone direct to the loudspeakers for most applications. You should always mute the Master output when using the microphone.

The mixer is generally a preset device and is not used to start or stop sound sources. The CD selection of tracks, for example, will normally be controlled from the CD Player software which starts automatically if you have enabled AutoPlay. Other devices will be manually controlled

70

separately — a cassette recorder used at the Line input, for example, will inevitably have to be manually controlled.

Playing other sound files

SoundBlaster can work with files that contain speech or music in digitised form, compressed so that a reasonable amount will fit even on a floppy disc. You will find a selection of Microsoft WAV files in the folder C:\WINDOWS\MEDIA to give you something to listen to. An important point to remember is that most of the WAV files you can get in collections are very brief — single chords or sound effects. These are sometimes referred to as Voice files, but the sound can be music, speech or noise effects — anything at all.

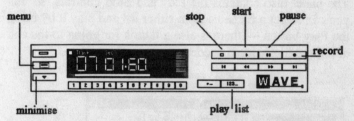

You can listen to these sounds, provided that the Wave input is enabled in the Mixer, by using the Creative Wave program, illustrated, or its equivalent for your sound card. For a SoundBlaster card, the Creative Wave panel is obtained using Start — Programs — Accessories — Multimedia — Creative Sound — Creative Wave.

The wave player will by default operate on a set of sound files in order, playing each one. The files are contained in a track list, and you can click on the Play button to find if there are any files currently in your track list. If your sound card is a SoundBlaster you may find the files s_16_44.wav and s_8_22.wav in the list, so that clicking on play will sound these two (a car starting, and a synthesiser chord) in sequence.

Multimedia explained

- The numbers indicate the conversion system. The file s_16_44 is recorded using 16-bit numbers sampled 44,000 times per second, full CD quality. The file s_8_22 is recorded using 8-bit numbers sampled at 22,000 times per second.

Playing all the files in a set is not always what you want, and there is a simple way of hearing selected sound files. Click the button for the play list (labelled 1.2.3), and look at the panel that appears. This contains the current play list on the left hand side, and has a space on the right hand side for files that you add by using the *Folder* button. Clicking this button allows you to browse for files, such as the C:\WINDOWS\MEDIA set.

The panel also contains the Play and Stop controls, so that you can select a filename from either list and play it by using the Play button — there is also a button for going to the end of a large file, seldom needed.

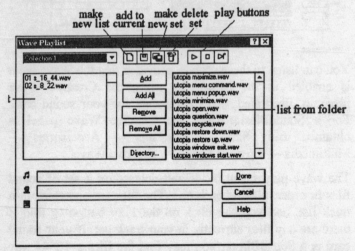

You can click the appropriate icon to start a new Collection — any existing files will be shown by default as *Collection 1*. With a new collection started, you can transfer files to the

Play List, then click the *Make New Set* icon to save these in a new collection, for which you have to provide a filename such as *Collection 2*. You might prefer to use a name that reminds you of what the files sound like.

Associating WAV files

The built-in Windows system allows you to associate sounds in WAV files with Windows events, and for events associated with Windows programs. The events that are covered for Windows itself are :

Asterisk	Close program	Critical Stop
Default sound	Exclamation	Exit Windows
Maximize	Menu command	Menu popup
Minimize	New mail notification	Open program
Program error	Question	Restore down
Restore up	Start Windows	

The association is done by using the Windows Control Panel and double-clicking on the Sound icon. This brings up the Sounds Properties panel as illustrated on the next page. You can click on a Windows event, then on a WAV file, and use the Preview button to check what the sound is like.

The Browse button allows you to look for sound files so that you can seek and listen to a sound you might need. In addition, you can import a complete sound scheme which contains sound files for each Windows event, avoiding the need to specify each one separately. When you click the arrowhead at the side of the Schemes box you will see a list that typically consists of:

Jungle	Windows default	Musica
No sounds	Robotz	Utopia

and you can click a scheme to apply it to all of your events. You can then override this for selected events if you want. Another option is to select a sound for each event that you want, and to save this as a scheme, clicking the Save As button and supplying a filename.

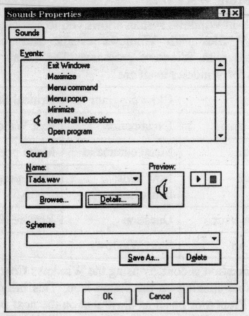

You can also provide a sound for Explorer when the Recycle bin is emptied, and for Sound Recorder and Media Player when these programs are opened or closed. Other programs that use Windows may also appear in the list — for example, the accounts program Quicken can have up to seven actions marked by sounds.

- Whether to have these sounds or not is very much a personal decision. Some users like them, others cannot stand them, and some of us like to use a few for items such as arrival of Email.

The sound card

Soundo'LE

This utility is in the same SoundBlaster set as the Creative Mixer Windows Mixer, and it provides, among other things, for playing the WAV type of files. To do this, you click on the File menu item and then on Open. You will see a folder listing, and you have to select the folder where your WAV files are stored — if they are in the same folder as Soundo'LE then no change is needed. The illustration shows the Soundo'LE panel with part of the Open file panel alongside.

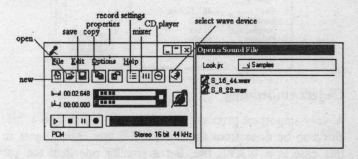

When you click on a name in the Open panel, you can use the Soundo'LE windows and click on the right-arrowhead (Play) button to start the playback. The actions of the buttons are illustrated above. The bars marked as L and R correspond to the volume indicator of a tape recorder, and the extent of illumination will vary as a waveform is played. If you have the example shown here of s_16_44.wav you can try this to hear the full stereo effect of an engine starting.

By using the *Properties* button, you can see the set of statistics for the wave. This example, the engine starting indicates how much memory is needed for digital sound — for this 16-bit sample using a sampling rate of 44 kHz, it needs 467,192 bytes of storage. The other options of Soundo'LE are illustrated by the captions on the buttons.

75

Multimedia explained

Note that you can provide a name and a description for a WAV file if you want to recognise it more easily.

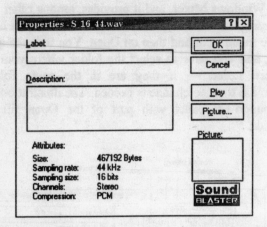

Object embedding

A very important process, embedding an object into a file, can also be done from the Soundo'LE box. The Object in this case is a WAVE file, but a smaller one than the car starting, the Chimes.WAV file from the C:\WINDOWS\MEDIA folder. This can be linked or embedded in text, such as text written using Windows Wordpad, Word (or any other word processor that uses Windows). There are two possible processes, Object Linking and Object Embedding, and the OLE that appears in the title of the utility is made up from the letters of Object Linking and Embedding.

Linking means that one file called Chimes.WAV will be linked to the Wordpad file, but will remain separate. Editing the Chimes.WAV file, or renaming another file to this name, will alter what is linked into the Wordpad file. If you embed the Chimes sound, its file becomes part of the WRITE file and is saved and loaded along with it, making the file that much bigger. The Chimes.WAV file is a separate entity and changes in that file do not affect the Write file.

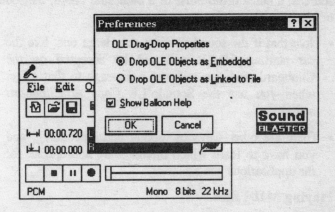

In the illustration, the Edit menu has been clicked to show the result of using Options — Preferences. The choice is to use Embedding or Linking, and in the example, Embedding has been used. If the OK button is now clicked, any sound file that is copied and pasted will be embedded.

To carry out this action, click on Edit — Copy Sound as an Object, which will place the sound file on the Clipboard. If we now open a Wordpad file, we can place the cursor where we want the sound file to appear. Now click on Edit and on Paste Special. The notice shows the file that is to be embedded, the source, which is the Soundo'LE program, and the cursor on Soundo'LE object (since you can select a variety of objects to paste in). The result of all this is an icon, a microphone symbol, that appears in the text to indicate a sound object.

Now when you are reading the text, double-clicking on the microphone icon will allow you to hear the sound (the default mixer settings always allow WAV files to be played, but if you have muted this channel there will be no sound). The sound can be more elaborate, and we shall look at ways of recording your own voice as a WAV file to place into text in this way. You can, of course, record sound from other sources, a quick drum burst or a orchestral chord, the sound of breaking glass, whatever you want.

- Note that if the sound file is a very large one, like the car starting file, it will not be accepted on the Clipboard, and you will get a message to that effect when you use the Soundo'LE *Copy to Clipboard* action.

- There are other ways of linking and embedding, and you have to learn which methods are appropriate for the applications you are using.

Playing MIDI files

MIDI files refer to files that use the standardised MIDI (Musical Instrument Digital Interface) format for connecting electronic instruments to computers, and such files bear the MID extension. Unlike the WAV files, which are digitised sound files, MID files are instructions to instruments, and these can be used by a utility program to send instructions to the Sound Blaster card, so playing the sounds. The MIDI files can be found on the C:\CREATIVE\CTSND\SAMPLE sub-folder.

- The advantage of using a MIDI file is that it can be very much smaller than a digitised sound file, even for a fairly long piece of music. The disadvantage is that you cannot generate MIDI files for yourself unless you have a keyboard with a MIDI connection, or software that allows the computer to generate MIDI files.

The MIDI player follows exactly the same pattern as the Creative Wave utility, so that a detailed description of the panel, following, is unnecessary. As for the Wave utility, you can click on File — Open to reveal a *Play* list, which the Midi Player will play in full. On the Play list panel, however, you can as before select an item and play it using the player buttons on the panel. The illustration shows the Creative Midi panel along with the Play list panel.

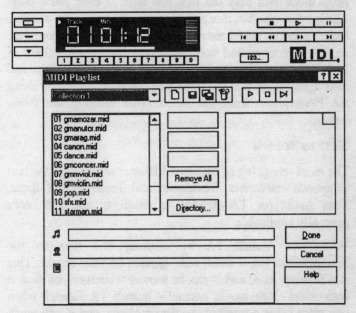

- Note that playing from the Play list will give only a short portion of the melody, because the Play list is of limited length. You can, however, use this to note the track number for a piece that you have sampled in this way, and which you can then play from the Creative Midi player panel.

The normal method of using Creative Midi is to compile your own track list, which might consist of only one item. If you delete all entries in a play list, and then use the Folder button to find the folder (such as SAMPLES) of MID files, these files can be opened and you will see the list on the right hand side of the panel. You can then select one or more files to add to the play list on the left, and these will be the files that are played.

Multimedia explained

You can opt for three playing modes, indicated by icons in the Creative Midi panel. The first is simple *Repeat*, which will play your list over and over again until you stop it. The *Intro* mode will play the first few bars of each piece only. Lastly, the *Shuffle* mode will play the tracks in random order. You can select more than one mode to be on together, so that if you wished you could play the first few bars of each item in random order, and keep playing them over and over again. Note that the Intro length can be altered by using the *Preferences* from the menu (after clicking the menu button).

Text to Speech

The most intriguing of the Sound Blaster utilities are the text to speech converters, TextAssist and Texto'LE. Of these, Text Assist (or TA Reader) is easier to use and more generally applicable.

When you launch TA by clicking this item in the SoundBlaster list, a small icon appears on your screen. This is a floating icon, and it can be moved wherever you find it convenient. You would normally launch TA Reader when you were using a word processing package, and it will work with any of the common packages, such as Microsoft Word.

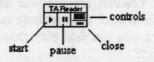

You can start the reading action by clicking the start button on the TA Reader toolbar, and by default this will start reading your text from the start. As an alternative, you can select some text, and when you use the Start button, only the selected text will be read. Once reading starts, the Start button changes to a square shape so that it can be used as a Stop button. The Pause button can be used if you want to stop the reading and later resume at the same place by clicking the Pause button again.

You can remove the TA Read toolbox by double-clicking on the small rectangle (close button), and clicking on the larger rectangle above it will bring up the *Controls* panel, controlling volume, rate of reading and pitch. This allows you to gain some control over the sound of the voice.

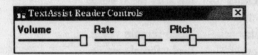

These controls are as much as you normally need for TA Reader, but they can be supplemented if needed by another menu, the *Reader* menu. On some applications that include a System menu, the item Reader will appear and can be clicked. On Windows 95, once TA Reader has been launched, you will find a TA Reader button in the Taskbar. Clicking this with the right-hand mouse button will bring up the usual Close, Maximise, Minimize type of menu, but with an additional item named Reader. Click this to see the Reader menu.

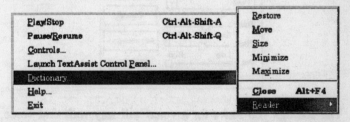

This menu contains several items that are simply alternative methods of carrying out the actions of the toolbar, but it also contains the *Launch Control Panel* and *Dictionary* items. These offer ways of giving you much more control over how TA reader operates.

Multimedia explained

This other Control Panel contains a list of names, representing speakers' voices. The default set is Betty, Dennis, Frank, Harry, Kit, Paul, Rita, Ursula and Wendy. The deepest man's voice is Harry, but Rita comes close in depth. The official descriptions of the voices are:

Paul	Standard male voice
Harry	Deep male voice
Frank	Older male voice
Dennis	Breathy male voice
Betty	Standard female voice
Rita	Deep female voice
Ursula	Light female voice
Wendy	Whispery female voice
Kit	Child voice

For each voice you can control the Rate, Pitch and Volume.

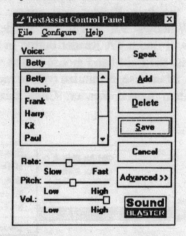

The settings you make for a voice will stay with that voice, so that you can associate a different voice for each application that you want to hear spoken. A typical applications list is: Cardfile, CCMail, Notepad, Progman, Winfile, WinWord, and Write. Note that several of these are Windows 3.1 applications that are no longer used in Windows 95, and modern replacements, such as WordPad for Write, will not work with TA Reader in its present form, though Word 8 is supported, as also is Notepad.

- If, after trying to get an unsuitable application to read, you get messages to the effect that *All Channels are in use*, close TA reader and restart it to clear the channels.

There are several advanced controls that can also alter the voices, and you obtain this set by clicking on the *Advanced* button. This brings up a set of controls, starting with a *Gender* choice. This, and the other controls are intended primarily to allow you to create a new voice, but they can also be used to alter the existing voices. The categories of voice characteristics are listed as *Head size*, *Smoothness*, *Richness* and *Laryngealization* (huskiness), and since no description in words can illustrate, try altering each of these in turn while a voice is speaking.

The other item in the Control Panel is *Dictionary*, and this is important because it controls how each word is pronounced. Though the pronunciation of words is generally quite good, there is certain to be some word that TA Reader has not encountered before and which will be mis-pronounced. Proper names are the main source of problems, closely followed by technical terms (like TA Reader, for example!).

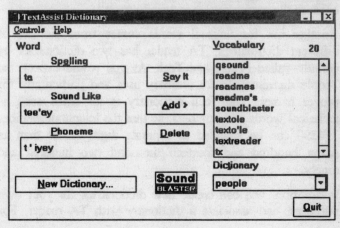

Multimedia explained

The dictionary is used after you have heard some text spoken and you have identified the words that are causing problems. Select one of these words, then click on the *Dictionary* option in the Control Panel list. You will see three items labelled as *Spelling*, *Sound Like* and *Phoneme*. The spelling space contains the word you have selected, and initially the Sound As space will be blank. The Phoneme space contains the characters that determine how a word is pronounced, and though this looks odd initially you will see after some practice how the groups of letters (phonemes) are sounded and how the apostrophe is used to separate groups.

In fact, you do not need to worry about the phonemes, because the *Sound Like* space is used to convey your interpretation of a sound. When you type characters into the Sound Like space, these will be converted into the appropriate Phonemes which will then appear in their own space. In the example I have typed tee'ay as a suitable sound-alike for TA, and I could also have used tee ay (with a space rather than the apostrophe), or tee a (with two spaces).

Once again, this is something that needs some experience along with a bit of trial and error, to get the precise pronunciation that you want for these words. You may find that remarkably few words need to be edited in this way, because the pronunciation is usually good.

Another aid for unusual words comes from the use of different dictionaries. TA reader has two dictionaries by default, called People and Tech. As you would expect, the People dictionary is for ordinary uses and particularly for proper names. The Tech dictionary is for items such as technical words and numbers, so that the telephone number 714290 can be sounded as separate digits rather than as seven hundred and fourteen thousand two hundred and ninety.

In addition, you can create new dictionaries for your own purposes, and associate a dictionary with TA reader. For example, if you want to make use of the Tech dictionary, open the Control Panel and on the menu click Configure — Dictionary. You can then select the Tech dictionary and click on the OK button to confirm this selection. This dictionary will continue in use until you change it.

- There are also minor changes that you can make, such as changing the colour of the TA reader toolbar.

Texto'LE

The Texto'LE utility is another form of reader, and it can also be configured to sing (there are examples supplied) if you like that sort of thing. Its main aim, however, is to allow you to create text that can be inserted into another document in Texto'LE form, meaning that when the icon is clicked the stored text will be spoken, and also viewed. Like TA reader, Texto'LE works well with some of the Windows 3.1 programs such as Write, and it will also work with the WordPad program of Windows 95, but is not best suited for Word 8 (Word 97).

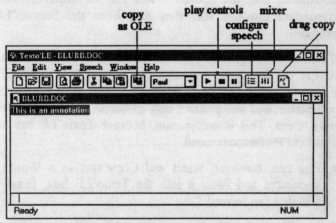

The Texto'LE window, illustrated here, has a menu bar and a toolbar, and its straightforward use can be illustrated using the tools only. Most of the tools are familiar, such as the new file, open file, save, magnify, print set, along with cut copy and paste. Texto'LE also uses a special copy command for sounded text, with its own icon, and this has been labelled *Copy as OLE* on the illustration. There is a corresponding icon labelled *Drag Copy*, and when selected text has been copied as an OLE object, this icon can be dragged to your Write or WordPad page to be embedded. The icon then appears in Write or WordPad as a picture.

- For some applications, including Word 97, this dragging action will not work, and you will have to use the Paste Special menu choice for that application. When Word 97 is used, Paste Special will paste in the sounded text in the form of a blank rectangle with no icon.

Once the text is pasted in, double-clicking on it will produce the text in its Texto'LE window, and the spoken version (assuming your sound card is correctly set up and the loudspeakers switched on). This insert is saved with the document, and the spoken insert can be used in other computers provided that they also have the Soundo'LE program.

Texto'LE can use only plain text files, the type recorded as ASCII or Text type, and with the extension letters TXT. Files of the DOC type from Microsoft Word are not acceptable, and will produce only gibberish if you attempt to open them. This is unfortunate, because Texto'LE has an excellent Preferences menu.

- You can, however, select and Copy text in a Word document and Paste it into the Texto'LE box, from which it can be read.

As the illustration shows, you can opt for *Clause* or *Word* punctuation. Word punctuation uses a pause after each word, which can be useful if you are taking notes or having difficulty with the sound of the speech. If you specify *All punctuation*, the speaker will use the words comma, semicolon, period, and so on, to emphasise where the punctuation marks are. The most useful option is the default of *Clause speech* mode and *Some punctuation*, as illustrated.

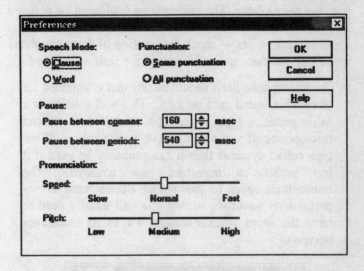

A particularly useful feature is that you can specify the pause time for a comma and a period (full stop), and the defaults of 160 ms and 540 ms are sensible. The unit used here is the millisecond, one thousandth of a second, so that these times are 0.16 seconds and 0.54 seconds respectively. The remaining options are for *Speed* and *Pitch*.

Microphone recording

Both the Windows and the SoundBlaster utilities provide for recording short sound files for yourself, using the WAV format, and whatever compression you specify. Before you can use these, you must invoke the mixer to ensure that the correct input (Line or Microphone) is selected, preferably at full gain. If you need Microphone input you must use the

Multimedia explained

Creative Mixer, because the simple Windows mixer is not set up for a microphone input.

The input can be any of these provided, but for the sake of explanation we'll concentrate on the most difficult input to use, the microphone. The microphone lead must be plugged into the sound card (be careful if your sound card has several identical jack points — check the position of the microphone input with the diagram in the manual for your sound card.

- The microphone itself should be one that is intended for use with a sound card on a PC. This will usually be a fairly sensitive type of microphone called an electret microphone. If you already have a microphone of the type called dynamic then it can probably be used if it has suitable a miniature jack connector. The microphone input to the Sound Blaster card is not particularly sensitive, so that you will usually need to have the input volume control set to its maximum position.

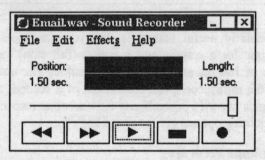

The Windows sound recorder is illustrated here, at the end of a 1.5 second recording. This recorder is obtained by using Start — Programs — Accessories — Multimedia — Sound Recorder, and it uses the usual set of conventional tape-recorder symbols complete with the (round dot) recording control.

To record from the microphone:

1. Make sure that the Mixer output is de-selected (no dot). If this is not done the sound input at the microphone will be amplified and output through the speakers, and this will usually cause a feedback whistle.

2. Make sure that Mic input is enabled, and the Mixer is set for maximum Mic input volume.

3. Bring up the Windows Sound Recorder. Click Edit — Audio Properties and set the Preferred Quality for Recording to Radio Quality. This is a reasonable compromise between high (CD) quality and low (telephone) quality.

4. Prepare the microphone, and click on the record dot on the Sound Recorder. The seconds counter will start and you can make the sounds you want to record.

5. The display shows an oscilloscope-type graph of sound amplitude. Ideally, your maximum amplitude should fill the height of this window — this may not be possible for a microphone recording.

- Keep it short — the display shows the time but gives you no indication of how large an amount of memory you are using.

When you have finished, click on the square *Stop* button on the Sound Recorder. Now use the File menu to click on *Save As* and name your WAV file. You can rewind (press on the << icon, and then on >) to hear the sound replayed. If you hear nothing, check that your mixer settings have enabled the wave output.

- You should store your WAV file in the Windows/Media folder so that it can be easily accessed for associating with Windows actions.

Multimedia explained

- When you have more experience, you can choose one of the compression systems that is offered. The default is PCM, but you can also use GSM 6.10, IMA ADPCM, Microsoft ADPCM, and MSN Audio.

It is very difficult to make satisfactory recordings from a microphone, and considerable practice is needed before you find the correct microphone position (try around 4" from your mouth) along with suitable settings for recording and playback volume controls. It is usually better to speak across the microphone than directly into it, and you will have to speak fairly loudly.

You can edit the results, particularly if you start or end with a second or more of silence. By stopping playback at the critical point you can opt to use *Delete before Current Position* or *Delete after Current Position* so as to eliminate these pauses (which can consume a lot of storage space).

The least-satisfactory aspect of Windows Sound Recorder is the time and the amount of hard drive activity it takes to get started on a recording. By the time it starts you are either unprepared or you have gone off the whole idea. It is very difficult to achieve reasonable sound quality, and you have to be careful to remember to reset (rewind) the recorder before you make another attempt. On the merit side, you have more control over the recording, with the ability to add sound into an existing file, add echo, alter the speed (increase or decrease, affecting pitch)

You can also use the Soundo'LE utility of SoundBlaster which seems to give much better results than Sound Recorder. Using the maximum volume setting with Radio quality produces a reasonable quality of sound with not too much effort. The menus of Soundo'LE allow you easy access to the Mixer and to fixing settings of gain, sampling rate and compression method. Editing is not quite so simple, and the Wave Editor is started by clicking on this option from the Edit menu of Soundo'LE.

The Editor shows the sound as a waveform, and allows you to select a portion that can be cropped to remove silences. The File menu is used to open the WAV file. Initially the sound wave appears below the editing box, and you have to use View — Fit Wave in Window to see the view shown here. You can then select a portion of the display by dragging the cursor, and cut or delete it as you please.

This Editor is ideally suited to more advanced work with sounds, beyond the scope of this book, but the illustration shows that it can be used in a very simple way to remove a silent portion of a wave by selecting this portion and deleting it, just as if it were text or graphics.

silent part selected for deletion

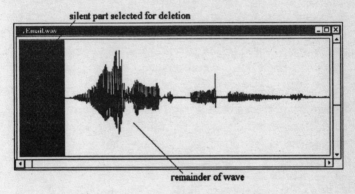

remainder of wave

7 Adding Hardware

The sound card

If you have bought a computer that does not feature sound, and you want to add this facility, there is no great problem about installing the sound card for yourself, particularly on the modern type of PC machine. If your PC runs Windows 95, and is stated to be compatible with Plug'n'Play (PnP) devices, then installation is easy. For an old machine, you need instructions that are relevant to the age of the machine, and you would be better to try to buy a sound card of about the same age as the computer. The descriptions that follow assume that you are using a reasonably modern machine. The main decision is then whether to try to use an assortment of bits and pieces that you have seen advertised, or to use an add-on sound package.

A typical sound-card package will consist of the card or board itself, two (sometimes three) loudspeakers (not always of high quality) and (sometimes) a microphone. There is usually a MIDI interface either built into the card or available as an add-on, and additional software such as the Creative software we have featured earlier in this book which can be used to replace or supplement the software supplied in Windows 95/98. The stereo amplifier that is needed for a reasonable sound output is almost always contained in one of the loudspeakers (the right-hand one). The card is plugged into a slot inside the PC, and will need to be connected to the CD-ROM drive if you have one (or are installing one at the same time).

In selecting an add-on sound system, you should consider the quality of sound from the loudspeakers before anything else, because you may find it difficult to live with poor-quality sound. The lower-cost packages are certain to omit a microphone, and, more important, may omit software that allows sound files to be compressed so as to take up less disc space. The software is the next important item, and should be suitable for your requirements. One standard item, as we have seen, should allow you to add narration to documents or images, and another piece of software that is often included is a voice synthesiser which will read text from a spreadsheet or a word-processed document (usually contained in the Windows clipboard). This latter application can often be, on its own, justification for adding a sound card because it has indisputable business uses — it can be very useful, for example, for proof-reading letters or other text if you don't want to be watching a screen at the time. Some cards come only with software suitable for games, and should be avoided if you have serious applications in mind.

Installing a sound card

Add-on devices are fitted to a PC machine by using the plug-in slots on the motherboard inside the casing. Looking at the back of your computer you will see the existing set of connectors along with some metal blanking plates that cover the vacant slots.

Turn the power off, and wait for a minute. Remove the power input cable from the computer, and then remove the cover so that you can see inside. When you open the casing you will see the other side of the blanking plates, and for each blanking plate there will be a 'slot', a set of electrical connections in the form of a long thin socket. The metal blanking plate is unscrewed from the rear of the casing so that connections can be made to whatever card you plug in, and the same

hole for
retaining screw

notch to hold
lower end

fixing screw is used to hold the new card in place. Boards (or cards) come in several types, and for a modern machine the two important types are ISA and PCI. The ISA (industry-standard architecture) slots will accept cards of the older type, right back to the type used on the first-ever PC machines. The PCI slots are used on Pentium PC computers, and are incompatible with the older type. Sound cards fit into the ISA type of slots.

- Some 386 and 486 computers were fitted with VLB slots along with the ISA type, and these are incompatible with the other two slot types.

Before you can think of installing a sound card, you need to check that there is room inside the machine — modern computers do not provide many ISA slots. If your computer contains only the usual disc interface card and a video card, with nothing else, fitting the sound card should be simple and straightforward, because these other cards use the PCI slots. If, however, you have items such as extra parallel ports installed these will use ISA slots. If you have no spare ISA slots you will have to decide which card to remove in order to fit your sound card. The illustration shows the shape of a typical sound card.

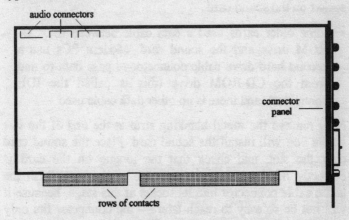

audio connectors

connector panel

rows of contacts

- At one time, sound cards had to be configured, and contained sets of connectors called *jumpers* that needed to be adjusted. If you are installing a modern Plug'n'play card on a modern Pentium computer, there will be no jumpers and no need for adjustments. If you are installing an old type of sound card on an old machine, consult the manuals for details of how to set the jumpers.

Your sound card will have a set of internal connectors (audio connectors) that connect with the CD-ROM drive. A special cable is needed, and this is another good reason for buying a combination package rather than piecemeal. The usual connectors are labelled as Mitsumi, Sony and Panasonic, and one of these will be suitable for the type of CD-ROM drive you are using. If this connection is not made, you cannot play audio CDs through your sound system, except by way of the front socket on the CD-ROM drive.

Now take a look at where you will insert the sound card, remembering that this must be one of the long ISA slots. Place the card temporarily over the slot (do not push it into the slot yet) and check that the little audio cable from the CD-ROM drive will reach. Plug the data connector into the socket on the sound card.

• Some older cards used a data cable between the CD-ROM drive and the sound card. Modern PCs use a second hard drive cable connector to pass data to and from the CD-ROM drive (this is called the IDE connector), and there is no other data cable used.

Now remove the metal blanking strip at the end of the slot where you will install the sound card. Place the sound card over the slot, and check that the tongue on the card is correctly lined up with the aperture of the slot. Push the audio cable connector into its socket at this stage, because it will not be so easy to reach later — the connector fits only one way round. Gently push the card down, rocking it slightly to help open the spring contacts, until the card slips into its holder. You can now clamp the card into place with the screw that was used to hold the blanking strip — do not force the card into position or over-tighten the screw because the purpose is only to ensure that the card does not pop out of place.

You can now replace the cover of the computer and turn the machine so that you can see the connectors on the rear of the sound card — the illustration shows a typical set.

You can now plug in connectors to the rear of the sound card, from the outside of the computer. The main connector is for the loudspeakers and this connection is made by way of a jack plug pushed into the appropriate socket.

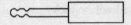

Check with your sound card manual before you make this connection, because there are usually several connection points all of which are jacks (sometimes called jill sockets).

The loudspeaker jack is of the stereo type so that both speakers are connected by inserting one jack. If you don't intend to use speakers you can plug stereo headphones into the same jack, but remember that the jack fitted to the Sound Blaster is the 3.5 mm size, and your headphones, unless they are of the Walkman type, may use a ¼" jack. Suppliers such as Tandy or Maplins can supply adapters to link a ¼" jack plug to a 3.5 mm socket.

If you connect to an existing hi-fi system rather than to loudspeakers which were part of a bundled kit, you will have to sort out connections for yourself. You will need an adapter which has a stereo jack plug (or whatever connector the sound card uses) at one end and a DIN plug or phono plugs (whatever your hi-fi needs) at the other.

Multimedia explained

The other connectors for the sound card may not be needed at present. These are for sound inputs, games, and MIDI connections. The microphone connector is usually a 3.5 mm jack, and is normally a mono jack rather than a stereo one. If you have a microphone (take a look at the low-cost dynamic microphones in the Maplin catalogue) then it can be plugged in now — this does not interfere with other inputs because the software allows you to control which input is being used.

The Line connector allows you to connect to devices such as a cassette recorder, an external CD player (if you have no CD-ROM drive), a synthesiser or the output of a radio. If you connect to the output from the pre-amplifier stage of a hi-fi you can select the sound source with the pre-amplifier. As before, you will need adapters, because the connectors on these sound sources will not be jacks.

- Remember that you cannot control with software an external CD player that is connected through the line input.

The large connector on the sound card is a 15-pin D-type which serves for both games (a joystick connection) and MIDI interface. On the Sound Blaster card a single joystick can be plugged in, and dual joysticks can be connected by way of a splitter cable. The MIDI interface needs additional hardware on some Sound Blaster cards and this is packaged with suitable software for managing MIDI files.

Once the sound card is installed you can adjust the position of the cables so as to ensure that none of them is likely to be trapped when the lid is closed. If you have already installed the CD-ROM drive then all the hardware work is now completed and you can shut the lid. What follows is software, and the usual pattern of software is of one installation program which installs short programs (drivers). In addition to adding drivers, the installation program will alter two important files, AUTOEXEC.BAT and CONFIG.SYS. Unless these alterations are made (and the installation program for CD-ROM will already have made some alterations) then there is no prospect of any sound output from the sound card.

- The use of sound from DOS is rather more complicated than from Windows, and is not covered in this book because most multimedia users will work exclusively from Windows 95 or Windows 98.

Unwanted noise

This, particularly in the form of hiss, is a common complaint with inexperienced users of any sound system when you try to make recordings for yourself. Any recording system works well only when the volume of sound input is high enough. This is because all electronic circuits generate some noise, which is heard as a hiss when a recording is played back with the volume control set to a high level. Whatever you are recording should be at a high enough level to drown the hiss, so that the most obvious way to avoid hiss on playback is to make the recording at as high a level as is possible. Distortion will be caused if the recording level is too high, so you have to find a suitable level for yourself. Software which controls inputs will always provide an AGC action — this sets the volume control automatically so that the recording level is kept high enough to avoid hiss but low enough to avoid distortion.

- The low sensitivity of the microphone input to the Sound Blaster card makes noise a problem on recordings unless you speak close to the microphone and with a loud voice.

Another source of unwanted noise is the use of unwanted inputs. If all the inputs to the sound card are connected, there may be interfering signals from the other inputs, and even if no connections are made there can be noise signals at these inputs. Use the Mixer software, see earlier, to ensure that only the wanted inputs are used. If you encounter hiss on

Multimedia explained

sound that you have not recorded for yourself, use the Treble Cut control of your hardware to reduce this. On some games, sound was recorded using 8 bits only, and this sound will inevitably cause hiss which can only be reduced, not eliminated.

Noise will also be a problem if you are using too high a volume level on playback. This is particularly likely if you have several sets of volume controls. For example, if you have the Master volume control on the Mixer, the CD volume control on the mixer and the hardware volume control(s) on your sound card or active speakers all set to maximum, noise in the form of hiss is almost inevitable, and when you play sound it will be much too loud.

CD-ROM Drives and specifications

At the time of writing, fast CD-ROM drives (typically ×16 to ×24) were quite inexpensive. You should avoid older slow drives that are offered as a bargain, because these are not likely to be of the Plug'n'play type, and can be a headache to get working. In addition, most multimedia discs are now designed round the faster units. The illustration shows the shape of a typical modern drive which fits into a standard half-height 5.25" bay as was once used for the older type of floppy disc drive.

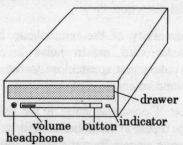

The front panel contains the end of the CD drawer, an operating button, a headphone socket and volume control, and an activity indicator light. When a CD is to be inserted, you press the button and an inner tray slides out to allow the CD to be placed on a recess. When this inner shelf is re-inserted by pressing the button again, the disc will start to spin, and if you have enabled *AutoPlay*, you will see a screen display for a multimedia CD or hear the sound if this is an audio CD.

• Note that you need software to replay audio CDs, because the CD-ROM player has no hardware controls for such tasks as finding tracks, making selections or even starting and stopping. The only operation built in to the hardware is to eject the tray and return it.

Because most CD-ROM drives for internal fitting (meaning that they fit inside a computer in the same way as a conventional disc drive) are so similar, a typical description will serve to show how to go about this task. The software that accompanies the drive will usually be on a floppy, and will have running instructions on its label.

Installing a CD-ROM drive

In order to add an internal CD-ROM drive, you need to have a 5¼ inch drive-bay free. You should preferably also have a sound card installed if you want to use multimedia. The drive bays are the deep horizontal slots in the front of the casing of the computer, and when they are not in use they are covered by metal or plastic. On some machines the hard drive will be fitted in the lowest of the drive bays, but many modern cases locate the hard drive elsewhere in the casing. Unless you have specified a machine with other drives (such as a tape drive), there will probably be no other 5¼ inch units, so that all the bays of this size will be free for use

Do not assume that a CD-ROM drive will be provided with mounting brackets at exactly the same places as the drive-bay, though these positions are usually standard on PC clones. You should enquire when you order the drive what provisions are made for mounting it on the style of casing you are using.

- Most modern CD-ROM drives use an IDE type of connector that is provided on the hard drive cable. Check when you order a drive that is uses this type of connection (some use the SCSI system which is suitable only if your computer uses this type). Check also that your computer uses the EIDE system that allows more than one type of drive to be connected to the hard drive cable, and that the existing cable has a spare connector.

The drives are provided with mounting holes at the side, rather than the sprung pads that are used for magnetic disc drives. This makes it easy to fasten them into the standard type of bay which has slots cut in the sides for the mounting bolts. The drive bay normally has slots at the sides to allow for to-and-fro adjustment of a drive, and two sets are usually provided at different heights in the bay. These should fit the mounting positions of the CD-ROM drive without any problems.

The fastening is by way of small bolts fitting into the threaded holes. In no circumstances should you consider drilling the casing of a CD-ROM drive in order to mount it in any other way. You should also handle the drive by its casing, not holding its weight on any other points. In particular, avoid handling the connector pins at the rear of the drive. Be careful also not to lose the bolts, because they are not easy to replace.

Installation work

Before you start, check the drive package to make sure you have all of the mounting bolts, any adapter that is needed, cables (which may be packed with the sound card, but are more usually with the CD drive) and instructions. The power cable for the CD-ROM drive will be one of the existing set that is used for the hard drive and floppy drive. The power supply usually is fitted with six or more connectors so that one should certainly be spare, but check that it will reach the CD-ROM drive. You may need to cut one of the plastic cable-ties in order to pull the cable connector over so that it reaches the drive.

Check also that you have the necessary tools — a Philips screwdriver (possibly also a plain-head type) and a pair of tweezers are usually needed. The bolts are either 6-32 UNC x 0.31 ($^5/_{16}$") or metric M4 x 0.7-6H. If you need spare UNC bolts you will need to contact a specialist supplier, but the M4 metric types can be bought from electronics suppliers such as the well-known Maplin Electronics or RS Components.

At this stage, check with your manual for the CD-ROM drive if any jumpers or switches need to be set. The modern Plug'n'play system usually ensures that no such settings are necessary, and if you see jumpers or switches this might indicate an old model of drive. Remember that once the drive is in place, any adjustment points will be impossible to reach. Use tweezers to manipulate these devices.

Switch off the computer if it has been running, wait for a minute, and remove the main cable. Open the cover — some hinge out of the way, others need to be removed completely.

You can now install the CD-ROM drive. Handling the drive by its casing, place it into the mounting bay and check that the slots in the mounting bay match with the fixing positions in the drive. Take the unit out again, and insert the audio cable connector. This is a small 4-way connector, smaller than a telephone connector, which fits only one way round. Feed the cable through the mounting bay first, and then push in the drive unit gently.

Place the bolts by hand and tighten evenly. Check as you tighten the bolts that the drive is positioned correctly. The

Multimedia explained

CD-ROM drive will need to have its front panel flush with the computer front. Installation is not a particularly skilled operation, though experience with a Meccano set as a child is helpful.

Problems arise only if the mounting pads on the drive do not correspond with openings in the bay, or if you manage to lose a mounting-bolt. A mounting-bolt that falls inside the drive casing or the computer casing can usually be shaken out, or you can use the flexible grabs that are sold in tool shops. Do not use a magnet to retrieve a bolt from a disc drive casing (don't bring a magnet anywhere near a computer at any time). Do not attempt to make use of other bolts, particularly longer bolts or bolts which need a lot of effort to tighten (because they are ruining the threads in the drive). It is better to mount a drive with only three bolts rather than to add one bolt of the wrong type. There is no great amount of strain on these fastenings.

There are two sets of cables required for any CD-ROM drive, the power cable and the data cable set. The power cable is a simple four-core (thick wire) type with a four-way connector (some drives use only two connections of the four). This connector is made so that it can be plugged in only one way round. The same power cable is used for floppy drives and for hard drives, and modern 386 and 486 machines usually provide four or five plugs on the cable. The plug is a tight fit into the socket and usually locks into place. The socket for the power plug is obvious. The small data cable is for audio signals and will connect to a corresponding socket on the sound card.

The main data cable that connects from the IDE controller card to the CD-ROM drive is of the flat type, usually ending in a 40-pin plug at the CD-ROM drive end. This plugs into the matching connector on the controller card at one end and into the drive at the other, with no complications. Look for one strand of the cable being marked, often with a coloured or speckled line, to indicate pin 1 connection position. This makes it easier to locate the connector the correct way round. Do not assume that one particular way round (such as cable-entry down) will always be correct, or that a card connector will have its pin 1 position the same way round as it is on another card. Check carefully with illustrations in the leaflets that come with the units.

• Remember that if you have bought different units in different places there will be no guarantee that the connectors will match — this is why you are strongly recommended to buy a package from one source.

Now tighten up any mounting screws that you may have had to loosen so as to slide the CD-ROM drive into place. Check everything again — it's always easier to check now than later. Replace the cover of the computer, push in the power cable connector, and get ready to install the software.

Software

When a CD-ROM drive, whatever the type, has been installed so that all the relevant steps described above have been carried out, you can install the software that will make it work. Simply installing the CD-ROM drive and connecting up will not activate it because the computer needs a program running to control the drive and without the program, a driver, nothing happens. Make sure once again that all cables are plugged into their correct places and the lid shut, then switch on the power. If the monitor is separately powered make sure that it is plugged in and switched on. You should hear the high-pitched whine of the hard disc drive motor start and settle to its final speed and the machine should boot up normally. Before you start installing software, you can check that the turntable for the disc will eject. Press the eject button — and keep your hand out of the way as the tray pops out. Pressing the button again or pressing the tray gently in will make it wind in all the

Multimedia explained

way. This checks that the power supply to the CD-ROM is working, and once the software is installed all should be well.

The software consists of short drivers and will be supplied on a 3.5" disc. The disc will usually contain a README.TXT file and you should print this out as soon as possible, preferably **before** you install the software. As usual, this installation disc is placed in the A: drive, and it often carries brief instructions about its use.

The usual method is that you use the Start button of Windows 95/98 and then click on RUN. You then type A:\INSTALL (and then click on the OK button). Some software may require you to type A:\SETUP rather than A:\INSTALL — check with the leaflets that are packed with the drive. The rest of the process is then automatic.

- The really valuable information you need is the letter that will be used for the CD-ROM drive. This is usually D, but a higher letter will be used if you have any other drive that uses the letter D. It does not matter what letter is used, but you have to know what it is to be able to type in this information for software that used CD-ROM. You will usually see the letter in one of the panels that appears during installation.

Appendix A

The Public Domain Software Library (PDSL)

The PDSL exists to supply discs of programs that are virtually free for inspection, and the only cost to the user is the cost of copying the discs. PDSL can supply on a range of disc formats, and in some cases are virtually the only source of software for some exotic machines. All of the programs are either public domain or shareware. The stock has now been extended to include a set of CD-ROMs.

Documentation for each program is included as a disc file, usually with the DOC or TXT extension. There are many other suppliers of the same software items, but PDSL was among the first and provides a more full description of the contents of its discs. Like all other reputable PD and Shareware dealers, it also warrants, as far as is possible, that none of its software is pirated commercial software. PDSL is a member of the Association of Shareware Professionals.

A **public domain** program is one for which the author has surrendered all copyright, allowing the program to be copied freely by anyone who wants to use it. Many public domain programs are short utilities, and you would normally buy them on a disc that contained 20–50 such items. Other PD programs are distinctly longer, and though some of them do not have the polish of a commercial program they must have represented hundreds of hours of effort. The writers are often professional programmers working at a hobby topic and glad to share the results of their efforts.

Shareware is a rather different concept. The author of a shareware package is hoping to sell directly to the user, cutting out the huge overheads that are involved in having a program manufactured and distributed commercially. In the early days of shareware, the programs were full working versions, and the poor response by way of payment was a severe blow to authors, particularly in the UK, where users were always less willing to pay for programs than in the USA where the idea started.

It has become more common now for shareware programs to be limited to some extent, perhaps running on only a single video card, or unable to use a printer or to create disc files. The user can run the program to a sufficient extent to see if it is likely to be useful, and will have lost very little if it is not. Registering with the author can be done directly (it is easy to phone an author in the USA and quote a credit card number) or by way of the PDSL if this can be arranged. The current catalogue contains many programs of particular interest to DTP users, including clip-art, graphics conversion and editing programs, printer utilities, vector-line drawing programs, etc.

Registration can often be done at various levels, with the minimum level entitling you to a copy of the program with all limitations removed. The documentation will be, as for PD items, as a DOC or READ.ME file on the disc. At a higher fee, a full manual is provided and the user is entitled to upgrades at nominal cost.

The address for PDSL is:

Winscombe House,
Beacon Road,
Crowborough,
E. Sussex, TN6 1UL
Tel: (01892) 663298
Fax: (01892) 667473

Appendix B

Specialised Suppliers
Electronics components and kits

Maplin Electronics plc,
P.O. Box 3, Rayleigh,
Essex SS6 8LR
Tel. for Sales: (01702) 554161
Tel. for Enquiries: (01702) 552911
Fax: (01702) 553935

Cricklewood Electronics Ltd.,
40 Cricklewood Broadway,
London NW2 3ET
Tel: 0181 452 0161 or 0181 450 0995
Fax: 0181 208 1441

Multimedia systems and packages

Evesham Micros Ltd.,
Unit 9, Richards Road,
Evesham,
Worcs. WR11 6TD
Tel: (01386) 765500
Fax: (01376) 765354

SMC Computers,
253–257 Farnham Road,
Slough,
Berks. SL2 1HA
Tel: (01753) 550333
Fax: (01753) 524443

Manufacturers

Creative Labs. (UK) Ltd
Delta House,
264 Monkmoor Road,
Shrewsbury,
Shrops. SY2 5ST
Tel: (01743) 248590
Fax: (01743) 248199

Appendix C

Printing out a README file

Many items of hardware and software now dispense with manuals, and rely on suplying README files, particularly on CD. Often a README file is too long and too detailed to take in when you read it on the screen, and you would prefer to use a printed version. There are several methods of achieving this, all of which start with requiring you to have a printer connected to the LPT1 port, switched on, and ready on line.

From Windows, switch to Windows Explorer. You can select the file by clicking on it, and then click on the *File* menu, and on the *Print* item. There will be a message of confirmation and by clicking on the OK box of this message you will start the printing process.

The only snag is that some README files may use more characters per line than your printer is set for. You may be able to set the printer for a smaller font, which is the easiest way of tackling the problem, but another option is to use a word-processor such as Windows WordPad or Windows Notepad, to read the file and convert it into a page format that suits your printer. A bonus of using this method is that you can print what you want, cutting out unnecessary information. Windows Notepad will read only the smaller files, but Write can tackle larger ones. If you have Microsoft Word, it will make an even better job of dealing with large README files.

Appendix D

Glossary of Terms

- To save space, this list is confined to the terms that are applicable mainly to multimedia work, covering text, sound and graphics. Words that are used purely in connection with Windows or other aspects of computing are not included.

256 Colours: The minimum requirement for a VGA screen driver if multimedia packages are to be enjoyed fully. This will require a video memory of at least 1 Mbyte. Modern machines should all be equipped with suitable hardware, but may not possess the necessary driver software.

80486: The minimum standard of machine on which multimedia can be enjoyed. Faster machines are desirable.

A-D: Analogue to digital conversion, required to convert a sound (or other waveform) into a digital signal that can be recorded and processed digitally.

Active loudspeakers: Loudspeakers, one of which contains an stereo amplifier and power supply, so that they can work with small input signals, requiring no power from the computer nor any amplification in the sound card. Such loudspeakers can also be used along with portable cassette players in place of earphones.

AGC: Automatic Gain Control, a system used to prevent overloading of an amplifier. The use of AGC will help to prevent hissy recording (due to the input being too low) or gross distortion (because the input is too high) and should always be used when a microphone is the input source.

Airbrush: A tool used in painting programs to give an effect of speckled colour rather than solid lines or areas.

A-Law/MU: A system for compressing digital sound files.

Multimedia explained

Alignment: The matching of two lines or points so as to be at the same distance from an edge or another point. Used of ruler guides, lines of print, edges of graphics and other items that must be positioned correctly with respect to existing features of a document.

Aliasing: The generation of spurious frequencies in an analogue to digital conversion. Aliasing is caused by using a sampling rate that is less than twice the highest frequency of signal present. For example, if a 15 kHz signal is sampled at 25 kHz, there will be as strong 5 kHz component, equal to the difference between 25 kHz and 2 x 15 kHz.

Amplitude: The overall size of a wave measured to its peak. The amplitude of a sound wave is a measure of the loudness of the sound.

Analogue: An electrical representation of a wave that uses an infinite number of signal levels between maximum and minimum (usually zero). Analogue recording depends on using a reproduction of the sound wave mechanically, magnetically, or optically.

Arpeggio: A set of notes played rapidly in succession that, if sounded together, would make a chord.

Aspect ratio: The ratio of width to height for a screen. Most VDUs use the TV standard of 4:3, and this is reflected in the number of pixels used in vertical and horizontal directions. Some high-cost DTP systems use a 17" or 21" monitor of A4 aspect ratio.

Associate: To nominate a filename extension as one created by an application, so that TXT might be associated with a word-processor, SKD with a CAD program, PUB with a DTP program, AVI with a video file and so on.

Associate sounds: A Windows method of making a sound audible for a given event, such as a chord sound when a file is closed.

114

Asynchronous: Not tied to a fixed rate of repetition. An asynchronous signal can occur at intervals which do not coincide with a fixed-rate clock pulse.

Attribute: One of the set of characteristics that the object has, such as width and depth, colour, border, text, picture, video, etc.

Audio: Referring to the frequency range of human hearing, in the range of 30 Hz to 20 kHz.

Audio cable: The cable used to connect a multimedia CD player to the sound card so that audio CDs can be played through the sound card.

Author mode: The mode in which a multimedia package allows you to create your own displays. Most packages have no author mode.

Autoplay: An action used in some multimedia presentations, allowing the presentation to start as soon as the software is loaded. The alternative is to require the user to click on a RUN command, or press a key combination.

Autosave: An action, used in word-processors and DTP programs, which makes a copy of the current publication (set of pages) file at intervals of 5 minutes to 30 minutes, adjustable by selection from the File menu.

Bandpass: An electrical filter circuit which passes a range of frequencies, rejecting frequencies below the lower limit of the band and above the upper limit. A 25 Hz to 15 kHz bandpass is often applied to audio signals.

Bar: The unit of phrasing in music, using a vertical bar to enclose each group of notes.

Bézier: A method of drawing complex curved shapes using a simple equation.

Multimedia explained

Binary: Using only two digits, levels or codes, as opposed to the scale of ten used in normal counting.

Binary file: A file that consists of binary codes for numbers in the range 0 to 255. Text files use numbers in the range 0 to 127 only. A binary file is meaningless when printed or displayed but can convey information to a program.

Bit: A binary digit, one single unit of data, expressed in number-code as 0 (off) or 1 (on). All computer storage systems use this type of coding because it corresponds to the most reliable use of electrical signals as off or on.

Bit-editing: A method of editing bit-map image picture files one bit at a time, usually by showing a magnified view on the screen.

Bit map: An image that consists of dots, with each dot represented by one bit in the memory of the computer. A large bit-map image with high resolution requires a large number of bits — at 300 dots per inch an A4 page consists of 8 million bits (about 1 Mbyte of memory), hence the requirement for a large memory in a laser printer.

Bitstream: A technique pioneered by Philips in which a binary number is represented by a set of signals of two possible levels. The average value of these signals corresponds to the analogue voltage which was encoded by the binary number.

BMP: The standard file extension for bit-map files created by MS Paint and other graphics applications.

Body text: The main text of a document as distinct from headings, captions, sub-headings, etc. Most or all of the body text will be in one type font and size, such as Times Roman 10 or 12 point.

Bold: A heavily printed version of a font which stands out in the text, used to draw attention to a word or phrase. Bold type is often wider than the normal type of the same font and size.

Border: The area around picture or text, which can be unmarked, lined, double-lined or otherwise marked.

Browse: To look aimlessly through a set of pages of text, pictures and sound. Browsing is often a way of finding unexpected items.

CAD: Computer Aided Design. A program which allows the computer to be used for producing technical drawings to any scale, using vector line methods.

Caddy: A holder for CD discs that is inserted into a CD player rather than inserting the discs directly. Seldom used now.

Caption: A title, usually for a picture or for an action-button in a page.

Capture: Conversion of a screen display to a file or to the printer.

CD: Compact disc, a recording made using optical markings on a plastic disc, formed and also read by a laser beam. The markings are digitally coded to represent samples of the amplitude of sound waves.

CD-ROM drive: A mechanism for playing a compact disc, containing a controlled motor (which must allow the disc to spin faster when the innermost tracks are being read), and the reading mechanism. This consists of a miniature laser whose light reflects from the surface of the disc, along with photocells that detect the reflected light.

CD-ROM: A CD disc that contains digital information which can be read by a suitable drive such as the low-cost Mitsumi or Panasonic drives. Some 600 Mbyte can be placed on a single disc. This is particularly useful as a way of distributing clip-art and large masses of information. It is also useful for multimedia work which can mix text, graphics and sound.

Channel, MIDI: The control code in a MIDI system for altering some particular instrument.

Character properties: The menu of text options for font, style, pattern, colour, tint, size, width and typestyle as used in word processor and DTP programs.

Chromakey: A video system that allows one picture to be inlaid over another, using colour as the basis for the overlay.

Clipboard: A portion of the memory of the computer, created by Windows, which is used to hold information (text or graphics) temporarily, used in Cut, Copy and Paste actions.

Compact disc: A plastic disc with a silvered surface which can carry digital information in the form of tiny pits on the disc surface, used for sound recording and for digital information (CD-ROM).

Compose program: A program that allows you to compose music. These are not so common as you would expect, and generally require you to have a considerable knowledge of music.

Compressed files: Files that have had all redundancy removed, so that they occupy less space on a disc. Picture and video files can be compressed, and compression is essential for video files if they are to occupy a reasonable amount of space.

Copy text: To make an invisible copy of a piece of (usually) text which can then be pasted (see Paste) visibly into another part of the document or into another document. See also Clipboard.

Copyright: The ownership of text or pictures by a writer or artist. Copyright usually extends to seventy years after the death of the originator, and until copyright expires it is unlawful to reproduce the text or picture without permission.

Crescendo: A rising volume of sound.

Crop: To trim the outline of an image. The Crop tool of a drawing program allows trimming to be done by selecting part of the picture. When the Crop action is completed, only the selected area will exist.

Cross-referencing: Providing references that in multimedia works, can be clicked on to bring up further associated information.

Crotchet: The basic timing unit of music.

Cut: To store a piece of (usually) text into memory and remove the visible text from the screen. The Cut material can be pasted (see Paste) into another part of the document or into another document. See also Clipboard.

D-A: Digital to analogue conversion, the essential transformation at the player which permits the sound wave to be reconstructed from the digital number data.

Data connector: The large connector between a CD-ROM drive and its interface (usually the IDE card or the IDE section of the motherboard).

Despeckle: A graphics program action that will clean up a picture by removing small dots that are not part of the main picture.

Digital signals: Signals that use only two digital levels, labelled as 0 and 1.

Digitiser tablet: A flat plate on which X-Y co-ordinate data can be created and sent to the computer. A drawing placed on such a plate can be stored in the computer by placing a stylus on each point of the drawing, if suitable software is present

Dither: (1) In digitised sound, the addition of random noise in order to avoid perfectly steady signal conditions. (2) In graphics, the simulation of colour by a pattern.

Diminuendo: Term used in music to mean a reduction of loudness (amplitude).

DIN plug: A standard type of plug, usually seen in its 5-pin version. The name comes from the initials of the standardising organising body in Germany.

DING.WAV: One of the Windows WAV files that makes a bell sound.

Dropin: A tape or magnetic disc error that causes a sound to appear on playback that was not originally recorded.

Dropout: A tape or magnetic disc fault in which a small piece of magnetic materials is missing or faulty, causing a loss of signal at that point.

DXF: A method of coding a vector drawing into text, used by CAD programs such as AutoSketch and AutoCAD to exchange information. Some graphics packages can read DXF files, as also can several word-processors and DTP programs.

Earphone stereo: Stereo sound as heard through earphones. This gives a much enhanced but rather artificial effect.

Edge Filter: A system used in a graphics editor to enhance the edges of an image.

Edit: To inspect text and graphics material so that changes can be made if required.

EFM: Eight to fourteen modulation, a method of re-coding a byte of data so that the 0s and 1s fall into a pattern that is more suitable for recording on tape or disc.

Embedding: Placing a file, such as a picture or sound file, into a receiving file (such as a text file). The embedded file remains as part of the host file and is recorded with it. Contrast this with a linked file.

Expansion slot: The socket (usually one of 4 to 8) within the computer which will accommodate a plug-in card that enhances the capabilities of the machine. A Pentium computer uses two types of expansion slots, ISA and PCI. One ISA expansion slot is normally used for the sound card.

Field: In TV, one half-set of picture scan lines, either the odd-numbered lines or the even-numbered lines

Filters: (a) In electronics, a circuit which will pass one range of frequencies, the pass-band, and reject all others (the stop-bands). (b) In graphics, an action that will modify the appearance of an image (see Edge filter).

Fill: To place colour or pattern into a closed area.

Flat: The sign that in written music lowers the pitch of a note by one semitone.

Font: A design of alphabetic or numerical characters, available in different sizes and styles (Roman, Bold, Italic).

Forte: Term in written music meaning loud.

Frame: (a) In TV, one complete set of picture scan lines, composed of two fields. (b) An outline into which an object, which can be text, graphics, table or any other entity can be placed. An object, or set of objects, in a frame can be treated as one entity and moved or otherwise processed as one.

Multimedia explained

Frame counter: A software device that counts the number of video frames (25 per second) so that the count number can be used for timing actions. You might, for example, opt to see frames 37 to 516 of a piece of video.

Frame grabber: A hardware addition to a computer that allows any frame of a video sequence to be captured and stored in digital form.

Frequency: The number of pulses or repetitions of a waveform per second.

Fundamental: The lowest frequency that is present in a musical note.

Gamma correction: A correction of picture shading to allow for the relationship between intended brightness and actual brightness of, for example, a monitor.

Genlock: A video editing system that allows computer-generated video pictures to be mixed with video from a camera or a video recorder.

GIF: A form of image file used in Clip-art.

Graphics board: The add-on board for the PC machine that determines what definition of images you can use on your monitor (if the monitor itself can cope). Enhanced graphics boards are needed for actions such as video playback.

Graphics resolution: The measure of detail in a picture, in terms of dots per inch. The higher the resolution the better the appearance, the longer it takes to print and the more memory it needs.

Group: A set of objects, each of which can be separately selected, but which have been placed into one large selection box to be dealt with together. Grouping is done by selecting one item and then holding down the Shift key while clicking on each other item.

Guides: The lines that can be placed over a page in word-processor or DTP programs and used to indicate positions for headings, indents, etc. The lines are obtained by clicking on the ruler, and can be dragged to any part of the page - they do not appear on the Pasteboard, and can be removed by dragging them off the page area.

Handles: The small black squares that appear surrounding an object to indicate that editing actions can be carried out on that object. By using the handles you can move an object, or alter its size, copy it, delete it, or change its characteristics.

Harmonics: Frequencies, part of a musical note, that are multiples of the fundamental. For example, a fundamental of 1000 Hz might have harmonics at 2000, 4000, and 8000 Hz.

Harmony: The sound of notes that are related harmonically, so that the overall effect is pleasant.

Hertz: The unit of frequency, one cycle of a wave per second. Named after Heinrich Hertz who discovered radio waves.

Highlight: A method of marking an icon or text, using a different shading or colour.

High pass: An electronic filter circuit which passes only frequencies above a limit, rejecting lower frequencies

Hiss: High-frequency noise.

Histogram: A bar-chart display.

Hyperlink: A piece of coloured text or an icon that can be clicked to produce some effect such as a sound, some new text, a picture, or a connection to the Internet.

Multimedia explained

Image coding: A method used to digitise an image into numbers 0 to 255 that can be recorded on disc or other media.

Imaging card: A hardware add-on card that can be used for capturing video images.

Interpolation: Addition of information by taking an average value between two adjacent items. Interpolation is one method used to correct missing portions of digitally recorded information.

Jack: A very old form of connector for sound signals, originating with the telephone system which at one time used ¼" jack plugs in exchanges. The 3 mm type is now more common, and all jacks are available as mono or stereo types. The socket is sometimes referred to as a jill.

Joystick port: A connector on a PC machine to which a joystick can be plugged for 'shoot-em-down' games.

Justification: Alignment of text. The name can be used to mean alignment of text so that each line has the same length. Some users prefer to call this right-justification, using the term left-justification for text with a ragged right hand edge. Full or right justification is done by altering the spaces between words.

Jumper: A clip-on connector between pins on a computer board, used to set up conditions. Jumpers should not be needed when Plug'n'play cards are used along with a computer running Windows 95 or 98.

Landscape: Paper positioning (orientation) with the long dimension of the sheet horizontal, making the width greater than the height.

Laser: Acronym of Light Amplification by Stimulated Emission of Radiation. A device which for an electrical input generates light of a single wavelength and with no sudden changes of phase, use for reading CDs.

Layering: The arrangement of objects in background or foreground. A box dragged over text, for example, will appear on the foreground layer and will hide the text until the *Arrange* option from the Edit menu is used to place the selected box in the background. Layer changing can be carried out only on a selected object.

Libris Britannia: A CD-ROM contains a huge collection of shareware programs.

Lifetime: The time for which an object is active in the sense of being visible (text or picture) or audible (sound).

Linear: Any system in which a graph of output plotted against input produces a straight line. A linear amplifier is one that would produce no distortion of the electrical signals into it.

Line: An input to a sound card intended for connection to external hi-fi equipment such as a record player, another CD-player, tape recorder or radio tuner.

Linking: Associating one file with another. For example, a picture file can be linked with a text file so that the picture appears in the text, but is not saved with it. This keeps the text file size down, but requires the image file to be available.

Lock: A sound-board software action that ensures that the left and right channel volume controls are kept in step so that the channels are not unbalanced. the lock can be removed if you want to work with unequal channels.

Loudness: The response of the ear to the amplitude of a sound. This is uneven, and the ear has its peak response at about 400 Hz. It is less sensitive to sound at low frequencies (below 200 Hz) and at high frequencies (above 4000 Hz).

Multimedia explained

Loudspeaker: An electrical device that converts electrical waves into sound waves of the same frequency.

Low pass: An electronic filter circuit which passes only lower frequencies, rejecting frequencies above the limit. A 15 kHz low pass filter is often used in audio work to attenuate or reject higher frequencies which could cause trouble in circuits.

Mains hum: The low-frequency noise signal caused by wiring in a amplifier picking up the mains signal at 50 Hz.

Marked strand: Applied to the strand of wire at one edge of a ribbon cable, indicating connection to pin 1.

Master volume: A mixer control which allows all input volumes to be controlled together. If the separate input levels have all been correctly set, only the master need be altered when you fade sound up or down.

Metafile: A form of vector graphics file which can be used in Windows applications.

Microphone: A device that converts sound waves into electrical waves of the same frequency and shape.

MIDI: Acronym of Musical Instrument Digital Interface, a system for connecting electronic musical instruments to each other and to a computer so that one performer can play several instruments.

Mixer: A device, which can be in hardware or software, that controls several sound inputs, combines the waves, and feeds them out through a master volume control to whatever outputs are required.

Modulation: The alteration of signals into a form that can be transmitted or recorded.

Monochrome: Of one single frequency, like the light from a laser. Also applied to black/white TV.

MPEG: Acronym of Motion Pictures Expert Group, a committee who have set up standards for the use of moving images in multimedia.

MSCDEX: A Microsoft program (memory-resident) that allows the use of multimedia devices.

Multimedia: Making use of text, pictures (still and moving) and sound together, under computer control.

Multimedia package: A set of programs that make use of the capability of the computer to show text and still or moving pictures along with sound, all stored in digitised form.

Multi-session: A CD-ROM player design that allows the reading of images that have been put on to the CD at different times (sessions), as when a CD is filled with images in sets of 24. All modern drives are of this type.

MUTE: Action of reducing sound volume to zero.

Negative Image: An image in which light and dark has been reversed, or colours changed to their opposites.

Noise: Unwanted signal of any kind, usually of random frequency and amplitude.

Noise immunity: A measure, usually in terms of volts, of the ability of a digital circuit to ignore noise signals.

Noise shaper: A circuit, used in bitstream D-A converters, whose action is to shift the frequency of noise in a digital signal so that on conversion the noise will be outside the audio range. This is done by reducing the number of parallel bits used to carry the data, increasing the number of serial bits and so the frequency of the digital signal.

Multimedia explained

Object: Any item of text, graphics or sound that can be considered as a single entity. An object can be manipulated when it is selected so that its selection handles can be seen

Object-oriented format: Used of drawing packages that use vector format, treating each line as a mathematical equation.

Optical: Making use of light, including infra-red and ultra-violet frequencies which are invisible to the human eye. The CD is sometimes described as an optical disc.

Oscilloscope: An electronic instrument, used for servicing and diagnosis, that can make electrical waves visible on a small TV type of screen.

Oversampling: A method of increasing the performance of a D-A converter by inserting additional pulses into the digital signal between the original pulses. The effect is similar to that which would be produced by using a faster sampling rate in the original recording.

Paint Shop Pro: A graphics editor, available as shareware, that allows a huge variety of file types to be read or saved, and a large number of graphics effects, such as filters, to be applied.

Paste: To copy a piece of text or graphics from the Clipboard into a window.

Paste Special: A Windows command that allows a file to be linked or embedded.

Pattern: The type of monochrome filling that can be used for a graphics box or circle shape in a graphics program.

PCM: Pulse-Code Modulation, a system of converting analogue signals to digital in which the amplitude of the analogue signals is converted to a binary number, rather than to pulse amplitude, pulse frequency or pulse position. The

CD and Mini Disc audio systems use PCM, but other coding methods are used.

PCX: A form of file coding for graphics information which compresses the information to a reasonable size. Used by PC Paintbrush (Zilog), the PCX type of file can be imported by most graphics programs

Phono plug: A coaxial plug developed in the U.S.A. for hi-fi use. Each channel of signal is carried in a screened cable terminated in a single phono plug.

Photo-CD: A system developed by Kodak for transferring photographic negatives into positive images in digital form on a CD. Using modern CD-ROM drives, the transfer need not be in a single session, allowing you to fill a CD even if you have only a few photos to use each time. The Photo-CD system also contains software for viewing and copying the images, subject to copyright.

Pixel: Acronym of Picture Element, meaning the smallest units (dots) from which a picture can be built up, usually referring to the screen. Each pixel must be addressable, meaning that the computer keeps a reference number (an address number) for each pixel so as to allow the pixel to be changed (change of colour or shading). Nothing smaller than one pixel can be displayed.

Point size: A printers unit of type size, equal to 1/72 inch, used in measuring type sizes.

Power cable: The four-core cable from the power supply box in the PC, with connectors for four or more drives.

Program mode: A software action in a CD player program that allows you to pick specific sections of the CD track to play in whatever sequence you want.

Pulse code modulation: see PCM

Multimedia explained

Quantization: Analysis of a waveform into a number of set levels, the essential preliminary to any analogue to digital conversion.

Quantum: A single unit of anything. Originally applied to the quantity called *action* (energy x time) in Planck's Quantum Theory, and used in digital work to describe a unit of signal level.

Queue: A set of files awaiting processing, as in some sound commands.

Quiet screen: A screen that does not show any messages during actions involving sound effects.

Readme: A file used in program distribution discs to contain information that has been added since the manual was printed.

Recording sound: On a PC, using the soundboard along with one of the sound utilities to make a digital file of sound from the microphone, from a record or a cassette.

Red Book: A data book which contains the specifications for the CD and other digital audio systems, provided to manufacturers who take out a licence for using the system.

Redundancy: The addition of excess information so that the loss of some data can be made up by using the rest of the data

Reed-Solomon coding: A coding system that uses redundancy to detect and correct errors in data transmission. This is used on music CDs to detect and correct errors that could be caused by scratches or dust.

Repeat points: The portions of a CD which will be the start of a repeat of playing.

Resample: A re-reading of original data, used by some graphics programs to correct an image after it has been re-scaled.

Root page: The main first page of a multimedia presentation, often containing a master index.

Rotation: A graphics program command to turn an image, graphics or text, through an angle. The object is selected, the Rotate tool chosen, and the mouse used on one corner of the selection box to rotate the box around its opposite corner. Holding down the Shift key causes the rotation to be done in 45° steps.

Ruler: A display of measuring units (usually inches or centimetres) along the top and down the left-hand side of the window. This makes it easier to position objects precisely, particularly when used in conjunction with Guides and Snaps. Used by word processors, DTP programs, and CAD programs.

Sampling: The system of measuring the amplitude of a waveform at fixed intervals so that the samples can be converted into digital signals.

Sampling rate: The number of samples of an analogue waveform taken per second to convert into digital form.

Scale: (a) In graphics, a scale means the size relationship between one quantity and another, often applied to dimensions. To scale an image means to alter its dimensions so as to make an enlarged or a reduced copy. (b) In music, a set of notes that can be used in writing a melody.

Scanner: A hardware input device which can read text or graphics images and convert them into machine-readable digital form. Simple scanners can be used to read line drawings, more complex scanners can create a digital form of a photograph. Additional software called OCR (optical character recognition) allows a full-page scanner to produce a file of ASCII codes from a piece of text, eliminating the need to copy the text by typing. Low-cost OCR used with a hand-scanner can take more time to get a copy than typing the words by hand.

SCART: A standard form of connector for TV receivers and video recorders that allows for video and sound signals to be passed between them and to other devices.

Script file: A file of instructions, particularly for a multimedia presentation.

SCMS: Serial Copy Management System, a form of coding used on DAT machines which prevents a digital tape from being used to create another tape and so mass-produce perfect copies.

SCSI: Small Computer Systems Interface. A method used to control a large number of disc drives and other devices on large computer systems.

SETUP: A program often included on a program distribution disc as a way of copying files to a hard derive folder. The files are usually in compressed form, and the SETUP program will expand them as well as copy them.

Sideband: A range of frequencies produced when a signal frequency is modulated or sampled.

Sidebeam: A part of the laser beam of a CD player, used to detect whether or not the main beam is aimed correctly. Two side-beams are used to ensure that the main beam is held in the centre of the track.

Sine wave: The simplest and smoothest form of wave. The name is used because the shape is that of a graph of the sine of an angle plotted against angle.

Single-medium: A program that uses only one aspect of computer possibilities, unlike multimedia.

132

Single-session: A recording made on to a CD blank that does not fill the disc.

Sixteen-bit number: A binary number that uses sixteen bits. This allows a range of number equivalent in ordinary terms to 0 to 65535.

Snaps: The action of moving precisely into place, applied to a graphics program. When Snaps is turned on, moving an object near a margin or guideline will make the object jump or snap into place. This avoids the problems of trying to position screen objects with the uncertain mechanical movement of a mouse.

Solarise: An image effect which partly inverts the image (turning black to white). This is named after the effect that is seen when a film is exposed to light while being developed.

Sound: A waveform of pressure in air or in dense materials. Audible sound uses frequencies of around 50 Hz to 10,000 Hz.

Sound Blaster: The name of the first sound board for the PC machine, which set de facto standards. All other sound boards should be Sound Blaster compatible.

Sound card: An add-on card that provides sound capabilities for the PC machine.

Sound editor: Software that allows digitised sound files (of the WAV type) to be edited, mainly to remove silences.

Sound wave: A pressure wave in air or in a more dense medium, usually in the frequency range of 50 Hz to 10,000 Hz.

Speech synthesis: Software that can produce the effect of a human voice, usually for reading text from a file.

Spray: A graphics program action in which dots of colour can be placed on the screen, as if by a spray gun.

Multimedia explained

Square wave: A wave shape that can be produced by switching a steady voltage on and off periodically. This waveform is rich in harmonics and is a good starting point for wave synthesis.

Stereo: Two (or more) channels of sound used to convey an illusion of a real source of music.

Swap file: Part of the hard disc used in the 386-Enhanced mode of Windows to swap with memory so that the memory is not overloaded. Any machine running multimedia should preferably use a permanent swap file so that no time is wasted in creating a new file when one is needed.

Synthesiser: A device that can generate electrical waveforms, and alter them so as to imitate real musical instruments when the waves are converted into sound waves. Since the synthesiser is a purely electronic device, it can be computer controlled through a MIDI link.

TADA.WAV: One of the sound files of Windows that plays a triumphant chord.

Teletext: The television information service (BBC or ITV) that transmits data in the frame intervals of the TV signal. Most TV receivers can detect this information and place it on screen, but none can send it to a printer. An add-on card for a PC allows you to capture Teletext as well as TV pictures and to save and/or print the information.

Text to speech: Software that works along with a speech synthesiser chip to allow a text file to be read out.

TIF: Tagged Image Format graphics file, developed by Aldus for their PageMaker DTP program. Was intended to be a standard, but too many variations now exist.

Tint: The proportion of the selected colour, as a percentage, used for a colour fill or a printed character - the remainder is white.

Trace Contour: A graphics program action that will trace out the outline of a picture, removing any filling.

Track Address: A number that can be used to locate any part of a CD surface.

Transducer: A device that will convert one form of energy to another. Familiar examples are the microphone (sound to electrical energy) and the loudspeaker (electrical energy to sound).

Transparent object: An object which can be clicked on, but which is transparent and can be laid over some other object.

VDU: Visual Display Unit, another name for a monitor display.

Vector graphics: Images, also called object-oriented, which do not consist of dots (bit images) but of instructions such as 'draw a line from point 22,36 to point 25,39'. Images which use vector graphics can be expanded or shrunk with no loss of resolution, and the printed resolution of a vector graphics image depends on the printer resolution, not on the resolution of the original drawing device. Vector graphics are produced by Computer Drawing packages (CAD programs) and by business-oriented graphics packages. Some of the WMF files of Windows are also of this type.

VGA screen: Video Graphics Array. The most recent IBM graphics adapter for high resolution and colour. A VGA adapter makes a machine eminently suitable for DTP work. For multimedia work, the 256-colour screen is preferred, and it is an advantage to use both higher resolution and more colours.

Multimedia explained

Video: Relating to images, applied to image recording and transmission, particularly of moving images.

Video player: Any machine for replaying video images, but when a video player is referred to in multimedia work it usually means a video CD player.

Voice annotation: A sound file attached to text. The software will usually place an icon (such as a microphone or loudspeaker image) in the text, and clicking on this will play the sound file.

WAV: The digital sound file type developed by Microsoft and used in Windows.

Waveform: The graph of voltage or current plotted against time for an electrical signal.

White noise: A noise signal in which all frequencies are present to an equal extent, not weighted in any way (as pink noise would be).

WMF: Abbreviation of Windows Meta File, a method of coding pictures so that they can be scaled up or down without losing resolution.

Zoom: A graphics, word-processor or DTP action that allows you to see a magnified view of a screen page. Typically, the magnifying-glass tool of a Toolbox will zoom into and out of a section of a page when it is double-clicked, or the 1:1 icon in the Status bar can be clicked for a full-screen view; the page icon for the normal page view.

INDEX

1

16-colour graphics driver. 31

4

4.00.950B Windows version
.... 12

5

5¼ inch units *101*

A

acknowledgement 19
acoustic feedback 70
active loudspeakers 58
adapter, audio 97
ADC 60
add drive *101*
add-on sound system 93
advanced controls, Reader 83
advantages, bitmap 24
adventure games 6
advice 22
air pressure waves 55
airbrush 42
All Channels are in use
   message 83
amplifier 58
amplitude 55
analogue 59
annotate text 6
applications list, reader 82
artwork, PCX 27
ASCII code 1
associating sounds 73
Attribute 38
audio cable connector *103*
audio CD 2

audio connectors 96
Autoplay 65

B

basic requirements 6
batch conversion 43
Bézier tool 41
binary code 60
bit-editing 39
bitmap 23
bitmap images 26
bitmap sizes 24
blanking plates 94
Borders 45
box, text 42
Browse button 73

C

CAD programs 25
Capture action 44
captured colour images 30
catalogues 22
CD Audio control 65
CD drawer *100*
CD player 61, 63
CD storage 2
CD-ROM 2
church organ 56
clipart 26
Clipboard 30
collections, programs 11
colour printer 23
compressed file 33
compression methods 3
compression methods, sound
   62
compression systems 33
computer chess 6

Multimedia explained

Control Panel, Reader......82
controls, TA.....................81
conversion, signal............60
Copy and Paste................19
copying text 19
copyright..........................19
cost and compatibility........7
Creative Midi 79
Creative Mixer 68
cross-references................4
curve drawing 41

D

DAC 61
data cable.......................*104*
default font......................42
despeckle option..............47
device-dependent bitmap . 24
Dictionary, Reader 83
digital..............................59
digital sound......................2
Digital Workshop 43
digitised files...................71
dilate..............................47
distortion.........................*99*
DIY installation................7
DMA 12
DOC files.........................86
DrawPlus 25, 49
drive bays *101*
drive letter......................*106*
DXF file...........................25
dynamic microphone 88

E

ear response 57
eardrums 55
earphones........................63
editing graphics...............33
EIDE system *102*

electret microphone 88
electronic instruments......78
embedding........................76
emboss 47
enabling DMA.................13
encyclopaedia....................4
erase image 37
eraser 35
erode 47
external amplifier 58

F

fast CD-ROM drives......*100*
fast machine 8
fastening, drive...............*102*
file conversion program ...33
Filters, PSP.....................46
flag key 15
Flip 37
frequency 56
fuzz image.......................47

G

games...............................6
games connector..............98
gamma correction 47
graphics package 26
grey scale 48
grey scale illustration.......30
greyscale images 46
Grid 39
Grolier Encyclopædia 20

H

handle 51
hard drive capacity............9
hardware volume control .65
headphones.......................6
hertz unit 56
hi-fi system connection....97

high CD drive speed 10
High Colour 23
high pitch 56
highlight/shadow 48
hiss 99
Histogram 44
Hutchinson Encyclopædia
    .... 21, 31
hyperlink 19
hyperlinks 5

I

icons, player 67
IDE controller *104*
image manipulation, ... 43
image coding 23
images, clipart 27
inputs, sound card 63
installation program... 15, 98
installing sound card 94
internal drive *101*
Internet 5
Intro mode 80
Inverse 38
ISA 94

J

jack points 88
jack sockets 63
jerky animation 10
jill socket 70
jumpers 95

L

lasso selection 36
Libris Britannia 15
line width 40
linking 76
loudness 56
loudspeaker jack 97

loudspeaker positioning ... 58
loudspeaker quality 93
low pitch 56

M

Magnifier tool 39
Maplin 70
Maplins 97
master volume setting 65
median 47
microphone 6, 55, 58
microphone use 87
Microsoft Photo Editor 43
MIDI 78
MIDI interface 93, 98
mixer 63
mono sound 57
monochrome image 23
mosaic 47
mounting brackets, drive *101*
MPC standard 3
MSPaint 24
multimedia 2
multimedia CDs 11
multimedia encyclopaedia.. 4
multimedia PC 6
multimedia sound 61
music CD playing 65
Mute boxes 65

N

negative image 48
new software on CD 11
node editor 51
noise *99*
noise, CD-ROM drive 10

O

object 76
object-oriented format 25

Multimedia explained

old drives 10
other graphics formats 27

P

package, multimedia 7
package, sound 93
Paint Shop Pro 24, 42
paintbrush tool 42
paint-roller tool 41
palette pattern 42
pause, word 86
PCI 94
PCX 33
PCX format 27
PDSL 15
Pentium processor 8
permanent swapfile 9
Phoneme 84
PhotoEditor 24
photographic editing 43
Photo-real 23
pitch 56
pixels 23
PKUNZIP.EXE 28
plain text files 86
Play List 68
player, MIDI 78
Plug'n'play 95
Plug'n'Play (PnP) 93
poorly-designed programs 10
poor-quality sound 93
posterize 47
power cable, drive *102*
Print icon. 21
print text 21
program collections 15
program distribution 11
pronunciation 6, 83

R

RAM memory 8
range, musical sounds 56
Reader menu 81
README.TXT file *106*
recording, digital 59
rectangular box selection . 36
Repeat 80
Resample action 46
re-scaling 27
rotate 52
Rotate 37
rubber banding 41
running MS-DOS programs
.... 19

S

sampling rate 61
sampling wave 60
scaled images 25
Schemes box 73
SCSI system *102*
Select All option 19
selection process 36
Serif DrawPlus 25
setup action 14
shareware 19
Shuffle 80
sine wave 55
single-session drive 10
single-speed drive 10
Skew 37
slot 94
software *105*
Solarise 48
sound 55
sound waves 55
Sound Blaster 63
sound card 58, 63, 93
sound files 11

140

Sound Like box 84
Soundo'LE 75
speakers' voices 82
speed 8
speed, CD-ROM drive 10
spray 42
Start button 15
statistics, wave 75
stereo sound 57
storage space 1
straight-line patterns 40
Stretch 37
suitable machines 8
swapfile 9

T

Tandy 97
Tandy shops 70
Taskbar list 19
text 42
Text Assist 80
text only CD 22
text reader use 6
text to speech converters .. 80
Text tool 52
Texto'LE utility 85
Thumbnail 39
TIF 33
time, speech pause 87
tools, DrawPlus 50
tools, drive fitting *103*
track data 67

U

Undo 37, 44
unwanted noise *99*
utility programs 17

V

vector editing 26
vector format 25
virtual memory 9
VLB 95
voice characteristics 83
voice messages 6
voice synthesiser 94

W

Walnut Creek CD-ROM .. 16
warp tool 52
WAV file 89
WAV files 71
Wave Editor 90
Windows 95 8
Windows clipboard 24
Windows Metafile WMF . 25
Windows mixer 64
Windows Paintbrush 33
WINZIP utility 28
WMF files 53
WordPad 86
word-processor 5
Write 86

Z

ZIP files 28
Zoom 39

Notes

Notes

Multimedia explained

Notes

813.54 MOR
week
loan ✓
0 -50

The Voices of Toni Morrison

The
Voices
of Toni
Morrison

Barbara Hill Rigney

Ohio State University Press
Columbus

Library of Congress Cataloging-in-Publication Data

Rigney, Barbara Hill, 1938–
      The voices of Toni Morrison / Barbara Hill Rigney.
         p.   cm.
      Includes bibliographical references and index.
      ISBN 0–8142–0555–0 (pbk.: alk. paper)
      1. Morrison, Toni—Criticism and interpretation. 2. Feminism and
literature—United States—History—20th century. 3. Afro-American
women in literature. I. Title.
PS3563.08749Z84   1991
813´.54—dc20   91–16092
                                                                        CIP

Text design by Hunter Graphics.
Cover design by Donna Hartwick.
Cover illustration: Aminah Robinson, "Woman Resting," Sapelo Island Series,
1985. Collection of the artist. Courtesy of Esther Saks Gallery.
Type set in ITC Galliard by G&S Typesetters, Austin, TX.
Printed by Bookcrafters, Chelsea, MI.

The paper in this book meets the guidelines for permanence and durability of
the Committee on Production Guidelines for Book Longevity of the Council on
Library Resources.

Printed in the U.S.A.

9 8 7 6 5 4 3 2

For Kim, Julie, Kris, Sky, and Papa

I gratefully acknowledge the time and the encouragement provided by the College of Humanities and the Department of English at The Ohio State University, the support of my editor, Charlotte Dihoff, and the invaluable assistance and advice of both colleagues and students, most particularly Murray Beja, Erika Bourguignon, Grace Epstein, Michael Hitt, Sebastian Knowles, Marlene Longenecker, and James Phelan.

Contents

Introduction   *1*

1   Breaking the Back of Words: Language and
Signification   *7*

2   Hagar's Mirror: Self and Identity   *35*

3   "The Disremembered and Unaccounted For":
History, Myth, and Magic   *61*

4   Rainbows and Brown Sugar: Desire and the
Erotic   *83*

Afterword   *105*

Notes   *109*

Bibliography   *115*

Index   *125*

Introduction

... what is important is to disconcert the staging of representation according to *exclusively* "masculine" parameters, that is,
according to phallocratic order. It is not a matter of toppling
that order so as to replace it—that amounts to the same thing
in the end—but of disrupting and modifying it, starting from
an "outside" that is exempt, in part, from phallocratic law.
                                        —Irigaray, *This Sex Which Is Not One*

From her vantage at the intersection of race and gender, Toni
Morrison represents an exemption from "phallocratic law"; her
own language and her theory of language, as she has demonstrated in her five novels and explained in a number of essays and
interviews, reflect a consciousness that she writes both from and
about a zone that is "outside" of literary convention, that disrupts
traditional Western ideological confines and modifies patriarchal
inscriptions. While no American writer, regardless of race or gender, can be considered as totally outside of the dominant signifying structure, there is nonetheless an area on the periphery, a zone
both chosen and allocated, which represents a way of seeing and
of knowing that disconcerts and finally discounts the very structure which excludes it. Mapping that zone as Morrison delineates
it most radically—through language, through a rendering of history, through a reinscription of identity, and through the articulation of female desire—is the concern of the following study,
which seeks to place Morrison's works within the context of a
black feminine/feminist aesthetic and to define that aesthetic in
terms of contemporary feminist and African American critical
theory.

According to French feminist theorists Hélène Cixous and
Catherine Clément in *The Newly Born Woman*: "It is impossible
to *define* a feminist practice of writing, and this is an impossibility
that will remain, for this practice can never be theorized, enclosed,
coded—which doesn't mean that it doesn't exist. . . . It will be
conceived of only by subjects who are breakers of automatisms,

1

by peripheral figures that no authority can ever subjugate" (313). Morrison is surely one of these "peripheral figures" in terms of the dominant culture, central though she is to the contemporary literary scene. For Morrison—as is also true for many other contemporary African American women writers, including Alice Walker, Toni Cade Bambara, and Gloria Naylor, to name three— gender is not separate or separable from racial identity; while their arguments are for liberation from racial and gender oppression, both race and gender themselves are always seen as liberating points from which to construct a language or to create a literature that is political in form as well as in subject matter. As Morrison consciously writes the black text, so she also defines herself as "valuable as a writer because I am a woman, because women, it seems to me, have some special knowledge about certain things. [It comes from] the ways in which they view the world and from women's imagination. Once it is unruly and let loose it can bring things to the surface that men—trained to be men in a certain way—have difficulty getting access to" (Lester, 54).

In Morrison's texts, to be "other," i.e., black and female, is to have privileged insights, access to that "special knowledge" she both inscribes and describes repeatedly in her novels. In keeping with the paradox that is also her fictional text, Morrison celebrates "otherness" but simultaneously also resists participation in what art sections of the popular press are currently calling "artistic tribalism" and "the cult of otherness." Morrison has said of African Americans: "We are not, in fact, 'other.' We are choices. And to read imaginative literature by and about us is to choose to examine centers of the self and to have the opportunity to compare these centers with the 'raceless' one with which we are, all of us, most familiar" (1990, 208). She writes, finally, she says, about that which "has something to do with life and being human in the world" (Tate 1989, 121). Perhaps, as Morrison illustrates, it is possible to be both "other" and "human in the world" without, at the same time, serving the gods of traditional Western humanism.

For Morrison's fictions *do* represent otherness, in which fact lies their great strength, for from her very marginality she presents a mirror to the larger culture as well as to the African American culture, and the image contained there is often a revelation. For Morrison, to recognize the other as one's "self," to come to terms with one's own otherness, to enter willingly the forbidden zones of consciousness (and unconsciousness) that lie through and beyond the mirror of gender and race, is to become more fully human, more moral, and more sane. Often Morrison presents this psychic zone in terms that emphasize rather than minimize its cultural otherness, for she guides her reader through metaphoric jungles, through representations of the conjure world,[1] and through images of an Africa of the mind that is repressed but never totally lost or forgotten, a part of the unconscious which surfaces in racial memory, particularly for African Americans.

Perhaps Elaine Showalter is generally correct in her argument that the anthropologically defined "wild zone"[2] of female space within the literary text is, at least for most women writers, a "playful abstraction: in the reality to which we must address ourselves as critics, women's writing is a 'double-voiced discourse' that always embodies the social, literary, and cultural heritages of both the muted and the dominant" (1985, 263). But Morrison invites her own inclusion into a very much less abstract and not always so playful wild zone, a place where women's imagination is "unruly and let loose," as she herself describes it, and where language is subversive, where the female body claims the power to articulate itself, where silence speaks and the unconscious becomes the conscious.

Largely outside the myth of American homogeneity, freer than most American theorists of the thumbprint of patriarchal discourse in spite of their acknowledged debts to such theorists as Derrida, Lacan, and Foucault, the French feminist theorists are those who most pointedly seek to investigate the feminine language, who have begun to map the "wild zone," and who might provide a metaphoric structure by which to approach the nature of Morrison's marginality and her difference. For Morrison does write what the French call *différence*, that feminine style that opens the closure of binary oppositions and thus subverts many of the basic assumptions of Western humanistic thought. The important metaphor that pervades the works of such theorists as Luce Irigaray, Julia Kristeva, Hélène Cixous, Catherine Clément, Marguerite Duras, and Monique Wittig, is in fact that of marginality, of blackness as symbolic of radical dissidence and linguistic revolution. Duras, for example, defines feminine writing as "an organic translated writing . . . translated from blackness, from darkness . . . from the unknown, like a new way of communicating rather than an already formed language" (quoted by Marks, 174). Cixous, too, in "The Laugh of the Medusa," aligns herself with all women, whom she perceives as victimized by but victorious over white patriarchy: "We the precocious, we the repressed of culture, our lovely mouths gagged with pollen, our wind knocked out of us, we the labyrinths, the ladders, the trampled spaces . . . we are black and we are beautiful" (310). Women, write Cixous and Clément in *The Newly Born Woman*, are "the Dark Continent" (68). "Blackness" as metaphor, for Morrison as well as for these French theorists, embraces racial identity *and* a state of female consciousness, or even unconsciousness, that zone beyond the laws of white patriarchy in which female art is conceived and produced.

Ann Rosalind Jones sees many aspects of French feminisms as limited in political application, the constitution of "an energizing myth" (372) rather than an agenda for change, but she also defends the works of French feminists as "an island of hope in the void left by the deconstruction of humanism"; they represent "a powerful alternative discourse . . . to write from the body is to recreate the world" (366). The following study also frequently employs the language of contemporary French feminists when that becomes useful—not as a defense or even as an analysis of their works, certainly not as a limiting construct on Morrison's own politically and artistically powerful voice, but as "an island of hope," as an alternative discourse, a radical way to approach the radical aspects of Morrison's fictions, a means of interpreting and translating the double-voiced discourse which is Morrison's text. Like the powerful Eva in *Sula*, Morrison herself speaks "with two voices. Like two people were talking at the same time, saying the same thing, one a fraction of a second behind the other" (61).

Feminist scholars of African American literature are also fully aware of the philosophical two-step necessary to approach the double voices of writers like Morrison, and it is they, most specifically, who warn of the dangers involved in subsuming racial difference into the category of the feminine. Some scholars have expressed their concern that all theory as practiced in the academy today is largely inappropriate for the interpretation of African American literature in general. Barbara Christian, in "The Race for Theory," for example, sees critical theory as "hegemonic as the world it attacks. I see the language it creates as one that mystifies rather than clarifies our condition, making it possible for a few people who know that particular language to control the critical scene" (1988, 71). Morrison herself has questioned the validity of the application of traditional critical paradigms to African American texts, suggesting that they may "constitute a disguise for a temporal, political and culturally specific program" (1990, 202). Even within the context of her fiction, Morrison extends a subtle warning about the nature and relevance of critical scholarship as applied to her work. In her earliest novel, *The Bluest Eye*, she depicts Elihue Micah Whitcomb, alias Soaphead Church, who advertises himself as "Reader, Adviser, and Interpreter of Dreams" (130), and who comes from "a family proud of its academic accomplishments and its mixed blood" (132):

> Little Elihue learned everything he needed to know well, particularly the fine art of self-deception. He read greedily but understood selectively, choosing the bits and pieces of other men's ideas that supported whatever predilection he had at the moment. Thus he chose to remember Hamlet's abuse of Ophelia, but not Christ's love of Mary Magdalene; Hamlet's frivolous politics, but not Christ's serious anarchy. . . . For all his exposure to the best minds of the Western world, he allowed only the narrowest interpretation to touch him. . . . A hatred of, and fascination with, any hint of disorder or decay. (133–34)

As the following chapters will attempt to document, Morrison's own fictions include more than a bit of controlled disorder and a great deal of serious anarchy, and these are aspects any scholar must consider despite her or his own self-deceptions and predilections, from which none of us is totally free.

The criteria necessary for the "sane accountability" in the consideration of texts by African American women that Barbara Smith requests in "Toward a Black Feminist Criticism" (1985, 183) involves a refusal to separate categories like race and gender, to view a writer like Morrison in the context of "both/and" rather than "either/or," and to perform, as Beloved does, "A little two-step, two-step, make-a-new-step, slide, slide and strut on down" (*Beloved*, 74). The following study seeks to represent that new-step, which is the cultivation of a common ground for theory, race, and gender.

1

Breaking the Back of Words: Language and Signification

> The most valuable point of entry into the question of cultural (or racial) distinction, the one most fraught, is its language—its unpoliced, seditious, confrontational, manipulative, inventive, disruptive, masked and unmasking language.
> —Morrison, 1990, "Unspeakable Things Unspoken"

A consideration of language is primary in the development of theoretical paradigms as these relate to all literatures, but particularly to the African American feminine/feminist text. This is especially true in a critical approach to Toni Morrison's works, for, like the Sibyl of mythology, Morrison scatters her signs, her political insights, and it is only through an analysis of her language that we can reconstruct an idea of the political and artistic revolution constituted in her work. "Confrontational," "unpoliced," hers is the language of black and feminine discourse—semiotic, maternal, informed as much by silence as by dialogue, as much by absence as by presence. Morrison seems to *conjure* her language, to invent a form of discourse that is always at once both metaphysical and metafictional.

One of the freedoms Morrison claims in her novels is to move beyond language, even while working *through* it, to incorporate significance beyond the denotation of words, to render experience and emotion, for example, as musicians do. Morrison says that she wishes to accomplish "something that has probably only been fully expressed in music. . . . Writing novels is a way to encompass this—this something" (McKay, 1). The enigma of freedom itself, to be discovered at the margins of the dominant culture, can best be expressed, Morrison writes, through the analogy, even through an imitation, of music:

> The pieces of Cholly's life could become coherent only in the head of a musician. Only those who talk their talk through the gold of curved metal, or in the touch of black-and-white rectangles and taut skins and strings echoing from wooden corridors, could give true form to his life . . . and come up with all of what that meant in joy, in pain, in anger, in love, and give it its final and pervading ache of freedom. Only a musician would sense, know, without even knowing that he knew, that Cholly was free. Dangerously free. (*The Bluest Eye*, 125)

Like the blues-singing women who populate her fiction, like the prostitute Poland in her "sweet strawberry voice" (*The Bluest Eye*, 49), or like Claudia's mother who can sing "misery colored by greens and blues" and make pain sweet (*The Bluest Eye*, 24), so Morrison also sings her novels (and anyone who has heard Morrison read from her work will know this is literally as well as metaphorically true). Images of music pervade her work, but so also does a musical quality of language, a sound and rhythm that permeate and radiate in every novel.

Pilate, for example, "sings" throughout *Song of Solomon*, in which both the motif of music and the musicality of language are so crucial. The solution to Milkman's quest is found in the words and the rhythms of a song, the same song his aunt Pilate sings on the first page of the novel, and his rediscovered grandmother is significantly named "Sing Byrd." The duet sung by Pilate and Reba at Hagar's funeral is spontaneous, yet staged, theatrical, an operatic performance, typical of the way these particular women have always communicated among themselves. All Pilate's words are musical, rhythmic, as the young Milkman realizes: "Her voice made Milkman think of pebbles. Little round pebbles that bumped up against each other. Maybe she was hoarse, or maybe it was the way she said her words, with both a drawl and a clip" (40).

And if *Beloved* is not, as Morrison writes, "a story to pass on" (274), then it is certainly one to be sung. Morrison describes "the sound of the novel, sometimes cacophonous, sometimes harmonious, [which] must be an inner ear sound or a sound just beyond hearing, infusing the text with a musical emphasis that words can do sometimes even better than music can" (1990, 228). Sethe often recounts her "rememories" in the form of songs, made-up ballads for her children, which constitute a transmission of history and of culture, but it is also her conversation, even her thoughts, which are musical. Beloved's own voice is "gravelly" with "a song that seemed to lie in it. Just outside music it lay, with a cadence not like theirs" (60). All women's songs, Morrison indicates, are "just outside music"; often also they are codes, ways to break an enforced silence; they constitute a protest. Cixous writes, in "The Laugh of the Medusa," "In women's speech, and in their writing, that element which never stops resonating, which, once we've been permeated by it, profoundly and imperceptibly touched by it, retains the power of moving us—that element is the song: first music from the first voice of love which is alive in every woman" (312). And also in Morrison's terms, music and the singing of women have a power beyond words, a transcendent meaning that can provide "the right combination, the key, the code, the sound that broke the back of words . . . a wave of sound wide enough to sound deep water and knock the pods off chestnut trees" (*Beloved*, 261).

Certain men, too, are permitted the expression of song in Morrison's fiction. Milkman, who, in addition to his other failings, "knew no songs, and had no singing voice" (*Song of Solomon*, 340), learns to sing only on the last page of the novel when, at Pilate's request, he sings loud enough to wake the birds, although not the dying Pilate. Sixo, in *Beloved*, who needs no Pilate because suffering has been his teacher, confronts death with his hand on the mouth of a rifle and singing a song; it is the song which tells the white captor that Sixo is free in his soul and that he cannot be taken alive. All the songs at Sweet Home are expressions of a desire for freedom in which "yearning fashioned every note" (40). In Alfred, Georgia, Paul D sings his passion in songs that are "flat-headed nails for pounding and pounding and pounding" (40). Dancing "two-step to the music of hand-forged iron," Paul D and the other chained convicts

> sang it out and beat it up, garbling the words so they could not be understood; tricking the words so their syllables yielded up other meanings. They sang the women they knew; the children they had been; the animals they had tamed themselves or seen

> others tame. They sang of bosses and masters and misses; of mules and dogs and the shamelessness of life. They sang lovingly of graveyards and sisters long gone. . . . Singing love songs to Mr. Death, they smashed his head. More than the rest, they killed the flirt whom folks called Life for leading them on. Making them think the next sunrise would be worth it; that another stroke of time would do it at last. (108–9)

These songs, like those sung by women, are subversive, "garbled so they could not be understood," and they speak the lost language of Africa, the language of Sethe's mother "which would never come back" (62), and a heritage of freedom.

Like music, but even less intelligible, far more mystical, is Morrison's recurrent evocation of a sound that transcends language, a primal cry that echoes from prehistory and also breaks "the back of words." The Word of the father and even of God is rewritten by the women of *Beloved*, who know that "In the beginning there were no words. In the beginning was the sound, and they all knew what that sounded like" (259). As we also learn in *Song of Solomon* along with Milkman, this metaphysical sound, this transcendence of language, is

> what there was before language. Before things were written down. Language in the time when men and animals did talk to one another, when a man could sit down with an ape and the two converse; when a tiger and a man could share the same tree, and each understood the other; when men ran *with* wolves, not from or after them. And he was hearing it in the Blue Ridge Mountains under a sweet gum tree. And if they could talk to animals, and the animals could talk to them, what didn't they know about human beings? Or the earth itself. . . . (281)

What Milkman hears here and from Pilate, what Sethe echoes, is the "mother tongue," which, according to Kristeva, is "beyond and within, more or less than meaning: rhythm, tone, color, and joy, within, through, and across the Word" (1980, 158).

Karla Holloway and Stephanie Demetrokopoulos write in *New Dimensions of Spirituality* that "Black women carry the voice of the mother—they are the progenitors. . . . Women, as carriers of the *voice*, carry wisdom—mother wit" (123). Throughout Morrison's novels, women are the primary tale-tellers and the transmitters of history as well as the singing teachers; only they know the language of the occult and the occult of language and thus comprise what Morrison has called a "feminine subtext" (1990, 220). In *The Bluest Eye*, Claudia and her sister Frieda are spellbound by the rhythmic conversation of women, the sound of which is more important than the sense, moving far beyond language and even beyond music:

> Their conversation is like a gently wicked dance: sound meets sound, curtsies, shimmies, and retires. Another sound enters but is upstaged by still another: the two circle each other and stop. Sometimes their words move in lofty spirals; other times they take strident leaps, and all of it is punctuated with warm-pulsed laughter—like the throb of a heart made of jelly. The edge, the curl, the thrust of their emotions is always clear to Frieda and me. We do not, cannot, know the meanings of all their words, for we are nine and ten years old. So we watch their faces, their hands, their feet, and listen for truth in timbre. (16)

Perhaps it is the fluidity, the *jouissance*, in black women's speech that is so musical, so erotic, and that accomplishes "truth in timbre." Again in *The Bluest Eye*, Morrison not only describes but recreates the effect of musical language:

> They come from Mobile. Aiken. From Newport News. From Marietta. From Meridian. And the sounds of these places in their mouths make you think of love. When you ask them where they are from, they tilt their heads and say "Mobile" and you think you've been kissed. They say "Aiken" and you see a white butterfly glance off a fence with a torn wing. They say "Nagadoches" and you want to say "Yes, I will." You don't know what these towns are like, but you love what happens to the air when they open their lips and let the names ease out. (67)

Female speech, as Morrison renders it, is equivalent to what Cixous calls the "eternal essence," that feminine quality of bringing language down to earth and making it "playful." It also corresponds to Kristeva's definition of the semiotic in *Polylogue* as "a distinctive, non-expressive articulation. . . . We imagine it in infants' cries, vocalizing, and gestures; it functions in adult discourse as rhythm, prosody, word plays, the non-sense of sense, laughter" (14).

Mary Helen Washington maintains that there is a "generational continuity" among black women in which "one's mother serves as the female precursor who passes on the authority of authorship to her daughter and provides a model for the black woman's literary presence in this society" (147). Similarly, according to Kristeva, the "symbolic" as a form of communication is merely an acknowledgment of the language and the law of the father; it constitutes the repression of the "semiotic" which remains the province of the preoedipal phase, the world of the mother passed down to her daughters. According to Temma Berg as she interprets French theory in *Engendering the Word: Feminist Essays in Psychosexual Poetics*, "The fluidity of the preoedipal union with the mother offers the daughter an image of her body and of the language she needs to learn to use. Defined by woman's sexual difference, woman's language would be fluid, disorderly, sensual" (9). And, according to Berg and other theorists, and I think according to Morrison as well, the use of such language "will lead to the subversion of the closure of traditional Western metaphysics" (9).

In all her novels, Morrison implies the primacy of the maternal and the semiotic in the economy of language in order to achieve signification and a higher form of poetic (and also political) truth. As Kristeva writes in *Desire in Language*, "this relationship of the speaker to the mother is probably one of the most important factors producing interplay within the structure of meaning as well as a questioning process of subject and history" (137). Beyond the male "I" and outside of the metaphysics of binary opposition of Western humanism lies Kristeva's "she-truth" of the semiotic and, also, Morrison's mother-wit of the conjure woman, the expression of which is so central in her novels. Kristeva writes, in *Desire in Language*:

> No language can sing unless it confronts the Phallic Mother. For all that it must not leave her untouched, outside, opposite, against the law, the absolute esoteric code. Rather it must swallow her, eat her, dissolve her, set her up like a boundary of the process where "I" with "she"—"the other," "the mother"—becomes lost. Who is capable of this? "I alone am nourished by the great mother," writes Lao Tzu. (19)

As Cixous also says of the writer of feminine discourse, "There is always within her at least a little of that good mother's milk. She writes in white ink" (1986, 312).

What most wrenches the heart about Pecola in *The Bluest Eye* is not her poverty and her madness, but her motherlessness and her silence.[1] There is no adequate mother to teach her the feminine language, no preoedipal bonding to help her love herself and her body. As surrogate, she has only the "three merry gargoyles" (47), the "whores in whore's clothing" (48), to sing to her or to tell the stories that unmask the lie of the other story contained in the Dick and Jane reader, the unmusical and finally nonsensical words of which begin each chapter. The prostitutes and their stories cannot save Pecola, but they provide the only laughter in her life, and that laughter is yet another primal sound which transcends language, "like the sound of many rivers, freely, deeply, muddily, heading for the room of an open sea" (45).

Just as Pecola haunts the upstairs apartment of the three whores, seeking the laughter and the maternal space, so Milkman, living as he does in the oedipal nightmare of his family, seeks out the preoedipal arrangement of Pilate's family of women and also Pilate's mother-wit, the forbidden fruit of her knowledge, the orange she peels, the fruity wine she sells, and the perfect egg she offers. She wears a black dress and sits "wide-legged," suggestive of a birth position, and Milkman recognizes immediately that she transcends the law and the language of the father: "with the earring, the orange, and the angled black cloth, nothing—not the wisdom of his father nor the caution of the world—could keep him from her" (36). Her words are hypnotic, beyond language, and Milkman is charmed, bewitched, enthralled: "The piney-winey smell was narcotic, and so was the sun" (40). And Pilate teaches Milkman about language, that there are "five or six kinds of black. Some silky, some wooly. Some just empty" (40). As Pilate is the language-giver, she is also Milkman's spiritual mother, and on a literal level is responsible for his birth, having administered the aphrodisiac which united his parents and having made the voodoo doll which kept his father from killing him in the womb; she is also the primal mother, as Charles Scruggs notes, comparable to "the only other woman in history without a navel, Eve" (320).

The forbidden fruit Pilate gives to Milkman is a knowledge which is both more and less than that he seeks, his quest being information about his past and the past of his ancestors. She (and also the ageless Circe, another Eve figure and also a tale-telling woman) directs him to the maternal space of a cave in which he might discover gold, a bag of bones, an echo, or the ghost of his grandfather, but certainly the treasure of knowledge, even if the significance of that knowledge is lost on the unprepared boy. This cave, like the watery tunnel in *Sula* in which so many citizens of Medallion, lured by Shadrack's song, lose their lives, is an obvious womb symbol, but also more complex than that. For Morrison, the relationship with the mother is always ambiguous, revelatory yet destructive, even for women; but the male desire to return to the womb, to reenter the mother, is more often negatively associated with a surrender of consciousness or a death wish: "a big man can't be a baby all wrapped up inside his mama no more; he suffocate" (*Sula*, 62).

Death also is the dominant image in the first pages of *Tar Baby*, as the significantly named Son tries to birth himself from the sea, struggling from the vortex through "water, blood-tinted by a sun sliding into it like a fresh heart" and then darkness: "He knew he was in a part of the world that had never known and would never know twilight" (2). At the end of the novel, beaten by a world in which there is no place for him, abandoned by Jadine, Son returns to the mother, reenters the womb symbolized by the swamp that the Haitians have named "Sein de Vieilles. And witch's tit it was: a shriveled fogbound oval seeping with a thick black substance that even mosquitoes could not live near" (8), just as he has been directed by the conjure woman, Thérèse, who retains the archaic language and whose ancient breasts still give milk, images that link her also with the primal mother.[2]

What Milkman finds in the pit of the cave to which Pilate has directed him in *Song of Solomon* is even more negating and, to him, even more totally terrifying than the probable annihilation that Son runs so eagerly to meet. Milkman finds, not the bag of gold he has anticipated, nor the values of the father which such wealth represents, but that "There was nothing. Nothing at all. And before he knew it, he was hollering a long *awwww* sound into the pit" (255). This also is the birth cry, the primal scream that represents pain, that triggers bats, that greets the "too bright" light of the world.

The space of the mother is as equally ambiguous and problematic for a number of theorists as it is for Morrison; Kristeva, for one, although she celebrates both the biological condition and the metaphorical implications of motherhood, warns that women

must challenge the "myth of the archaic mother." Woman, Kristeva writes in "Women's Time," "does not exist with a capital 'W',
possessor of some mythical unity—a supreme power, on which is
based the terror of power and terrorism as the desire for power.
But what an unbelievable force for subversion in the modern
world! And, at the same time, what playing with fire!" (205).
Playing with fire, indeed, as Plum learns in *Sula* as he feels the
benediction, the blessing of the kerosene on his skin, the love of
the mother who strikes the match.

Existence in maternal space is less a problem for Morrison's
female characters, most of the central figures living in the houses
of their mothers and their grandmothers, comfortable with the
female worlds and the matriarchal social structures these houses
represent. Inevitably, the houses themselves exude exoticism, just
as do the women who live in them. The "house of many rooms"
(*Sula*, 26) in which Sula lives with Eva and Hannah is as whim-
sically constructed, with gratuitous stairways and doorways, as
the lives of its inhabitants, and it is a testament to female power
and autonomy in its refutation of male logic and practicality.
Similarly, Pilate's house, which she shares with Reba and Hagar,
is defined as female space; empty of furniture, on the edge of the
black community and therefore of both the black and the dominant cultures, it is characterized by the pervasive presence of sunshine and the smell of pine trees. Baby Suggs's house in *Beloved*,
where Sethe comes to live with her daughters, is inhospitable to
males in general; Sethe's sons flee its confines on the first page of
the novel, and it is not the baby ghost alone that at first prevents
Paul D from entering and, finally, from being able to sleep or live
at 124 Bluestone Road; for, as the first sentence of the novel
makes clear, "124 was spiteful" (3).

As we shall also see in later chapters, this pattern of women
living communally, which Morrison depicts with such frequency,
is an arrangement that is not unusual given the historical and so-
ciological realities of African American economic exigency. However, the persistence of the female triad as image in Morrison's
fiction has also to do with an inquiry into the dangerous secrets
of women's lives, their ways of knowing, and especially into their
language and the wisdom and truth it expresses. The semiotic
may be equated with the instinctual desire for the mother, the
unconscious wish to enter the *chora* which is the maternal space,

that same space which Berg defines as "the space of the unconscious, the common language of the dream, the poetry we all read/write" (13). According to Berg, the "woman's language" as defined by French theorists is that which "enables us to reenter Plato's cave, from which the 'good' male philosopher has expelled us. The cave becomes the womb, the womb from which we seek consciously to escape and to which we struggle unconsciously to return" (9).

Ambiguities, as we have seen, are inherent in the image, and in Morrison's novels the maternal space, even for women, is fraught with danger as well as with desire. Sula's death, for example, is still a death, imbued though it is with the erotic potential of union with the mother. Curled into a fetal position, lying in her grandmother's bed and in her grandmother's room, thumb in her mouth, Sula reenters the womb of death:

> It would be here, only here, held by this blind window high above the elm tree, that she might draw her legs up to her chest, close her eyes, put her thumb in her mouth and float over and down the tunnels, just missing the dark walls, down, down until she met a rain scent and would know the water was near, and she would curl into its heavy softness and it would envelop her, carry her, and wash her tired flesh always. (128)

For the child, Denver, in *Beloved*, the womb space is at first sweet and full of secrets. Just outside of her mother's house, a ring of trees forms a narrow room, a cave of "emerald light": "In that bower, closed off from the hurt of the hurt world, Denver's imagination produced its own hunger and its own food, which she badly needed because loneliness wore her out. *Wore her out.* Veiled and protected by the live green walls, she felt ripe and clear, and salvation was as easy as a wish" (28–29). Eventually Denver leaves the female space of Sethe's house—her "salvation" lies after all in a confrontation with a larger world—but not, however, until she has learned the mother tongue, drunk the mother's milk, mixed though it literally is with blood. Such relationships are also potentially damaging for the mother as well as for the daughter; Sethe's other daughter's desire to reenter the womb almost kills the mother. Although Sethe is a willing host, the community women are correct in believing that "Sethe's dead daughter, the one whose throat she cut, had come back to fix her. Sethe was worn down, speckled, dying, spinning, changing shapes and generally bedeviled" (255). That which Beloved has sought in Sethe is the maternal space, the "loneliness that can be rocked. Arms crossed, knees drawn up; holding, holding on, the motion, unlike a ship's, smooths and contains the rocker. It's an inside kind—wrapped tight like skin" (274).

In *Beloved* it is the daughter who is the primary aggressor, but Denver is haunted also by a memory of maternal violence: "Her eye was on her mother, for a signal that the thing that was in her was out, and she would kill again" (240). Fear of maternal aggression, for both men and women, is as justifiable in Morrison's novels as it is in the work of a number of psychoanalysts, including Nancy J. Chodorow in *Feminism and Psychoanalytic Theory*: "cemented by maternal and infantile rage, motherhood becomes linked to destruction and death" (85). However, for both Morrison and Chodorow, female children are more likely than their brothers to survive, even benefit, from the encounter. While all children, Chodorow argues in *The Reproduction of Mothering*, are originally and essentially "matrisexual" (95), girls experience the preoedipal phase as less threatening than do boys: "Because of their mothering by women, girls come to experience themselves as less separate than boys, as having more permeable ego boundaries" (93). Chodorow quotes Freud's statement in "Female Sexuality": "One insight into this early pre-Oedipal phase in girls comes to us as a surprise, like the discovery in another field of the Minoan-Mycenaean civilization behind the civilization of Greece" (92).[3]

Morrison, too, renders this phase poetically, and in her novels it is not merely a phase but a condition of living, there being no interruption by the father in most instances, no violation of the feminine world of mothers and daughters by the oedipal law. And, always in Morrison, this preoedipal state encompasses space that is forbidden by the fathers; it is erotic, beyond masculine "law" and order, a wild zone.[4] As we have seen, she depicts it in Eva's house in *Sula*, in Pilate's house in *Song of Solomon*, in Rosa's house in *Tar Baby*, but never so graphically as she does in *Beloved* when, after Paul D leaves Sethe's house, it becomes a veritable witch's nest, a semiotic jungle in which language itself defies convention and the laws of logic; voices merge and identities are indistinguishable:

> I am Beloved and she is mine. . . . I am not separate from
> her there is no place where I stop her face is my own and I
> want to be there in the place where her face is and to be look-
> ing at it too a hot thing . . . she is the laugh I am the
> laughter I see her face which is mine . . . she knows I want to
> join she chews and swallows me I am gone now I am her
> face my own face has left me I see me swim away a hot
> thing I see the bottoms of my feet I am alone I want to be
> the two of us I want to join . . . a hot thing now we can
> join a hot thing. . . . (210–13)

It is not surprising that Stamp Paid cannot enter the house, for what he hears from outside is "a conflagration of hasty voices— loud, urgent, all speaking at once so he could not make out what they were talking about or to whom. The speech wasn't nonsen- sical, exactly, nor was it tongues. But something was wrong with the order of the words and he couldn't describe or cipher it to save his life" (172).[5] What Stamp Paid hears and what excludes him is the mother tongue, the feminine language, which, accord- ing to Cixous and Clément is "the resonance of fore-language. She lets the other language speak—the language of one thousand tongues which knows neither enclosure nor death" (317).

Later, Stamp Paid decides that what he has heard is the "mumbling of the black and angry dead," a natural response to white people, who, he says, believe that "under every dark skin was a jungle. Swift unnavigable waters, swinging screaming ba- boons, sleeping snakes, red gums ready for their sweet white blood. In a way, he thought, they were right. . . . But it wasn't the jungle blacks brought with them to this place from the other (livable) place. It was the jungle whitefolks planted in them. And it grew. It spread" (198). Stamp Paid is only partly right; it is not merely a black jungle he intuits, but a black *woman's* jungle, a linguistic wilderness, the mumbo-jumbo of the conjure world, "the thoughts of the women of 124, unspeakable thoughts, un- spoken" (199). When, finally, Denver understands that she must extricate herself from this preoedipal stew or starve to death, it is like stepping "off the edge of the world" (239).

Also in the case of the motherless Jadine/Jade in *Tar Baby*, guilt-ridden and haunted as she is by her visions of the African mothers and by her own departure from the values they represent, the dark womb is a source of hysteria. Sheer panic is her reaction to being sucked into quicksand in the same swamp on Isle des Chevaliers into which Son is later to run so eagerly; that pit of "moss-covered jelly" is no source of poetic truth for Jadine, but instead represents the possibility of a terrifying death, suffocation in "slime"; it is the locus of worms, snakes, and crocodiles (156). In Eloe, Florida, that island of African culture in America, and in Rosa's house, that image of maternal space, Jadine is similarly oppressed and terrified, suffocated in a tiny, womblike room where she wakes to find "the blackest nothing she had ever seen. . . . It's not possible, she thought, for anything to be this black. . . . She might as well have been in a cave, a grave, the dark womb of the earth, suffocating with the sound of plant life moving, but deprived of its sight" (216–17). Morrison indicates, however, that Jadine's hysteria is a result of her own inability to choose an identity, whether black or white, and her aversion to maternal space is both cause and symptom for her fragmentation. Jadine never sings, and her conversation is "educated," too white, too superficial, too removed from the mother tongue. As Ondine tells her: "Jadine, a girl has got to be a daughter first. She have to learn that. And if she never learns how to be a daughter, she can't never learn how to be a woman" (242).

Not focused upon but powerfully present in its intimations, one of the significant silences and potent gaps in *Sula*, is Helene Wright's rejection of the preoedipal bond, her refusal to recognize in language her relationship with the Creole-speaking prostitute in the canary-yellow dress who is her mother. Nel is enchanted by the dress, the gardenia smell, and the exotic language, but Helene rejects them all: "I don't talk Creole. . . . And neither do you" (23). Perhaps Nel's cry in the last lines of the novel, a primal scream beyond and above language, a cry Jadine has forgotten but that Beloved well remembers, is a reinstatement of the semiotic from which her own mother has separated her as well as herself: "It was a fine cry—loud and long—but it had no bottom and it had no top, just circles and circles of sorrow" (149).

Sula's own similar "howl" experienced at the moment of orgasm is also a primal scream with its origins in the mother-tongue. According to Mae Gwendolyn Henderson: "It is through the howl of orgasm that Sula discovers a prediscursive center of experience that positions her at the vantage point outside of the dominant discursive order. The howl is a form of speaking in

tongues and a linguistic disruption that serves as the precondition
for Sula's entry into language" (33). Henderson further theorizes
that Sula's cry constitutes a "womblike matrix" in which "soundlessness can be transformed into utterance, unity into diversity,
formlessness into form, chaos into art, silence into tongues, and
glossolalia into heteroglossia" (35–36). Sula's howl is like Pilate's
toward the end of *Song of Solomon*, a statement of the loss of Hagar but also of universal loss, a cry for "Mercy!" that resonates
from the unconscious, from the "jungle" part of Pilate's mind:

> Suddenly, like an elephant who has just found his anger and
> lifts his trunk over the heads of the little men who want his
> teeth or his hide or his flesh or his amazing strength, Pilate
> trumpeted for the sky itself to hear, "And she was *loved*!"
> It startled one of the sympathetic winos in the vestibule
> and he dropped his bottle, spurting emerald glass and jungle-
> red wine everywhere. (323)

The primal cry, the loss of intelligible language, often effected
by the return, willing or unwilling, to maternal space, is as problematic and as fraught with danger and with the potential for hysteria for most French theorists as it is for Morrison. Alice Jardine
explains Kristeva's thoughts as follows:

> For Kristeva, the moments when women deny culture, reject
> theory, exalt the body, and so forth are moments when they
> risk crossing over the cultural borderline into hysteria. While
> recognizing hysteria as potentially liberating and as one of the
> major forms of contestation throughout our history, she also
> relentlessly emphasizes its very real limits: the fantasy of the
> phallic, all-powerful mother through which women reconnect
> with the very Law they had set out to fight. . . . (1980, 11)

Yet, even for Kristeva, the transformation of the symbolic order is
necessary, and she repeatedly argues that women must let what
she calls the "spasmodic force of the unconscious," experienced
through the link with the preoedipal mother figure, prevail and
disrupt their language in order that they may emerge sexually and
politically transformed.

Hysteria itself can function as an agent of such transformation. For Cixous in "Castration or Decapitation?" "The hysteric
is a divine spirit that is always at the edge, the turning point, of
making" (47). If hysteria results in silence, that, too, is a form of

discourse: "Silence: silence is the mark of hysteria. The great hys-
terics have lost speech, they are aphonic, and at times have lost
more than speech: they are pushed to the point of choking, nothing gets through. They are decapitated, their tongues are cut off
and what talks isn't heard because it's the body that talks, and man
doesn't hear the body" (49).

All of Morrison's works are about silence as well as about
language, whether that silence is metaphysical or physically enforced by circumstance.[6] All African Americans, like a great many
immigrants to America, write and speak in a language they do
not own as theirs. Women too, perhaps, speak generally in a language not their own but which belongs to a male culture. Historically, the dominant culture has enforced black and female silence through illiteracy as well as through hysteria, through the
metaphoric and actual insertion of the bit in the mouth which
inevitably results in "the wildness that shot up into the eye the
moment the lips were yanked back" (*Beloved*, 71). The point of
Morrison's novels, in fact, is to give a voice to the voiceless, to
speak the unspeakable on the part of the speechless, to tell just
"how offended the tongue is, held down by iron" (*Beloved*, 71).

Pecola Breedlove in *The Bluest Eye*, for example, does not tell
her own story or even speak much beyond monosyllables. Among
the poignant scenes in the novel is that in which Pecola confronts
the white owner of the candy store and can only point or nod
in the direction of the Mary Janes she covets. "Christ. Kantcha
talk?" he demands, and, in fact, Pecola cannot talk; her almost
perpetual silence prefigures the condition of hysteria in which she
ends, "picking and plucking her way between the tire rims and
the sunflowers, between Coke bottles and milkweed, among all
the waste and beauty of the world—which is what she herself
was" (159). Pecola's silence, broken only in her insane discourse
with an imaginary friend who reassures her that in fact her eyes
are blue and therefore beautiful, surely is intended to represent
the muted condition of all women as well as the powerlessness of
children in the face of cruelty and neglect, and to indict a dominant culture that values speech over silence and presence over
absence.

Because Pecola is so effectively muted, the novel is narrated
by Claudia, who recognizes her complicity and that of the rest of
the community of Lorain, Ohio, in contributing to Pecola's hys-

teria through its almost malicious refusal to provide either love or charity. Even though Claudia's narration is most often in present tense and she presents herself as a child, the reader accepts that the teller is working through memory, is now grown and capable of the poetic and sophisticated imagery she commands. Yet, still, Claudia doubts her own authenticity; occasionally the present tense is interrupted by interjections: "But was it really like that? As painful as I remember?" (14). In her summation at the novel's end, Claudia wonders whether she has not "rearranged lies and called it truth, seeing in the new pattern of an old idea the Revelation and the Word" (159). Almost as if by way of correction, Pecola's story is also told by implication in the first-person narration of her mother, as well as by a disembodied and nameless omniscience, whose word we can never doubt. This narrator, like Claudia, and like Morrison herself in all her fictions, operates within a "new pattern of an old idea," a reinscription of the Word itself which is also, paradoxically, a silence.

Henry Louis Gates, Jr., writes that much of black literature is distinguished by the stylistic use of the trope that is not "the presence of voice at all, but its absence. To speak of a silent voice is to speak in an oxymoron" (1988, 167). As Gates theorizes, blackness, like silence, signifies absence as well as racial identity within the symbolic order. In *The Bluest Eye*, Pecola cannot be heard, but she also cannot be *seen* by the candy seller: "He does not see her, because for him there is nothing to see. . . . And it is the blackness that accounts for, that creates, the vacuum edged with distaste in white eyes" (42). What is *not* seen in this novel, so imbued with the significance of vision, is as important as what *is* seen. Because of her self-perceived ugliness and because others see her as ugly as well, Pecola wishes, even prays, to become an absence, to disappear: "'Please, God,' she whispered into the palm of her hand. 'Please make me disappear'" (39).

That which has disappeared, is absent, silent, or invisible— what Morrison calls "the void that is Pecola's 'unbeing'" (1990, 220)—pervades the novel: Pauline Breedlove's unhappy life is determined by the absence of a tooth rather than by the presence of the crippled foot she blames for her misfortunes; a lack of blue eyes and her inability to conform to white standards of beauty as represented by the chimera of an absent Shirley Temple contribute to Pecola's loss of sanity; rather than a cry or a word, there is silence, only the "hollow suck of air in the back of her throat" (128) as Pecola is raped by her father; the universal deprivation of the Dick-and-Jane-reader image of the pretty green and white house with the red door is the cause rather than the effect of historical suffering; the novel opens and closes with references to the marigolds that do *not* grow in 1941.

Sula, too, is a novel about absence as well as about presence, and, like *The Bluest Eye*, it inverts a system of thought and values that can entertain only the viability of presence. The very setting of the story, the neighborhood of the Bottom in Medallion, Ohio, no longer exists at the time of the telling, nor do its "nightshade and blackberry patches," nor the beech trees, nor Irene's Palace of Cosmetology, all having been replaced by the Medallion City Golf Course. More than nostalgia has been established by their absence, for now the Bottom is part of myth and memory, and, as such, it becomes a kind of center, a world navel, a cosmic omphalos, a "Medallion" in fact. The "nigger joke" told on the first page of the novel is really on the white man who thought he lied when he said that this land was "the bottom of heaven" (5).

Sula, the "central" character, is also defined by absence, having "no center, no speck around which to grow" (103). She is literally absent for ten years of the novel's action, her whereabouts only vaguely accounted for, and she dies three-quarters of the way through. Among the significant moments of her life is not the killing, however accidental, of Chicken Little, but her recognition of the "closed place in the water" where he has disappeared, the "something newly missing" (52). Even orgasm for Sula is defined by silence and by absence—a "howl" that is paradoxically "soundlessness," a transcendence of the "word"—and by a recognition of something missing or lost: "she leaped from the edge into soundlessness and went down howling, howling in a stinging awareness of the endings of things: an eye of sorrow in the midst of all that hurricane of rage and joy. There, in the center of that silence was not eternity but the death of time and a loneliness so profound the word itself had no meaning" (106).

For both Sula and Nel, life and its choices are defined more by what they are *not* than by what they are; being "neither white nor male, and that all freedom and triumph was forbidden to them, they had set about creating something else to be" (44). Shadrack, too, is defined by negation: "with no past, no language, no tribe, no source, no address book, no comb, no pencil, no clock, no pocket handkerchief, no rug, no bed, no can opener, no faded postcard, no soap, no key, no tobacco pouch, no soiled underwear and nothing nothing nothing to do" (10). Relationships, like that between Sula and Nel, or between Nel and Jude, are a matter of filling spaces, the "space in front of me, behind me, in my head" (124). Much more significant for Sula than Ajax's presence is his absence, which "was everywhere, stinging everything, giving the furnishings primary colors, sharp outlines to the corners of rooms and gold light to the dust collecting on table tops" (116). Where does Ajax go when he leaves Sula, or Jude when he leaves Nel, and where was Eva when she lost her leg? Morrison explains in "The Afro-American Presence in American Literature" that "invisible things are not necessarily 'not-there'; that a void may be empty, but is not a vacuum. In addition, certain absences are so stressed, so ornate, so planned, they call attention to themselves; arrest us with intentionality and purpose . . ." (1990, 210).

Most obviously in *Sula*, there is the absence of Eva Peace's leg, the other rendered more glamorous by "the long fall of space below her left thigh" (27); it is this missing limb which may well be responsible for Eva's attainment of money and therefore of power, but it is also her refusal to *tell* how and why she lost the leg that accounts for her status in the community and her mythic presence in the novel. Marianne Hirsch, in *The Mother/Daughter Plot*, argues convincingly that communication between mothers and daughters is always characterized by silence and based on "the unspeakable," and in *Sula*, "Eva's missing leg is the mark of maternal discourse in the novel and the key to its (thematized) ambivalence toward it" (179). According to Houston A. Baker, Jr., Eva's missing leg is itself a challenge to patriarchy and to capitalism, an "utterance of the *Non Servium*," a conversion of her body "into a dismembered instrument of defiance—and finance" (91).

In *Song of Solomon*, places as well as people are defined by what they are not: "Not Doctor Street" and "No Mercy Hospital" are both terms of passive resistance, defiance hurled in the teeth of white officialdom. But the most important absence in this novel is the smooth, bare space on the stomach of Pilate Dead, that place where a navel should have been. So dominant is this absence in her life that it dictates her position on the margins of her community, while it also defines her mythological status as a woman who gave birth to herself, who "began at zero" (149). Like the white spaces in Chinese paintings that define their shapes and designs, absence defines the form of this novel as well as Pilate's significance at its center. The "nothing" that Milkman Dead finds at the center of the cave, the center of maternal space to which Pilate directs him, is, in reality, everything, the perfect circle, the mystical zero without which numbers, and indeed all logic and knowing, are impossible.[7]

Clearly, the significant silences and the stunning absences throughout Morrison's texts become profoundly political as well as stylistically crucial. Morrison describes her own work as containing "holes and spaces so the reader can come into it" (Tate 1989, 125), testament to her rejection of theories that privilege the author over the reader. Morrison disdains such hierarchies in which the reader as participant in the text is ignored: "My writing expects, demands participatory reading, and I think that is what literature is supposed to do. It's not just about telling the story; it's about involving the reader . . . we (you, the reader, and I, the author) come together to make this book, to feel this experience" (Tate 1989, 125). But Morrison also indicates in each of her novels that images of the zero, the absence, the silence that is both chosen and enforced, are ideologically and politically revelatory. The history of slavery itself, Morrison writes in *Beloved*, is "not a story to pass on" but, rather, is something that is "unspeakable," unconscionable, unbearable. Among the heinous crimes of slavery was its silencing of its victims; how perversely ironic it is that "Schoolteacher" does not come to Sweet Home to teach literacy, but to take notes, to do scholarship on the measurement of black craniums. Ironic, too, is the fact that Schoolteacher's notes are taken in ink that Sethe, herself quite possibly functionally illiterate, has manufactured. Paul D cannot read the newspaper account of Sethe's crime, and, even in freedom, Denver must lurk outside and beneath the window of the reading teacher's house.

Morrison's characters are most frequently politically muted in spite of the lyrical language of the mother she always provides for them. They themselves do not articulate, or perhaps realize, the political ramifications of certain of their actions, but Morrison repeatedly translates the body itself into political "speech." Eva's act of self-mutilation in *Sula*, for example, is motivated by a will to survive, but the effect is also a statement indicting poverty and the conditions of life for black women. As Eva endures the amputation of her leg, so Sula slices off the tip of her own finger, ostensibly to protect herself and Nel from abusive white boys, but also effectively to issue a warning, to use her body as a language. And Sethe in *Beloved* trades ten minutes of sex for a single inscription, "the one word that mattered" (5), on her daughter's tombstone, thus almost literally translating her body into the written word. Sethe's motivation for murdering her child is, obviously, a desperate attempt to protect that child from what she considers a fate far worse than death; but, as we shall see in Chapter 3, Morrison renders this act also as the ultimate statement, the most significant transcendence of the word, an act of the body that, like slavery itself, is truly "unspeakable."

Silence exists also in the text of *Beloved* itself, as, according to Wilfred D. Samuels and Clenora Hudson-Weems, was the case in the original slave narratives, characterized by "not what history has recorded . . . but what it has omitted" (96). Samuels and Hudson-Weems quote Morrison as saying of slave narratives: "somebody forgot to tell somebody something. . . . My job becomes how to rip that veil" (97). But Morrison's own "veils," indicative of the kind of pain the writing of *Beloved* entailed, remain implicit in the text, which itself is a revision, an inversion, and, finally, a subversion of traditional value systems that privilege presence over absence and speech over silence.[8] The central paradox, however, is that the silence of women echoes with reverberation, speaks louder than words: "What a roaring," writes Morrison in *Beloved* (181).

Reverberation is that quality which characterizes all of Morrison's fictions—what is left unsaid is equally as important as what is stated and specified; what is felt is as significant as what is experienced; what is dreamed is as valid as what transpires in the world of "fact." And none of these conditions of being is rendered as opposite; there are no polarities between logic and mysticism, between real and fantastic. Rather, experience for Morrison's characters is the acceptance of a continuum, a recognition that the mind is not separate from the body or the real separate from that which the imagination can conceive. She writes from the maternal space, which is consciousness but also the unconscious, the dream world; but those dreams have substance, teeth, and they are part of a world conception in which terms like "fact" seem superfluous. In Chapter 3, we shall see that "magic realism" is not, for Morrison, an oxymoron. In an interview with Grace Epstein, Morrison talks about the significance of dreams, their practical value for winning at the numbers game when she was a child in Lorain, Ohio, and about how their validity was unquestioned, particularly by her mother, who "thought" rather than "dreamed" her sleeping experiences:

> It was like the second life she was living, so that dreamscape, then, becomes accessible, a separate part, and it's functional in some respects. As a child the problem is trying to establish what is real and what is not real. Since my dreams were real in the sense they were about *reality*, some dream life could spill over into the regular life; that's where the enchantment came from. (5)

All of Morrison's fictions partake of a dreamscape, contain a quality that is surreal at times, largely because of this refusal to mark dreams as distinct or separate from "reality."[9] There are some dreams—in *Sula*, for example, in which Hannah dreams her own death by fire as "a wedding in a red bridal gown" (63)— that serve as predictions; but these are exceptions. Narrative itself is dreamlike: diffused, fluid, always erotic. In one sense, Morrison's novels serve as the reader's own dreams, where that which is repressed, contained, becomes consciously expressed. Irigaray writes about the dream quality of the feminine text as a reflection of the feminine sensibility: "women diffuse themselves according to modalities scarcely compatible with the framework of the ruling symbolics. Which doesn't happen without causing some turbulence, we might even say some whirlwinds, that ought to be reconfined within solid walls of principle, to keep them from spreading to infinity" (1985, 106).

Morrison's language does, in essence, spread to "infinity," and the prevalent image of flight in all her novels is more than a symbol for freedom or for ambition. Airplanes, birds, anything that flies, become signifiers for the flight of language itself, for the movement beyond linguistic boundaries, for the untraditional style and structure of Morrison's work. Cixous writes, "Flying is a woman's gesture—flying in language and making it fly" (1986, 316). While Morrison's language soars in *The Bluest Eye*, little Pecola, without a language, can only aspire to a grotesque imitation of flight: "Elbows bent, hands on shoulders, she flailed her arms like a bird in an eternal, grotesquely futile effort to fly. Beating the air, a winged but grounded bird, intent on the blue void it could not reach—could not even see—but which filled the valleys of the mind" (158).

Morrison's male characters, too, imagine themselves in flight and are almost all in love with airplanes. Ajax in *Sula* loves his mother, and "after her—airplanes. There was nothing in between" (109). In the tradition of black literature since Richard Wright's *Native Son*, however, the privilege of flight, at least in airplanes, is mostly reserved for white boys. Black males, in Morrison, fly only metaphorically, and then only with the assistance and the inspiration of black women. According to Baker, in his aptly titled "When Lindbergh Sleeps with Bessie Smith," "flight is a function of black woman's conjure and not black male industrial initiative" (105). The only male character in *Sula* permitted flight pays with his life; Sula picks up Chicken Little and swings him out over the water, letting go (accidentally) at that precise moment when his joy is greatest: "His knickers ballooned and shrieks of frightened joy startled the birds and the fat grasshoppers. When he slipped from her hands and sailed away out over the water they could still hear his bubbly laughter" (52). Sula alone in this novel is capable of seeing "the slant of life that made it possible to stretch it to its limits"; she only has the ability to "free fall," to complete that action "that required—demanded—invention: a thing to do with the wings, a way of holding the legs and most of all a full surrender to the downward flight," and this act only can allow the flyer to "taste the tongue or stay alive" (103–4).

Song of Solomon opens with the image of attempted flight, as Robert Smith, ironically an agent of the North Carolina Mutual Life Insurance company, promises to "take off from Mercy and fly away on my own wings" (3). Pilate (Pilot?) does not save him (as the reader always hopes she might and believes she could), but she sings him to his death: "O Sugarman done fly / O Sugarman done gone," and he, at least, "had seen the rose petals, heard the music" (9). And Milkman Dead, born the next day in Mercy Hospital, the first "colored" baby ever to claim that distinction, must, Morrison says, have been marked by Mr. Smith's blue silk wings, for "when the little boy discovered, at four, the same thing Mr. Smith had learned earlier—that only birds and airplanes could fly—he lost all interest in himself" (9).

Years later, Milkman and his friend, Guitar, are amazed by the mysterious, even mystical appearance of a peacock over the building of the used car lot where they stand. As the bird descends, Milkman mistakes it for a female, but Guitar corrects him: "He. That's a he. The male is the only one got that tail full of jewelry. Son of a bitch." Milkman, in all his innocent conviction of male superiority, asks why the peacock can fly no better than a chicken, and Guitar, who wants to catch and eat the bird, answers, "Too much tail. All that jewelry weighs it down. Like vanity. Can't nobody fly with all that shit. Wanna fly, you got to give up the shit that weighs you down" (179–80).

Morrison permits Milkman at least one experience of actual flight, if only on a plane, but even then "the wings of all those other people's nightmares flapped in his face and constrained him" (222). Mostly, Milkman's flight fantasies are in the form of dreams, and they evoke womb images more than an idea of freedom:

> It was a warm dreamy sleep all about flying, about sailing high over the earth. But not with arms stretched out like airplane wings, nor shot forward like Superman in a horizontal dive, but floating, cruising, in the relaxed position of a man lying on a couch reading a newspaper. Part of his flight was over the dark sea, but it didn't frighten him because he knew he could not fall. He was alone in the sky, but somebody was applauding him, watching him and applauding. (302)

In order to truly fly, however, Milkman must give up his male vanities, "the shit that weighs [him] down"; it is necessary to placate the violated female essence of his universe, atone for his mistreatment of Hagar, apologize for his failure to recognize the humanity of his sisters and his mother, exorcise the influence of his father, and embrace the teachings of Pilate, who is surely the one applauding and watching in Milkman's dream.

Whether or not Milkman fulfills these requirements, becomes a better human being, and actually flies as a reward on the last page of the novel is a subject for a great deal of critical contro-

versy. According to Cynthia A. Davis, Milkman truly flies, and he
represents the traditional mythic hero:

> Milkman's life follows the pattern of the classic hero, from mi-
> raculous birth (he is the first black baby born in Mercy Hospi-
> tal, on a day marked by song, rose petals in the snow, and hu-
> man "flight") through quest-journey to final reunion with his
> double. And Milkman largely resolves the conflict between free-
> dom and connection . . . he finds that his quest is his culture's;
> he can only discover what he is by discovering what his family
> is. By undertaking the quest, he combines subjective freedom
> with objective fact and defines himself in both spheres. . . .
> Only in the recognition of his condition can he act in it, only
> in commitment is he free. (333–34)

But even among classical heroes, there is the possibility of failure
in flight, and Icarus always looms as example. At the opposite
extreme of interpretation from Davis's analysis is that by Gerry
Brenner, who argues that Morrison's treatment of Milkman is
purely ironic, and that her attitude toward his search for his "gene
pool" is one of disdain. Even the image of flight, in Brenner's
analysis, is pejorative, representing "man's prerogative—to escape
domestication, to fly from responsibility, in the name of self-
fulfillment or self-discovery or self-indulgence . . . he flies, indeed,
from the burdens of doing something meaningful in life, preferring the sumptuous illusion that he will ride the air" (119). Morrison herself indicates that her rendering of myth in this novel is
indeed ironic: "Sotto (but not completely) is my own giggle (in
Afro-American terms) of the proto-myth of the journey to manhood. Whenever characters are cloaked in Western fable, they are
in deep trouble; but the African myth is also contaminated"
(1990, 226). Also evidence that Morrison's rendering of Milkman's character is ironic can be found in her own statement: "I
chose the man to make that journey because I thought he had
more to learn than a woman would have" (McKay, 428).

Certainly women suffer as a result of the male desire for
flight. Milkman's ancestor, Solomon/Shalimar, was one of numer-
ous slaves from Africa who could fly; according to the story Milkman is told, Solomon launched himself into the air from a cotton
field one day, leaving behind his wife and twenty-one children.
The cry of the abandoned woman, another primal scream from

the jungle of female discourse, still echoes throughout the land in Ryna's Gulch, a testament to the irresponsibility of men and the proclivity of women to love them. Milkman, too, has abandoned every woman in his life, including the convenient Sweet, who warms the bed and bathes his body in the last sections of the novel. Pilate alone is the woman/mother who commands Milkman's respect and his love, for "Without ever leaving the ground, she could fly" (340).

Whether or not Milkman "rides the air" in the last lines, or whether he reenacts the suicide of Robert Smith on page one, jumping into space and delivering himself into "the killing arms of his brother," is, finally, ambiguous. Were Morrison to resolve this novel so neatly with Milkman's complete regeneration and reward, the reader's expectations about her recurrent and pervasive use of paradox, her refusal in every novel to adopt novelistic conventions about closure and resolution, would be disappointed. Significant to Morrison's great strength as a writer is the fact that her style is imbued with contradiction and saturated with breaches of narrative continuity. And, according to Irigaray, a feminine style of writing, is "always *fluid*," always "resists and explodes every firmly established form, figure, idea, or concept" to the point that "linear reading is no longer possible" (1985, 79–80).

As we shall also see in a later chapter on Morrison's rendering of history, concepts like linearity, progress, chronology, even development, are not primarily valuable in an analysis of her works, nor do they form a pattern for the structure of her novels. Morrison's structures are almost always circular, diffuse, organized by a radical standard of that which constitutes order. (This study, too, is deliberately arranged thematically rather than chronologically, in deference to Morrison's style and in an attempt to discount linearity as a value.) It would be worse than useless, for example, to talk about "plot development" in Morrison's novels; there is plot, certainly, but its revelation *culminates* or evolves through a process of compilation of multiple points of view, varieties of interpretation of events (and some of these contradictory), through repetition and reiteration. As there is no "climax," in the usual sense, so also there is no resolution, no series of events that can conveniently be labeled "beginning, middle, end." Cixous characterizes feminine writing in the following way: "A feminine textual body is recognized by the fact that it is always endless, without ending; there's no closure, it doesn't stop. . . . A feminine text starts on all sides, all at once, starts twenty times, thirty times, over" (1981, 53).

All of Morrison's novels embody a principle that defies closure: *The Bluest Eye* reveals in the second sentence that "Pecola was having her father's baby," and the rest of the text is an afterthought: "There is really nothing more to say—except why. But since why is difficult to handle, one must take refuge in how" (9). The "how," then, is explained from every perspective, including a historical one in which Pecola does not even participate as subject. Morrison explains her choice for the structure of this novel:

> I tell you at the beginning of *The Bluest Eye* on the very first page what happened, but now I want you to go with me and look at this, so when you get to the scene where the father rapes the daughter, which is as awful a thing, I suppose, as can be imagined, by the time you get there it's almost irrelevant because I want you to *look* at him and see his love for his daughter and his powerlessness to help her pain. By that time his embrace, the rape, is all the gift he has left. (Tate 1989, 125)

Morrison has also explained her intention of subverting the literary tradition of male rape fantasies through a use of feminine language: "It is interesting to me that where I thought I would have the most difficulty subverting the language to a feminine mode, I had the least: connecting Cholly's 'rape' by the white men to his own of his daughter. This most masculine act of aggression becomes feminized in my language, 'passive,' and, I think, more accurately repellent when deprived of the male 'glamor of shame' rape is (or once was) routinely given" (1990, 220).

Perspective and narrative responsibility in *Sula* are similarly "feminized" by being fragmented and multiple; the novel begins with a story from Shadrack's perspective, which has little, immediately, to do with Sula; Nel, and even Nel's mother, are also centers of consciousness at times only marginally concerned with Sula. Each event in the novel is similarly fragmented, related impressionistically, and thus this novel, like all of Morrison's works, subverts concepts of textual unity and defies totalized interpretation.

Tar Baby, too, has multiple centers, as well as multiple central characters whose histories are gradually revealed in fragments by a variety of sources. Secrets and silences and the failure of love comprise the province of each set of couples in the novel; Son and Jadine share the focus with Sydney and Ondine, Margaret and Valerian, and even with Thérèse and Gideon, all of whom lose identity in Morrison's concern for the central dyad, white and black, and even this opposition is blurred, merged, rendered less valid. Setting, too, in this novel is amorphous; whether the reader is in Isle des Chevaliers, Eloe, Florida, or in New York City ("if ever there was a black woman's town, New York was it" [191]), she is always in a world of myth, a place that is metaphorically "the end of the world" (7).

The same blurring of boundaries is true of *Beloved*, in which the personal history of Sethe and her daughters is revealed ever so gradually, fragmented into symbols, and, finally, becomes one with the history of all African Americans. Everyone tells or sings the story of slavery and the escape into a freedom that is also, paradoxically, still a form of slavery. And, each tale, each aspect of the monomyth, is retold, elaborated upon, rendered in circles and silences by every character in the novel; Sethe's recounting of her story to Paul D is accompanied by a physical act of making circles and is emblematic of all tale-telling in the novel: "At first he thought it was her spinning. Circling him the way she was circling the subject. Round and round, never changing direction, which might have helped his head . . . listening to her was like having a child whisper into your ear so close you could feel its lips form the words you couldn't make out because they were too close" (161). But the largest circle and the deepest secrets are those told us by that same enigmatic, pervasive omniscience which is Morrison herself.

Despite the ambiguity and the lack of resolution at the conclusion, *Song of Solomon* is, in form, more conventional than Morrison's other novels, styled as it is after the traditional bildungsroman and stressing as it does the education of a young man. Morrison has described her intentions with regard to the structure of her novels in the following way:

> The first two books were beginnings. I start with the childhood of a person in all the books; but in the first two, the movement, the rhythm, is circular, although the circles are broken. If you

> go back to the beginnings, you get pushed along toward the
> end. This is particularly so with *The Bluest Eye*. *Sula* is more
> spiral than circular. *Song of Solomon* is different. I was trying to
> push this novel outward; its movement is neither circular nor
> spiral. The image in my mind for it is that of a train picking up
> speed; and that image informs the language; whereas with *The
> Bluest Eye* and *Sula*, the rhythm is very different. (Tate 1989, 124)

It is quite likely that Morrison's use of traditional novel structure
in *Song of Solomon* is a deliberate subversion of the form itself, just
as she has indicated that the style of the opening pages is a mock
journalistic style (1990, 224). If, as was discussed earlier, Morrison's treatment of Milkman as a character is at least partially
ironic, then there is also the possibility that her "imitation" of the
bildungsroman, itself a gendered form, is parodic, carnivalesque,
yet another indication of Milkman's privileged status within the
realm of the symbolic, even though his quest, ultimately, is to
escape what is not, after all, a privilege but a limitation.

Morrison's ironies, however, are always gentle, meant to heal
rather than to wound, to correct rather than to punish. Her humor, like her use of language in general and like her departures
from stylistic tradition, is nonetheless subversive, often sexually
implicit (as we shall see in Chapter 4), certainly gendered. She
takes her novelistic pleasure and provides the same for her readers,
for her language is always a celebration of the laugh of the Medusa, even when her subjects are so serious, so tragic and intense,
that they turn us to stone.

2

Hagar's Mirror: Self and Identity

> One day Pilate sat down on Hagar's bed and held a compact
> before her granddaughter's face. It was trimmed in a goldlike
> metal and had a pink plastic lid.
>
> "Look, baby. See here?" Pilate turned it all around to show
> it off and pressed in the catch. The lid sprang open and Hagar
> saw a tiny part of her face reflected in the mirror. She took the
> compact then and stared into the mirror for a long while.
>
> "No wonder," she said at last. "Look at that. No wonder.
> No wonder."
>
> —*Song of Solomon*

Mirrors are dangerous objects in Morrison's fictions. What destroys Hagar is not merely Pilate's oppressive love (her gift of the
mirror being evidence of this) nor Milkman's failure to love, but
the vision of herself as *self* that the mirror reflects. The mirror lies
in telling her that she is not beautiful, for mirrors represent only
white standards of beauty;[1] but the greater lie is that illusion of
unified selfhood which mirrors also perpetrate, for the "self" in
Morrison's fiction, like her use of language discussed in the preceding chapter, is always multiple, contradictory, and ambiguous—if, in fact, a self can be said to exist at all.

An interesting parallel to Hagar's mirror-death exists early in
the same novel, at the point at which Milkman gazes at his own
face in the mirror with at least mild approval of the "firm jaw line,
splendid teeth" but largely unaware of what the narrator knows,
that the image "lacked coherence, a coming together of the features into a total self" (69–70). According to Cixous and Clé-

ment in *The Newly Born Woman*, when a man looks into a mirror, he "identifies and constitutes himself with the mirror. It reflects his image to him, *fixes* it as a subject and subjects it to the law, to the symbolic order, to language, and does it in a way that is both inalienable and alienating" (137). Milkman's "self"-analysis is juxtaposed, significantly, to the entrance of his father, who surely represents for Morrison an exaggerated and clearly parodic version of patriarchal inscriptions, including those of identity and selfhood, most particularly the fiction that "You have to be a whole man. And if you want to be a whole man, you have to deal with the whole truth" (70).

Clearly, there are no "whole truths" or "whole" men and women in Morrison's novels, at least not in any traditional fictional sense. Just as she challenges the dominant cultural view of language and signification (as was discussed in the preceding chapter), so Morrison also subverts traditional Western notions of identity and wholeness. Patricia Waugh, in *Feminine Fictions: Revisiting the Postmodern*, is not alone in her observation that the death of the self is characteristic of all postmodern fictions, which thus act to undermine traditional philosophies by contradicting "the dualistic, objective posturing of western rationality" (22). More central to the present concern is Waugh's argument that "for those marginalized by the dominant culture, a sense of identity as constructed through impersonal and social relations of power (rather than a sense of identity as the reflection of an inner 'essence') has been a major aspect of their self-concept long before post-structuralists and postmodernists began to assemble their cultural manifestos" (3). If this is true particularly for women, as Waugh maintains, how much more radical might be the deconstruction of the self as a concept in fiction by those doubly marginalized by race as well as gender?

French theorists are among those who in recent years have radically undermined notions of the unitary self, notions they attribute directly to Western humanism, which they see as totally and unmitigatedly male in origin as well as in values. Irigaray, for example, condemns what she and many others term phallocentric literature as the "endless litigation over identity with oneself" (118). She defines feminine language by contrast as inherently multiple, based on the complex biology of women:

in that "syntax" there would no longer be either subject or object, "oneness" would no longer be privileged, there would no longer be proper meanings, proper names, "proper" attributes. . . . Instead, that "syntax" would involve nearness, proximity, but in such an extreme form that it would preclude any distinction of identities, any establishment of ownership, thus any form of appropriation. (134)

Alice Jardine, whose theoretical focus is an interpretation of French feminisms, characterizes their works as a "whirlpool of decentering" in which "The notion of the 'Self'—so intrinsic to Anglo-American thought, becomes absurd. It is not something called the 'Self' which speaks, but language, the unconscious, the 'textuality of the text'" (1986, 563). Toril Moi also analyzes French resistance to concepts of selfhood in terms of Lacan and Derrida, and writes:

As Luce Irigaray or Hélène Cixous would argue, this integrated self is in fact a phallic self, constructed on the model of the self-contained, powerful phallus. Gloriously autonomous, it banishes from itself all conflict, contradiction and ambiguity. In this humanist ideology the self is the *sole author* of history and of the literary text: the humanist creator is potent, phallic and male—God in relation to his world, the author in relation to his text. History or the text become nothing but "expression" of this unique individual: all art becomes autobiography, a mere window on to the self and the world, with no reality of its own. (1985, 8)

As she has made clear in a number of interviews, Morrison does not write autobiography.[2] As the author has no self that is manifested in her fiction, so also Morrison's narrators are most often unidentifiable, anonymous, vehicles to transmit information and convey emotion rather than to provide moral interpretations or represent a personality.[3] Often these narrators disappear completely as one character or another steps forward to tell the story from a different point of view. But even these speaking characters reflect multiple and fragmented selves, which are sometimes undefined, inevitably amorphous, always merging with the identity of a community as a whole or with the very concept of blackness. Henry Louis Gates, Jr., has commented on the irony of African

American writers attempting "to posit a 'black self' in the very Western languages in which blackness itself is a figure of absence, a negation" (1984, 7).

For example, in *Sula*, that point at which Nel looks into the mirror and discovers her "me-ness" is almost as fraught with premonition of disaster as when Hagar peers into the pink and gold compact in *Song of Solomon*. For Nel, the mirror reflects, not a concept called Nel, but something other: "'I'm not Nel. I'm me. Me.' Each time she said the word *me* there was a gathering in her like power, like joy, like fear" (24–25). Nel's assertion of selfhood, whether an indication of false pride or merely an adolescent delusion, ends in the reality of her common identity with other women of the community. For Sula, at least, Nel has become one of those unindividuated women: "The narrower their lives, the wider their hips. Those with husbands had folded themselves into starched coffins, their sides bursting with other people's skinned dreams and bony regrets. Those without men were like sour-tipped needles featuring one constant empty eye" (105). In Morrison's fictions, identity is always provisional; there can be no isolated ego striving to define itself as separate from community, no matter how tragic or futile the operations of that community might be. Individual characters are inevitably formed by social constructions of both race and gender, and they are inseparable from those origins.

That early scene in *Sula* in which Shadrack attempts to discover an identity in the only mirror accessible to him, the water in a toilet bowl, confirms the idea that "self" lies in blackness rather than in any subjectivity or uniqueness: "There in the toilet water he saw a grave black face. A black so definite, so unequivocal, it astonished him. He had been harboring a skittish apprehension that he was not real—that he didn't exist at all. But when the blackness greeted him with its indisputable presence, he wanted nothing more" (11). Interestingly, in this novel, blackness is a *presence* rather than an absence,[4] a key to an identity that is always multiple, shared, a form of membership in community.[5]

Even Sula, although the novel is named for her, is not, strictly speaking, a protagonist, for she shares the novel's focus as well as a black identity with Nel, Shadrack, Nel's mother, Eva, and the community itself. Her identity, multiple as it is, is a reflection of community identity; when she absents herself from that community for ten years, she ceases to exist within the text itself. Her much-quoted assertion, "I don't want to make somebody else. I want to make myself" (80), is almost demonic in Morrison's terms, one indication of many of the moral ambiguities Sula represents. To "make" one's self, or at least to make of one's self a single entity, is impossible, for all selves are multiple, divided, fragmented, and a part of a greater whole.

Sula's birthmark, for example, interpreted by every other character in the novel as representing a variety of images, is not only a reflection of the characters of those interpreting, but is also a valid indication of Sula's own multiplicity.[6] Her mark is, in fact, a stemmed rose, a tadpole, a snake, an ash from her mother's burning body, all interacting to represent aspects of Sula's ambiguous essence. As Deborah E. McDowell writes in "The Self and the Other: Reading Toni Morrison's *Sula* and the Black Female Text," Sula's birthmark "acts as a metaphor for her figurative 'selves,' her multiple identity" (1988, 81). McDowell concludes, based on this argument, that "Morrison's reconceptualization of character has clear and direct implications for Afro-American literature and critical study, for if the self is perceived as perpetually in process, rather than a static entity always already formed, it is thereby difficult to posit its ideal or 'positive' representation" (81). Even beyond McDowell's conception of self-in-process, however, lies the possibility of self as negation, as illusion, as contradiction, as an aspect of "the something else to be" (44) which Nel and Sula create for themselves.

Even Sula's birthmark, potentially a sign of an individual self however fragmented and multiple, is rather an indication of relationship, being one of a series of marks, brands, or emblems that Morrison employs in most of her novels, not to "distinguish" individuals, but (as blackness itself is a mark) to symbolize their participation in a greater entity, whether that is community or race or both. The marks are hieroglyphs, clues to a culture and a history more than to individual personality. Whether the "mark" is Pauline Breedlove's crippled foot in *The Bluest Eye,* Eva's missing leg in *Sula*, Pilate's navel-less stomach in *Song of Solomon*, Son's rastafarian dreadlocks in *Tar Baby*, or the crossed circle mandala branded beneath the breast of Sethe's mother in *Beloved*, or even the choke-cherry tree scars on Sethe's own back, these represent membership rather than separation. If these marks distinguish at all, they distinguish a racial identity, for most are either chosen or inflicted by the condition of blackness itself, by the poverty that has historically accompanied blackness, or by the institution of slavery which "marked" its victims literally and figuratively, physically and psychologically. "If something happens to me and you can't tell me by my face, you can know me by this mark," Sethe's African mother tells her. And the child Sethe answers, "Mark me, too . . . Mark the mark on me too" (*Beloved*, 61). Whether this is the mark of Cain or the bloodstain of a Passover, a curse or an anointment, it denotes a sisterhood (and sometimes a brotherhood as well) of Africa, which in itself is a political statement both subversive and confrontational.[7]

The verbal equivalent of such marks is the name, which, also like marks, does not necessarily designate an individual self so much as a segment of community, an identity larger than self. As Morrison has said in an interview with Thomas Le Clair: "If you come from Africa, your name is gone. It is particularly problematic because it is not just *your* name but your family, your tribe. When you die, how can you connect with your ancestors if you have lost your name? That's a huge psychological scar" (28). Of least importance in Morrison's novels are those names which are a part of the dominant signifying order, those denoting ownership, appropriation, those originating in slavery, those which deny group identity and African origins. In *Beloved*, Baby Suggs recalls her slave name as Jenny Whitlow; only as Mr. Garner delivers her into freedom can she turn and ask him, "why you all call me Jenny?" Her lack of a name—"Nothing . . . I don't call myself nothing" (141)—is testament to the "desolated center where the self that was no self made its home" (140). Baby Suggs has no "self" because she has no frame of reference by which to establish one, no family, no children, no context: "Sad as it was that she did not know where her children were buried or what they looked like if alive, fact was she knew more about them than she knew about herself, having never had the map to discover what she was like" (140).

Similarly, Paul D is one of a series of Pauls, identified alphabetically by some anonymous slaveholder, while Sixo is presumably the sixth of an analogous group.[8] Stamp Paid, born Joshua under slavery, has, however, chosen and devised his own symbolic name, which represents a rejection of a tradition of white naming as well as a celebration of freedom. His name is also and more specifically a symbol of freedom from debt; because he suffered under slavery and because he "handed over his wife to his master's son" (184), he has paid in misery any obligation to humanity, he believes, although his continued activity as a conductor on the Underground Railroad would indicate otherwise. All African Americans are, in essence, "Stamp Paid," Morrison implies.

Sethe's name is one of the few in this novel chosen by a mother, and that name is a mark of blackness and of acceptance into tribe and culture. As Nan tells the "small girl Sethe," "She threw them all away but you. The one from the crew she threw away on the island. The others from more whites she also threw away. Without names, she threw them. You she gave the name of the black man" (62). Whether this name is derived from that of the Egyptian god, Seth, or from the biblical Seth, it represents, like most of the names that Morrison designates as chosen, a sense of heritage and a context of relational identity.

And, Beloved, whose birth name we never learn, takes her identity from the single word on her tombstone and from the love her mother bears her, the paradox of which is reflected in the novel's epigraph from *Romans*: "I will call them my people, which were not my people; and her beloved, which was not beloved." Finally, Beloved has no identity other than that merged with the "Sixty million and more" of the dedication, all those who suffered the outrage of enslavement; her consciousness is a group consciousness, her memory a racial memory of the Middle Passage. All names in Morrison's fictions, finally, are, like that of Beloved, names of the "Disremembered and unaccounted for, she cannot be lost because no one is looking for her, and even if they were, how can they call her if they don't know her name?" (275).

Early in *Song of Solomon*, Macon Dead considers that he might have a better sense of the identity for which he futilely strives throughout the novel, mainly through an accumulation of wealth and an approximation of white bourgeois standards of living, if he could locate his ancestral context: "Surely, he thought, he and his sister had some ancestor, some lithe young man with onyx skin and legs as straight as cane stalks, who had a name that was real. A name given to him at birth with love and seriousness. A name that was not a joke, nor a disguise, nor a brand name" (17). For three generations, the Macon Deads have borne a name, the drunken mistake of a white bureaucrat, which is both a brand and a joke that continues throughout the novel: "You can't kill me. I'm already Dead." Although Milkman's nickname is so ignominiously earned, also a joke, and his character so ironically ambiguous, formed as it is by a parody of patriarchy, his ultimate dignity lies in his final realization of the importance of "Names that bore witness" (333).

Morrison's epigraph to the novel reads, "The fathers may soar / And the children may know their names," but it is, finally, also the names of the ancestral mothers which bear witness. Pilate's ambiguous name (inherently subversive in its anti-Christian intimations), selected by that family custom of placing a finger on the first word in an opened Bible (even though, in Pilate's case, the namer was unable to read), is so critical to her that she places the written inscription of it in a box that she wears strung through her earlobe, not because her identity as an individual is threatened, but because the name itself is a connection with family, with tradition and history. Even the young Milkman knows that Pilate's box contains the magic knowledge of all names: "Pilate knows. It's in that dumb-ass box hanging from her ear. Her own name and everybody else's" (89).

Pilate carries her name with her, just as she carries a rock from every state in which she has lived, to provide continuity in an otherwise random and dispossessed existence. Son in *Tar Baby* suffers a similar dispossession and also attempts to protect the name that will provide the only coherence he is capable of achieving:

> Oh, he had been alone so long, hiding and running so long. In eight years he'd had seven documented identities and before that a few undocumented ones, so he barely remembered his real original name himself. Actually the name most truly his wasn't on any of the Social Security cards, union dues cards, discharge papers, and everybody who knew it or remembered it in connection with him could very well be dead. Son. It was the name that called forth the true him. The him that he never lied to, the one he tucked in at night and the one he did not want to die. The other selves were like the words he spoke—fabrications of the moment, misinformation required to protect Son from harm and to secure that one reality at least. (119)

The primary significance of the name Son is, again, not to denote an individual self ("He did not always know who he was, but he always knew what he was like" [142]), but to place that self in a context of relationship: Son is a son of Africa and also a son of the American black male experience, the "Nigger Jims . . . Staggerlees and John Henrys. Anarchic, wandering, they read about their hometowns in the pages of out-of-town newspapers" (143). Like Pilate and any number of Morrison's other characters, Son is dispossessed, permanently "out-of-town," his name being his only connection with community and black tradition.

Most of the other characters in *Tar Baby* have at least two names, which Morrison indicates is symbolic of their fragmentation. Lost between the white and black worlds, Jadine is Jadine to her aunt and uncle but a more exotic Jade to the white Streets who have educated her and imbued her with their questionable values.[9] Ondine is Nanadine to Jadine, but Ondine to the Streets, just as Sydney is Sydney to the person he calls Mr. Street, years of intimacy not being sufficient to challenge racial and class protocol. Thérèse and Gideon are the generic Mary and Yardman to the Streets and, ironically, even to Ondine and Sydney, whose "superiority" as "Philadelphia Negroes" depends on such distinctions. Son at one point ponders Gideon's identity: "It bothered him that everybody called Gideon Yardman, as though he had not been mothered" (138). There is some justice in the fact that Margaret Street, white but as powerless as anyone else in her relationship to Valerian (whose name is that of a Roman emperor), also has multiple names—Margaret Lenore/Margarette—wherein lies her essence, "under the beauty, back down beneath it where her Margaret-hood lay in the same cup it had always lain in—faceless, silent and trying like hell to please" (71).

Choosing one's own name, in certain tragic cases, can also represent a rejection of race and culture. Helen Wright in *Sula*, for example, abhors the circumstances of her own birth to a Creole prostitute; in order to "be as far away from the Sundown House as possible" (15), she exchanges her name, Helene Sabat, with its exotic associations with the witch's sabbath, for the prosaic Helen Wright, with its implications of both "rightness" and "whiteness." Her recurrent advice to her daughter, "Don't just sit there, honey. You could be pulling your nose" (24), is further evidence of her discomfort with a racial identity she perceives as

outside the limits of propriety and social acceptability by which
she has defined (and thereby circumscribed) her life.

Pauline Breedlove in *The Bluest Eye* provides yet another example of Morrison's concern with the significance of naming.
"Mrs. Breedlove" even to her husband and children, she is "Polly"
to the white family for whom she works, and the diminutive name
is totally appropriate in this case, for Pauline has diminished herself through her obsequious dedication to whiteness just as surely
as little Pecola is diminished by her desire for blue eyes. Thus
nicknames are often appropriate in Morrison's novels, denoting
truths about character, revealing secrets, determining how a person is viewed by a particular community. Elihue Micah Whitcomb, also in *The Bluest Eye*, is called Soaphead Church by the
community, a name mysterious to him but nevertheless reflective
of his perverted sexual preference for "clean" little girls: "His
sexuality was anything but lewd; his patronage of little girls
smacked of innocence and was associated in his mind with cleanliness. He was what one might call a very clean old man" (132).

It is universal folklore that to know a person's name is to have
power over that person, and this is the reason in Soaphead's mind
that God refuses to name himself: in his letter to God, Soaphead
challenges: "Is that why to the simplest and friendliest of questions: 'What is your name?' put to you by Moses, You would not
say, and said instead 'I am who I am.' Like Popeye? I Yam What I
Yam? Afraid you were, weren't you, to give out your name? Afraid
they would know the name and then know you? Then they
wouldn't fear you?" (142).

But the power greater than knowing a name is bestowing it,
for the act of naming another reflects a desire to regulate and
therefore to control. This is true throughout Morrison's fictions,
and it is a major point of contention for feminist theorists as well;
to be female, as to be black, is most often to suffer the oppression
of being named by another. Monique Wittig in *Les Guérillères*
uses a master/slave metaphor (which, when applied to Morrison's
texts, is ironically pertinent) to protest a male naming of women:
"unhappy one, men have expelled you from the world of symbols
and yet they have given you names, they have called you slave,
you unhappy slave. Masters, they have exercised their rights as
masters. They write of their authority to accord names, that it
goes back so far the origin of language itself may be considered

an act of authority emanating from those who dominate" (112). Kristeva, too, repeatedly counsels women writers to avoid nouns, meaning that they should resist the temptation to authority which naming represents and realize the extent to which subjectivity is constructed through the disposition of such power.

Matriarchal power, always ambiguous in Morrison's novels, as we have seen in the preceding chapter, includes the equally ambiguous power to name, and a primary example of this is Eva in *Sula*. That Eva murders her son is an extension of the symbolic fact that she has already emasculated and rendered him infantile by calling him "Sweet Plum." Tar Baby, Morrison implies, might have lived more effectively if Eva had not ridiculed his white skin and infantilized him in the same stroke with her whimsical naming. And surely the Deweys would have been at least somewhat more individuated, perhaps even normal in stature, if Eva had not reduced them, truncated their potential, through her assignment of the same name for all three: "What you need to tell them apart for? They's all deweys" (32). Finally, the name is not even capitalized, and "them deweys" become a "trinity with a plural name" (33), indistinguishable in their appearance as in their childlike behavior. As Morrison has said in an interview with Bettye J. Parker, "Eva is a triumphant figure, one-legged or not. She's playing God. She maims people. But she says all of the important things" (255).

The African mothers, the ancestor figures as Morrison often refers to them, are the primary namers in Morrison's novels, just as they are the transmitters of culture and the inventors of language, itself the operative agency of culture. It is they who always "say the important things." However, the ancestor women are not themselves individuated any more than other characters; they represent a group consciousness, a history as well as a culture, what McKay refers to as the "ineffable qualities of blackness." McKay quotes Morrison as explaining that her characters have ancestors, not "just parents . . . but timeless people whose relationships to the characters are benevolent, instructive, and protective, . . . [and who] provide a certain kind of wisdom" (1988, 2). One aspect of that wisdom is that the self is a relative concept, decentered rather than alienated, relational rather than objectifying.

This relational self, which constitutes such an important pattern in Morrison's fictions, derives at least as much from the strong bonding among her female characters as it does from racial

identification. The biological states of pregnancy and of motherhood itself, in Morrison's terms, are experienced as a splitting of
the self; in *Beloved*, Sethe recounts her feelings to Beloved: "You
asleep on my back. Denver sleep in my stomach. Felt like I was
split in two" (202). No father, no man, can understand, according
to Sethe, that this condition is less a splitting than a spreading, a
dissolution of boundaries, an embrace of multiplicity. Of Paul D's
reaction to the murder of her child, Sethe says, "Too thick, he
said. My love was too thick. What he know about it? . . . when I
tell you you mine, I also mean I'm yours. I wouldn't draw breath
without my children" (203). Perhaps the closest we can come in
theoretical terms to understanding Morrison's rendering of motherhood is in Kristeva's argument in "Women's Time":

> Pregnancy seems to be experienced as the radical ordeal of the
> splitting of the subject; redoubling up of the body, separation
> and coexistence of the self and of an other, of nature and
> consciousness, of physiology and speech. This fundamental
> challenge to identity is then accompanied by a fantasy of total-
> ity—narcissistic completeness—a sort of instituted, socialized,
> natural psychosis. The arrival of the child, on the other hand,
> leads the mother into the labyrinths of an experience that, with-
> out the child, she would only rarely encounter: love for an
> other. Not for herself, nor for an identical being, and still less
> for another person with whom "I" fuse (love or sexual passion).
> But the slow, difficult and delightful apprenticeship in atten-
> tiveness, gentleness, forgetting oneself. (1981, 26)

Cixous, too, sees motherhood as the ultimate subversion of male-
defined subjectivity; in "The Laugh of the Medusa," she writes:
"The mother, too, is a metaphor. It is necessary and sufficient that
the best of herself be given to woman by another woman for her
to be able to love herself and return in love the body that was
'born' to her. Touch me, caress me, you the living no-name, give
me my self as myself" (313).

In Morrison's mother/daughter relationships, no Lacanian
mirror (and the separation from the mother that mirror represents) interferes with the preoedipal relationship, that sometimes
destructive yet also potentially positive arrangement which occurs
in each one of Morrison's novels and the discussion of which pervades each chapter of the present study. Most Western psycholo-
gists, including Chodorow in *The Reproduction of Mothering*, see

a possible pathology in such an arrangement: Chodorow notes those cases in which "mothers maintained their daughters in a nonindividuated state through behavior which grew out of their own ego and body-ego boundary blurring and their perception of their daughters as one with, and interchangeable with, themselves" (1978, 100). While Morrison, too, sees such boundary confusion as problematic (see Chapters 1 and 4 in particular), she nevertheless renders her female family relationships as powerfully positive agents in the lives of black women.[10] "Dread of the mother" (Chodorow 1978, 183) occurs in Morrison, too, but is always mitigated by a love that is virtually erotic, a merging of identities that transcends Western ideas about self and other, about subject and object.

Sula, for example, is primarily and inevitably one of "those Peace women" (35), linked inextricably to her mother and grandmother, with both of whom she shares personality traits and behavior patterns. Sula, like Hannah, "went to bed with men as frequently as she could" (105), and, like Eva, Sula is also a murderer, her participation in the drowning of Chicken Little almost as damning as Eva's act of burning Plum. Sula's passive pleasure in watching her mother burn—"not because she was paralyzed, but because she was interested" (67)—is no less dispassionate than Eva's self-mutilation, her sacrifice of her leg for insurance money to feed her children. Even this mutilation, the use of one's own body as sacrifice and also as political statement, is echoed by Sula's act of cutting off the tip of her finger to protect herself and Nel and to threaten the abusive boys who terrorize them. Like Eva and because of Eva, Sula has "no center, no speck around which to grow . . . no ego. For that reason she felt no compulsion to verify herself—be consistent with herself" (103). According to Cynthia Davis, it is Sula's rejection of her mother, and ultimately of Eva as well, which is that factor determining her lack of center, her "'splitting of the self,' a denial of facticity that can produce a centerless hero like Sula" (1990, 22).

The same relationship characterized by ambiguity exists in *Song of Solomon* among Pilate, Reba, and Hagar. The daughter, Reba, like Hannah in *Sula*, is relatively inconsequential, content to live obscurely in her more powerful and protective mother's shadow; the more intense relationship and more obvious doubling occurs between grandmother and granddaughter. Pilate and

Hagar form a continuum of "wildness," each a "wilderness girl," each manifesting the jungle of the female essence, like "every witch that ever rode a broom straight through the night to a ceremonial infanticide as thrilled by the black wind as by the rod between her legs" (128). Pilate's love for Hagar, finally, is more destructive and more tragic than Hagar's love for Milkman, and Hagar is "My baby girl" (322–23) to the moment of her death, locked but secure in the matriarchal realm that is her existence.

The merging of identities in the preoedipal bonding of the female triad is universal in Morrison's work but most pronounced in *Beloved*, the relationship among Baby Suggs, Sethe, and Denver giving way to that inverted trinity of Sethe, Denver, and Beloved, who become "us three," the "hand-holding shadows" on the road (182). The first thing we learn of Beloved's manifested presence at 124 Bluestone Road is the shattered mirror (3), highly significant as a prefiguration of the shattering and merging of identities that will occur throughout the novel. Even before Beloved's actual physical appearance, she is part of the trinity that represents both love and destruction, the empty white dress kneeling beside Sethe which Denver sees through the window: "The dress and her mother together looked like two friendly grown-up women—one (the dress) helping out the other" (29). But always the hands that begin with a caress end by attempting to strangle: "Putting the thumbs at the nape, while the fingers pressed the sides. Harder, harder, the fingers moved slowly around toward her windpipe, making little circles on the way. Sethe was actually more surprised than frightened to find that she was being strangled" (96). After Beloved arrives in the flesh, manifests herself on the tree stump outside 124, the three women live together, virtually at the end of the world, on the edge of consciousness and experience, sharing identity as they share the pair-and-a-half of ice skates on a mystical winter night when, repeatedly, "Nobody saw them falling" (174–75). The preoedipal bonding is also symbolized by Sethe's preparation of the "hot sweet milk" (175) they share on their return from skating.

Denver is the first to sense the melting of identity, the merging that is her love for Beloved, whose blood she has drunk "right along with my mother's milk" (205). Believing that Beloved has left her and returned to her otherworldly existence, Denver realizes "she has no self. . . . She can feel her thickness thinning, dissolving into nothing. She grabs the hair at her temples to get enough to uproot it and halt the melting for a while. . . . She doesn't move to open the door because there is no world out there" (123). Beloved, too, finds herself melting, surrealistically disintegrating, as she surprises herself by pulling out one of her own teeth:

> Beloved looked at the tooth and thought, This is it. Next would be her arm, her hand, a toe. Pieces of her would drop maybe one at a time, maybe all at once. Or on one of those mornings before Denver woke and after Sethe left she would fly apart. It is difficult keeping her head on her neck, her legs attached to her hips when she is by herself. Among the things she could not remember was when she first knew that she could wake up any day and find herself in pieces. She had two dreams: exploding, and being swallowed. When her tooth came out—an odd fragment, last in the row—she thought it was starting. (133)

Beloved is, finally, "exploded right before their eyes" (263) according to community women, but not before there has occurred a merging of voices and minds as well as of bodies: "I am Beloved and she is mine. . . . She smiles at me and it is my own face smiling. . . . Your face is mine. . . . Will we smile at me? . . . She is the laugh; I am the laughter. . . . Beloved/You are my sister/You are my daughter/You are my face; you are me. . . . You are mine/You are mine/You are mine" (214–17). It requires all of Paul D's strength and all the power of a community of women to separate this triad, to disperse the ghost, to save Sethe's life, and to return Denver to a "real" world. Paul D, with his male energy and his love, restores Sethe to at least a kind of subjectivity; but we wonder, at the end (such is the power of Morrison's ambiguity), whether or not he is more killer than healer, whether he lies when he says: "You your best thing, Sethe. You are" (273).[11] The last word in the novel, after all, is "Beloved," relegated though she is to the dreamworld, the realm of dark water, the unconscious where the self is always split and illusory, where "the sound of one's own feet going seem to come from a far-off place" (274).

Beloved, then, is both self and other, and always, in Morrison's fictions, such dichotomies are suggested only to be invalidated, subverted, rejected. The dyad is as important imagistically and philosophically for Morrison as the triad, and doubling becomes as effective a way of questioning the concept of self as does a fragmentation of identity in the tripled preoedipal arrangement. Oppositions and polarities are created between and within the characters, but only to be blurred, obscured, and finally negated.

Shortly after Nel's discovery in the mirror of her "me-ness," she meets Sula, who dispels that claim to individuality; for Sula and Nel come to represent aspects of a common self, a construction of identity *in relationship*. "Nel was the first person who had been real to her, whose name she knew" (103), Morrison writes of this friendship cemented not only by time and proximity but by complicity, a common and recurrent recognition of the river "with a closed place in the middle," the place where Chicken Little, the male sacrifice to female power, has disappeared. For Nel, "Talking to Sula had always been a conversation with herself" (82), and, when Sula returns after Nel's marriage, "It was like getting the use of an eye back" (82).[12] Sula, too, is conscious of the power and strength that the relationship once assured for each, and she remembers "the days when we were two throats and one eye and we had no price" (126).

Although Morrison is obviously sympathetic to Nel's pain and loneliness, she nevertheless holds her more responsible for the interruption of this friendship than Sula; for, although Sula sleeps with Nel's husband,[13] Nel has broken faith by marrying him in the first place, by reordering priorities and values according to social standards and giving herself over "to the town and all of its ways" (104). Sula, on the other hand, "had no thought at all of causing Nel pain when she bedded down with Jude. They had always shared the affection of other people: compared how a boy kissed, what line he used with one and then the other" (103). Sula knows long before Nel finally realizes that "a lover was not a comrade and could never be—for a woman" (104), and that the truly relational self and the ultimate value lie in the fact that "We was girls together" (149).

Comfort with the merging of identities, however, is only possible for the women in Morrison's fictions, most of the male relationships, such as that between Milkman and Guitar in *Song of Solomon*, suffering in contrast.[14] Theirs is a brotherhood based not on intimacy and the merging of identity so much as on competition for dominance and a common need for protection in a world that is totally hostile to young black men and so preclusive of their dreams. As Railroad Tommy tells the young Guitar and Milkman, black manhood is a catalogue of thwarted dreams and frustrated desire, and the only thing they will not be denied is "a broken heart. . . . And folly. A whole lot of folly. You can count on it" (60). Guitar serves mostly as a foil for Milkman, and perhaps Melvin Dixon is correct in his observation that Guitar's very name characterizes, not latent musical ability, but his role as "instrumental in Milkman's development of character and cultural awareness" (133). Finally, however, the form of communication between Milkman and Guitar lies in violence rather than affection, a vague homoerotic attachment rathehan love. Guitar is a real threat to Milkman's very life when, in the final lines, Milkman flies, jumps, into "the killing arms of his brother" (341).

Guitar represents, however, the repressed and wild part of Milkman's self, just as Sula fulfills this role for Nel. Like Sula, and like a number of Morrison's other characters, Guitar has golden eyes, yet another kind of mark, analogous to those discussed above, which places him in a category outside that of ordinary experience and within the context of another kind of membership, here in the wild zone that is beyond the recognizably and socially acceptable area of the rational. Morrison has called her golden-eyed heroes "the salt tasters," and she sees their particular freedom as dangerous to society and to themselves, yet they are always attractive, compelling:

> They are the misunderstood people in the world. There's a wildness that they have, a nice wildness. It has bad effects in society such as the one in which we live. It's pre-Christ in the best sense. It's Eve. When I see this wildness gone in a person, it's sad. This special lack of restraint, which is a part of human life and is best typified in certain black males, is of particular interest to me. It's in black men despite the reasons society says they're not supposed to have it. . . . It's a kind of self-flagellant resistance to certain kinds of control, which is fascinating. Opposed to accepted notions of progress, the lock-step life, they live in the world unreconstructed and that's it. (Tate 1989, 125–26)

Cholly Breedlove in *The Bluest Eye*, with his "yellow eyes, flaring nostrils" (91) and his dangerous freedom, is one such character; Ajax in *Sula* is another; and so is Shadrack, "The terrible Shad who walked about with his penis out, who peed in front of ladies and girl-children, the only black who could curse white people and get away with it" (53). Son in *Tar Baby* also represents nothing so much as "Wildness. Plain straight-out wildness" (165). Sixo in *Beloved* is yet another manifestation of this same outlaw wildness, this unrepressed jungle that is actually a part of all Morrison's people, although most of them fail to recognize it: "Sixo went among trees at night. For dancing, he said, to keep his bloodlines open, he said. Privately, alone, he did it. None of the rest of them had seen him at it, but they could imagine it, and the picture they pictured made them eager to laugh at him—in daylight, that is, when it was safe" (25).

But, of course, there is no such thing as safety for Morrison's wilderness characters, and they are inevitably hunted down, separated from community, or even destroyed. They are not so much individuals as they exist in relation to a community, and their function is most often that of pariah, their purpose ultimately the purification of that community, as it was the biblical Cain's to be marked and banished into the wilderness, taking with him the sins of the world. Community for Morrison is always a force to be reckoned with, a character itself as powerful as any individual. Terry Otten sees this force as prescriptive, and allegiance to community as a prerequisite to survival: "In all Morrison's novels alienation from community, or 'the village,' invariably leads to dire consequences, and the reassertion of community is necessary for the recovery of order and wholeness" (1989, 93). Similarly, Keith E. Byerman defines the importance of community in *Sula* as crucial: "It establishes the forms of male-female, parent-child, individual-society, good-evil relationships. It creates rituals recognizing the mysteries of birth, sex, and death; it codifies acceptable attitudes toward power, whether personal, sexual, or racial. In other words, it makes the conventions that define life in the Bottom" (65). Morrison has written, in an essay entitled "Rootedness: The Ancestor as Foundation," "If anything I do, in the way of writing novels or whatever I write, isn't about the village or the community or about you, then it isn't about anything" (Evans, 339). Morrison defines community in terms of its fictional value as a Greek chorus: commenting on the action, serving as a guide for the reader from the "real" world into the fabulous, making things credible. But the community in Morrison's fictions is never benign, and like all of her characters, community itself is morally ambiguous, comprising as it does a force for conformity, a demand for sanity, an argument for rationality—none of which qualities are totally or always desirable for either Morrison or her wilderness characters.

The "we" in *The Bluest Eye*, for example, is wider in implication than the ostensible "we" of Claudia and her sister Frieda, for Claudia speaks for community as a whole, the black community of Lorain, Ohio, but also the world community. Claudia shares in a universal guilt for a failure of tolerance, an inability to love sufficiently or to love at all. There is a distinctly malicious quality to the town gossip (to which Claudia always listens), as well as a perverse pleasure in the misfortunes and misbehaviors of the few, such as the Breedloves, whose actions, and even appearance, render them pariahs, place them outside the community and, in fact, "outdoors":

> Outdoors, we knew, was the real terror of life. The threat of being outdoors surfaced frequently in those days. Every possibility of excess was curtailed with it. If somebody ate too much, he could end up outdoors. If somebody used too much coal, he could end up outdoors. People could gamble themselves outdoors, drink themselves outdoors. . . . There is a difference between being put *out* and being put *outdoors*. If you are put out, you go somewhere else; if you are outdoors, there is no place to go. The distinction was subtle but final. Outdoors was the end of something, an irrevocable, physical fact, defining and complementing our metaphysical condition. (17–18)

According to Claudia's Mama, "that old Dog Breedlove had burned up his house, gone upside his wife's head, and everybody, as a result, was outdoors" (17). As Davis explains, "The characters who are 'outdoors,' cut off from reassuring connection and definition, are profoundly frightening to the community, especially to a community dispossessed and 'peripheral'; it responds by treating the free person as another kind of scapegoat, using that 'excess' to define its own life" (1990, 14).

The community may be justified in many ways, but not for its virtual pleasure in the fact that Cholly—already excluded by his ugliness and his poverty, having always been outdoors, outlawed, outraged and outrageous, out of control—has raped his daughter, that she gives birth to his baby, and that she goes mad in the end: "After the gossip and the slow wagging of heads. . . .

Grown people looked away; children, those who were not frightened by her, laughed outright" (158). Cholly is sufficiently fortunate to die in the workhouse, but Pecola lives on on the periphery of the community, picking through its metaphysical and
metaphorical garbage, serving, as Roberta Rubenstein writes, as
"the dark shadow, the Other, that undermines both white and
black fantasies of female goodness, beauty, and upward mobility"
(130). Pecola is necessary to her community; she cleanses and
beautifies it by her own ugliness:

> All of our waste which we dumped on her and which she ab-
> sorbed. And all of our beauty, which was hers first and which
> she gave to us. All of us—all who knew her—felt so wholesome
> after we cleaned ourselves on her. We were so beautiful when
> we stood astride her ugliness. Her simplicity decorated us, her
> guilt sanctified us, her pain made us glow with health, her awk-
> wardness made us think we had a sense of humor. Her inarticu-
> lateness made us believe we were eloquent. Her poverty kept us
> generous. Even her waking dreams we used—to silence our
> own nightmares. (159)

Surely this community and the world it represents is culpable—
mean and small and narrow. The "we" implicates the reader as
well as Claudia, for, in some mistaken but seemingly universal
need for self-definition through comparison with an Other, that
which we create and then regard as inferior, "the thing we assas-
sinated" (160) is forever our own integrity.

The community in *Sula* is not a great deal more sympathetic,
characterized primarily by the "church women who frowned on
any bodily expression of joy (except when the hand of God com-
manded it)" (68) and convinced that "the only way to avoid the
Hand of God is to get in it" (56). Here, however, there is a dignity of endurance, for this community lives for the most part no-
bly in the face of its oppressions and sorrows, and its virtue is
defined in large measure by its tolerance of Sula. Morrison has
said that she sees the community in *Sula* as "nurturing," if for no
other reason than that "There was no other place in the world she
could have lived without being harmed. Whatever they think
about Sula, however strange she is to them, however different,
they won't harm her" (Tate 1989, 130). Nurturing or not, the
community is clearly still requiring the blood sacrifice of the pa-

riah for its survival. Not "outdoors" but nonetheless outside of
community, the Peace women are prime candidates, particularly
Sula whose birthmark is so obvious a symbol, a mark of the beast
or the rose of Christ, certainly referred to in Morrison's epigraph
from Tennessee Williams's *The Rose Tattoo*: "Nobody knew my
rose of the world but me. . . . I had too much glory. They don't
want glory like that in nobody's heart."

It is not merely Sula's blatant sexuality and promiscuity the
community abhors (they had tolerated the same behavior in
Hannah), but perhaps her "glory" lies in her prettiness (which
acts to separate her, much as did Pecola's ugliness) and her lack
of "any normal signs of vulnerability" (100). Perhaps Sula, like
most of the outsiders in Morrison's fictions, also represents an
aspect of community that it does not wish to confront, namely,
its own essence, its own unconscious, for Sula is a part of every
member, a part of an idea of blackness itself. As Morrison describes her in "The Afro-American Presence in American Literature," she is "quintessentially black, metaphysically black, if you
will, which is not melanin and certainly not unquestioning fidelity
to the tribe. She is new world black and new world woman ex-
tracting choice from choicelessness. . . . Improvisational. Daring,
disruptive, imaginative, modern, out-of-the-house, outlawed, un-
policing, uncontained and uncontainable" (1990, 223).

Sula is thus an intrinsic part of community just as she is a
part of an idea of God. She is the Jungian shadow, that last
unexplained quadrant of the crossed circle symbolic of mandelic
wholeness, the fourth face of the Holy Trinity without which Father, Son, and Holy Ghost are incomplete: "in their secret awareness of Him, He was not the God of three faces they sang about.
They knew quite well that He had four, and that the fourth explained Sula" (102). And, identifiable as pariah and as witch, Sula
purifies the community, makes it whole, encloses the "medallion"
or mandala that inspires the community's very name: "Once the
source of their personal misfortune was identified, they had leave
to protect and love one another. They began to cherish their husbands and wives, protect their children, repair their homes and in
general band together against the devil in their midst" (102). Although the community returns to its former amorality after Sula's
death, she remains for the people "the most magnificent hatred
they had ever known" (148–49), making good her own deathbed

prophecy: "Oh, they'll love me all right. It will take time, but they'll love me" (125).

At least one person in Medallion does love Sula; Shadrack, the Holy Fool to Sula's witch, an incarnation of the River God of African lore, is her counterpart and the recipient of a virtually mystical transferral of mission, symbolized by Sula's belt, which Shadrack keeps as a talisman, and by the exchange of a single word, one that denies death: "always." He recognizes in Sula a life principle; she is "his woman, his daughter, his friend" (135), and her female essence contradicts or at least balances his experience of war (Morrison's equivalent to the biblical fiery furnace in which the original Shadrack found his apotheosis) and his fear of death. In order to control that fear, to order death, Shadrack has instituted "Suicide Day": "If one day a year were devoted to it, everybody could get it out of the way and the rest of the year would be safe and free" (12). The community depends on the annual regularity of Shadrack's ceremonial bell-ringing and his ritual invitation to death; but it is not until just after Sula's death and their own moral backsliding has occurred that the people respond. Like the Pied Piper leading away the children of Hamlin in revenge for a bad debt, Shadrack leads a great many members of the community to their deaths in the abandoned tunnel, thus not only ordering death itself but also ridding the town of its "rats," its unconscious guilt, and thus purifying it, just as Sula has done, and Pecola and Cholly Breedlove before her.

Unless we consider the brief interlude in Eloe, Florida, there is no actual community depicted in *Tar Baby*; rather, there is a single house that is a melting pot of white and black and an island that isolates and renders this group unique in the world. But even this small number of people requires its scapegoats, its agents of purification and moral regeneration, its confrontation with the dark face of the other which is also the self. Son, manifesting himself from the sea, hiding in people's closets, shaking his dreadlocks, is, as Rubenstein suggests, "a demon from the white unconscious" (127), or, as Otten theorizes, "a serpent in paradise" (104). His function is to tear aside the veils, remove the masks that dominate as image in the novel,[15] expose the secrets of every other character, to force confrontation with "truth" in all its many manifestations. Because of Son's presence, Valerian's "innocence" is challenged and his inherent racism revealed; Margaret's deep secret that she tortured her infant son with pins

and cigarette burns is exposed; Sydney and Ondine's superior but
nevertheless subservient blackness is at least partially subverted;
and Jadine is introduced for the first time to her own blackness,
the superficiality of her choices of "Ave Maria" over gospel music
and Picasso over an Itumba mask (62). She is also radically con-
fronted with her own sexuality: "He had jangled something in
her that was so repulsive, so awful, and he had managed to make
her feel that the thing that repelled her was not in him, but in
her" (105). By the end of the novel and Son's return to the unconscious, symbolized by the maternal swamp, L'Arbe de la Croix
is in a shambles, riddled with truths, shattered, fallen, but somehow also redeemed.

No such redemption is possible for members of the black
community of Cincinnati who, in *Beloved*, live furtive lives, a few
short years and a few miles across the Ohio River being all that
separates them from the terrors of slavery. Like Pilate's house in
Song of Solomon, "just barely within the boundaries of the elabo-
rately socialized world of black people" (150), Baby Suggs's
house is also on the edge of community, the periphery of town,
the margins of social existence. Its isolation began the day on
which Sethe killed her daughter and the community deserted her,
simply removing itself from the guilt it surely felt for not having
warned Sethe of the slave catcher's approach, for not having sent
"a fleet-footed son to cut 'cross a field soon as they saw the four
horses in town hitched for watering while the riders asked questions. Not Ella, not John, not anybody ran down or to Bluestone
Road, to say some new whitefolks with the Look just rode in"
(157). Stamp Paid can only conclude that the community's failure
lies in "like, well, like meanness—that let them stand aside, or not
pay attention, or tell themselves somebody else was probably
bearing the news already to the house on Bluestone Road where
a pretty woman had been living for almost a month" (157).
Anonymous contributions of food, left at Sethe's door years later,
hardly constitute a retribution, nor does the army of community
women who march on her house to exorcise the ghost with their
singing. The community in *Beloved*, as in each of Morrison's novels, is no better or worse than the people who comprise it, not a
single one of whom, as Baby Suggs tells her assembly in the
wooded clearing, is "the blessed of the earth, its inheriting meek
or its glorybound pure. . . . O my people, out yonder . . ."(88).
One is tempted to define Morrison's pariahs as separate from

their communities and from the idea of community in general, to make them conform to that pattern of Western literature in which the artist/hero is portrayed as outside, above, and beyond his or her culture. For surely Morrison's pariahs are all artists, even though, like Sula, they lack an "art form" (105), or at least an art form that is approved by Western culture and definition. But when "art" itself becomes ubiquitous, pervasive, less an entity than a way of seeing and being in the world, as it does in Morrison's novels, then we begin to understand that the pariah as artist is part of the community as artist. Art itself, for Morrison, does not begin with the isolated and subjective individual expressing a unique talent, but rather with some more generous urge, some impetus that merges the artist with her or his world, and thus with community as well. For Morrison, art is an expression of black culture, a manifestation of that "precious, imaginative yet realistic gaze of black people" (1990, 226).

To be more specific is difficult, and perhaps "art," as Morrison considers it, ought always to be placed within quotation marks and defined by what it is *not*. Certainly, Jadine, who has studied "art history" at the Sorbonne, has a jaded view of art, one that precludes the value of African art, for example: "Picasso *is* better than an Itumba mask. The fact that he was intrigued by them is proof of *his* genius, not the mask-makers" (*Tar Baby*, 62). But also incorrect is that white, liberal view of black art which sees it as a reflection of a stereotypical concept of black life: "all grits and natural grace" (62), a combination of cowrie beads and Afro combs. Valerian and Margaret Street's always-absent son Michael, a "nice boy" whose mind is still in the grip of *The Little Prince*, is recalled as envisioning a business enterprise of African art and a resultant elimination of welfare status for the black artists he believes will contribute. According to Valerian (whose racial views are certainly no more progressive), Michael's "idea of racial progress is All Voodoo to the People," and Jadine agrees that he, and, by implication, other well-meaning but naive white people, want "a race of exotics skipping around being picturesque" (61). Jadine, of course, requires the same thing, threatened as she is by her own relation to blackness, as we see her in Eloe, camera intervening between her eyes and her vision, "having a ball photographing everybody. . . . 'Beautiful. . . . Fantastic. Now over here,' click click. . . . 'This way. Beautiful. Hold it. Hooooold it. Heaven,' click click click click" (216). Jadine herself, of course, is an "art object," a photographer's model who once graced the cover of *Elle* magazine, a white fantasy of blackness, and a parody of African art—diluted, depleted.

"Art," for Morrison, transcends appreciation for the African mask; rather, it is a quality of perception and the translation of that perception into language or music or color, all of which are indivisible, interrelated, synesthetic. By this definition, all of Morrison's characters, to relative degrees, are artists: tale-tellers, musicians, good cooks, conjurers. Even that least likely candidate for "artist," Pauline Breedlove in *The Bluest Eye*, deprived and finally depraved, is an artist in her soul, defining the world by its colors, its rainbows and its "streaks of green," and searching for order in the chaos of her experience:

> She liked, most of all, to arrange things. To line things up in rows—jars on shelves at canning, peach pits on the step, sticks, stones, leaves. . . . Whatever portable plurality she found, she organized into neat lines, according to their size, shape, or gradations of color. Just as she would never align a pine needle with the leaf of a cottonwood tree, she would never put the jars of tomatoes next to the green beans. . . . She missed—without knowing what she missed—paints and crayons. (88–89)

Pauline is like Sula, who "Had she paints, or clay, or knew the discipline of the dance, or strings; had she anything to engage her tremendous curiosity and her gift for metaphor, she might have exchanged the restlessness and preoccupation with whim for an activity that provided her with all she yearned for" (105). Pilate, too, is an artist in *Song of Solomon*, conjuring her world, brewing her wine, singing her spontaneous songs, telling her stories in magical ways, cooking her perfect eggs.

And every character in *Beloved* searches for color—and finds it in a colorless/meaningless world: "Winter in Ohio was especially rough if you had an appetite for color. Sky provided the only drama, and counting on a Cincinnati horizon for life's principal joy was reckless indeed" (4). According to Morrison, "The painterly language of *Song of Solomon* was not useful to me in *Beloved*. There is practically no color whatsoever in its pages, and when there is, it is so stark and remarked upon, it is virtually raw. Color seen for the first time, without its history" (1990, 229).

The orange square on Baby Suggs's otherwise colorless quilt and her recurring request for color in the abstract, "lavender . . . if you got any. Pink, if you don't" (4), Amy Denver's quest for "carmine" velvet, even Sethe's refusal to remember the painful life of color—"It was as though one day she saw red baby blood, another day the pink gravestone chips, and that was the last of it" (39)—all are indications of the artistic vision that can see color in a colorless world and *make* life meaningful even when historical events are so antagonistic as to invalidate aesthetic consideration.

Finally, it is Denver who will reinvent color and retell Sethe's stories, for art survives in spite of history. Denver is also Morrison's symbol for hope, for the bridge between alienation and community, for the survival of identity, associated as that always is with both race and gender. Along with Lady Jones, we look at Denver in the wildly colored clothes in which Sethe has dressed her with the recognition that "Everybody's child was in that face" (246).

3

"The Disremembered and Unaccounted For": History, Myth, and Magic

> You say you have lost all recollection of it, remember. . . . You say there are no words to describe this time, you say it does not exist. But remember. Make an effort to remember. Or failing that, invent.
>
> —Monique Wittig, *Les Guérillères*

Just as she reinscribes femininity and identity, Toni Morrison reinscribes a history that is less individual than racial and national; hers is also a psychic and a mythic history, a feminine subtext, the kind Cixous and Clément describe in *The Newly Born Woman* as "a history, taken from what is lost within us of oral tradition, of legends and myths—a history arranged the way tale-telling women tell it" (6).

All of Morrison's novels are, in a real sense, "historical novels," quasi documentaries that bear historical witness. Her characters are both subjects *of* and subject *to* history, events in "real" time, that succession of antagonistic movements that includes slavery, reconstruction, depression, and war. Yet she is also concerned with the interaction of history with art, theory, and even fantasy, for, in her terms, history itself may be no more than a brutal fantasy, a nightmare half-remembered, in which fact and symbol become indistinguishable. As we have seen in previous chapters, Morrison always moves beyond the dimensions of the given, beyond the recording of fact, into an area that is at the edge of consciousness and experience, an area Jardine in *Gynesis* defines

61

as "neither Reality, nor History, nor a Text. The Real dissipates that which is categorically unrepresentable, non-human, at the limits of the known; it is emptiness, the scream, the 'zero-point' of death . . . " (567).

Had it not been 1941, stated but also symbolized by the presence of a little white girl sitting in "a 1939 Buick eating bread and butter" that she refuses to share (*The Bluest Eye*, 12), Pecola Breedlove might not have undergone the extremities of poverty dictated by her depression epoch. Poverty, the way Morrison renders it, is a historical fact, documented by the necessity to gather coal along railroad tracks, by the "tired, edgy voices" of adults, by the persistence of mice and roaches, and by the hellish orange glow of steel mills in Lorain, Ohio (12). But, for Morrison, poverty is also a *place*, a state of being, a frame of mind, and its effects are catastrophic, taking their toll in human dignity and self-respect, finally even in sanity.

Ironically juxtaposed to the primary-school-reader vision of the pretty green house with the red door where Dick and Jane live with the smiling mother and the big father, Pecola's house is an abandoned store, a "gray box" that "does not recede into its background of leaden sky" but "foists itself on the eye of the passerby in a manner that is both irritating and melancholy" (30). And we also know intimately the interior of this house, which comes to signify all houses that manifest poverty: the coal stove, which is the only "living thing," and the furniture itself, which has been "conceived, manufactured, shipped, and sold in various states of thoughtlessness, greed, and indifference" (31). There is no bathroom, no privacy, no dignity; human energy is depleted on things that do not function. These are the facts on which the novel is based, dictated by the time in which it is set. But time is also rendered figuratively, poetically, like coats of paint, its passage recorded in the manner of "tale-telling women," its existence relegated to the realm of myth: "probably no one remembers longer, longer ago, before the time of the gypsies and the time of the teen-agers when the Breedloves lived there, nestled together in the storefront. Festering together in the debris of a realtor's whim" (31). Hysteria, Freud wrote, is a matter of *place*, but he might well have added that it is also a matter of *time*.

History, as well as hysteria, is, in Morrison's fictions, always a matter of both time and place. Ohio as a frequent setting occurs not only because she was born in Lorain but because of that state's significance in the history of African Americans. Morrison has said in an interview that

> Ohio is a curious juxtaposition of what was ideal in this country and what was base. It was also a Mecca for black people; they came to the mills and plants because Ohio offered the possibility of a good life, the possibility of freedom, even though there were some terrible obstacles. Ohio also offers an escape from stereotyped black settings. It is neither plantation nor ghetto. (Tate 1989, 119)

Locale is always deeply and historically significant for Morrison, whether the place is Lorain, Ohio, with its orange glow of the steel mills; or Milkman's Detroit, the Motown of the industrial north in *Song of Solomon*; or postslavery Cincinnati in *Beloved*, where life for black people centers around the pig yards:

> Cincinnati was still pig port in the minds of Ohioans. Its main job was to receive, slaughter and ship up the river the hogs that Northerners did not want to live without. . . . The craving for pork was growing into a mania in every city in the country. Pig farmers were cashing in, provided they could raise enough and get them sold farther and farther away. And the Germans who flooded southern Ohio brought and developed swine cooking to its highest form. Pig boats jammed the Ohio River. . . . (154–55)

Morrison's most exotic setting is Isle des Chevaliers in *Tar Baby*, literally at "the end of the world" (7) from Ohio; here, in the Caribbean, color, like life itself, is intense: "The island exaggerated everything. Too much light. Too much shadow" (57). But, like Cincinnati or like Lorain, even this gorgeous place, "the shore of an island that, three hundred years ago, had struck slaves blind the moment they saw it" (5), is founded on the backs of black laborers and the exploitation of human resources by white capitalists; in its modern configuration, Isle des Chevaliers is still a forum for racial tension, a link in the chain of black history that is synonymous with oppression.

Morrison's geography, urban though it usually is, inevitably includes a sense of the natural world, an indication that the passage of time has significance beyond the conception of recorded history. *The Bluest Eye*, for example, is ordered by the presentation

of a series of rooms or interior spaces, but also by the passage of
seasons from autumn to summer, the way a child perceives such
passage, what Morrison refers to as "seasons in childtime" (1990,
220). Just as she ironically contrasts the white myth of the Dick
and Jane reader with the reality of Pecola's life, so Morrison contrasts the great fertility myth of the seasons to the irony that marigolds won't grow in Lorain, Ohio, and that Pecola ends by spend-
ing her "sap green days, walking up and down, up and down, her
head jerking to the beat of a drummer so distant only she could
hear" (158). As is true in all of her novels, Morrison juxtaposes
the natural order with the failure of human social order. The last
image we have of Pecola is also one of ironic contrast: she haunts
the narrator and the reader with her perpetual existence "on the
edge of my town," which is also the edge of community, of culture, "among the garbage and the sunflowers" (160). Pecola exists
because of, within, and beyond history, a testament to society's
denial of responsibility and its failure to love what it chooses not
to see.

Sula, too, is a historical novel, its events carefully recorded
within the context of specific years that are significant because
they either denote or, even more powerfully, suggest the reality of
war. As Maureen T. Reddy has discovered, the prologue to the
novel recalls the Civil War in its legend about the "Nigger joke"
of the freed slave whose master gives him "bottom" land at the
top of the rocky hills surrounding the mythical Medallion, Ohio.
The next section, "1919," recounts the terrors of World War I as
perceived through the consciousness of a single soldier, Shadrack,
who is driven mad by the carnage he witnesses and whose presence, and therefore that of World War I, permeates the rest of the
novel; another section is titled "1941," suggesting but not docu-
menting yet another war; and the merest mention of the date
"1965" in the epilogue implies the reality of Vietnam. As Reddy
remarks, Sula is "a war novel, or, more precisely, an anti-war
novel," and "Peace" is not only Sula's last name but an ironic observation on the historical lack of any such thing (30).

While the characters of Sula, like those in other of Morrison's
novels, are victims of history, they are not, somehow, prisoners of
time, for they live simultaneously in memory and dreams and in
the sense of a future—however apocalyptic, however ironically
redemptive—a future, as Sula recites on her deathbed, "when all

the black men fuck all the white ones; when all the white women kiss all the black ones; when the guards have raped all the jailbirds and after all the whores make love to their grannies . . . when Lindbergh sleeps with Bessie Smith and Norma Shearer makes it with Stepin Fetchit" (125). Time in Morrison's works is always arbitrary, circular rather than linear. Even death, that necessary effect of time, can be transcended, as Sula lives on after death to change the lives of her community and manifest herself to Nel years later in the rustling of leaves: "'Sula?' she whispered, gazing at the tops of trees. 'Sula?'" (149). As Morrison said in an interview with Parker, "She doesn't stop existing after she dies. In fact, what she left behind is more powerful after she is dead than when she was alive" (254).

Ghosts, both actual and figurative, from a past that is both historic and mythic, also dominate the actions of all the characters in *Song of Solomon*, all of whom resurrect their fathers and seek the meaning of the present in the legends of the past. Morrison dedicates this book to "Daddy," and her epigraph reads, "The fathers may soar / And the children may know their names." The quest of Milkman Dead, assigned to him, in part, by his father, is ostensibly a quest for gold and for a personal history, a racial identity, which he believes will be realized only in the context of the ancestral fathers. As Genevieve Fabre documents, *Song of Solomon* is a literary example of genealogical archaeology:

> Its drifting and uninformed hero is caught in the ambiguities of a quest that presents itself as a succession of riddles; each recorded incident, act, or word is a new adventure that further complicates the overall puzzle. And the legacy—an ever elusive reality—takes on many serious or trivial forms: a name, a birthmark, a bag of bones, or a song. Each is presented as a possible clue or a new mystery. The deciphering of the enigma is seen as a game in which the character and the reader are jostled from one puzzle to the next. Answers are presented piece by piece through hints that create further suspense, and this accounts for the structure of this enigmatic narrative: a pattern of revelation and deception, or recognition and denial. (107–8)

However, as Fabre also indicates, history as science, as archaeology, is merely a game, the serious aspect of knowledge remaining, not in Milkman's rediscovery of a personal history, the source of which is Solomon and his flight back to Africa, but in Pilate's wisdom and her racial memory, her intrinsically African identity, indicated on page one where she is literally cloaked in the quilt of African tradition. Hers is a female way of knowing and interpreting the significance of history. It is *she* who resolves the quest, brings Milkman to knowledge (or at least a ray of enlightenment), and who teaches him to fly, or at any rate to acknowledge that flight, in a metaphoric sense although not in any historic one, is the prerogative of women. As even Macon Dead, who is farther from his ancestors and the values they represent than any other character in the novel, can intuit: "If you ever have a doubt we from Africa, look at Pilate" (54).

Tar Baby, like *Song of Solomon*, is set in a contemporary world, but, also like *Song of Solomon*, its focus is historic and its goal the rediscovery of an African past, lost through slavery and perhaps irretrievable except through myth, and then only at the risk of life and sanity. Isle des Chevaliers is now a white man's version of paradise, but it was once a two-thousand-year-old rain forest, "scheduled for eternity" (7), the memory of which is preserved in the pervasive and indomitable swamp and in the reported but undocumented presence of a race of blind horsemen who live there, descendants of those slaves mentioned earlier who "went blind the minute they saw Dominique" (130). Son, an avatar of the ancient world and a spiritual brother to the mythological horsemen, is as lost and confused in his modern world as Milkman is in his. And, like Milkman, Son requires a guide into the realm of myth; it is Gideon who tells Son the legend, but it is Thérèse, the ancient conjure woman, herself a descendant of the blind slaves, who sends him, finally, to his spiritual kinsmen:

> Hurry. . . . They are waiting. . . . The men are waiting for you. . . . They are waiting in the hills for you. They are naked and they are blind too. I have seen them; their eyes have no color in them. But they gallop; they race those horses like angels all over the hills where the rain forest is, where the champion daisy trees still grow. Go there. Choose them. (263)

Thérèse herself is the swamp-haunt, and—like Pilate and the ageless Circe in *Song of Solomon*, like Eva Peace and Ajax's "conjure woman" mother in *Sula*, like the healer M'Dear who presides over birth and death in *The Bluest Eye*, and like the wise Baby Suggs in *Beloved*—she is also the ancestor figure, the guide through a history that transcends recorded fact, the escapee from slavery, the remnant of Africa, the keeper of racial memory, the teller of tales, often the practitioner of voodoo; and she is also an embodiment of a female principle, a way of knowing that transcends the ontological. Morrison's conjure women live always on the edge of both black and white cultures, relegated and sometimes confined to the wild zone, their magical powers thus contained but never completely dissipated. Always in Morrison's novels, the "edge of culture," the "wild zone" just outside of and beyond history, is the province of women, mythic figures who are not themselves actors in history but necessary mediators between biology and history, conservators of myth.

Son, with his fearsome dreadlocks and his haunted past, is the son of Africa and of his ancestors; all he needs is the passage that Thérèse provides him. Jadine/Jade, however, is an orphan daughter, separated from her African history as well as from a female way of knowing. As Thérèse tells Son, "she has forgotten her ancient properties" (263). Yet, the ancestor women manifest themselves to her; they appear in dreams or in supermarkets; they carry snow-white eggs in "tar-black fingers" (39) (Pilate also gives to Milkman a perfect egg, again symbolic of female power), wear yellow robes and colored sandals, have eyes "whose force has burnt away their lashes" (39). They are transcendently beautiful, and they represent to Jadine "that woman's woman—that mother / sister / she" (39). Sometimes they hang from trees in the swamp, watching Jadine with disapproval—quiet, arrogant, "mindful as they were of their value, their exceptional femaleness; knowing as they did that the first world of the world had been built with their sacred properties" (157). These women have no tolerance for Jadine, who has compromised the ancient knowledge; they spit at her, chastise her, become the "night women" who thrust their withered breasts at her "like weapons" (225); they are "the diaspora mothers with pumping breasts" who "with a single glance from eyes that had burned away their own lashes, could discredit your elements" (248). These are the women who surge from the unconscious, more terrifying than history itself, for they represent a *lost* history, a racial identity retrievable only by a dangerous journey to the mother space, which is the area of unbearable dreams and incomprehensible myths, a dark continent of the mind.

Unlike Jadine, Sethe of *Beloved* does not choose her separation from the African mother who, in this novel, is also the literal mother, removed from her daughter by the historical fact of slavery, recognizable only as a bent back and a straw hat in a distant field. Hers is the lost language and the lost heritage which surface from Sethe's unconscious only on occasion in the forms of an image or a word; Sethe considers that her unborn baby bucks like an antelope, an image she later links with the ancestor figures, shadow dancers in her own foggy past and that of her race: "Oh but when they sang. And oh but when they danced and sometimes they danced the antelope. The men as well as the ma'ams, one of whom was certainly her own. They shifted shapes and became something other. Some unchained, demanding other whose feet knew her pulse better than she did. Just like this one in her stomach" (31). Sethe's connection in the present to the ancient myths and the African mothers is through Baby Suggs, herself a conjurer who is magic and prescient but also practical. To the people who gather in her clearing to hear her "call," she gives a history and the wisdom that "the only grace they could have was the grace they could imagine. That if they could not see it, they would not have it" (88). Baby Suggs spends her dying days looking for color and for meaning, depressed and worn out and hopeless. Like Sethe, she has lost sons and daughters; of her little girl she remembers only that "she loved the burned bottom of bread. Her little hands I wouldn't know em if they slapped me" (176).

The brutal realities of history are, in this novel, more antagonistic to the psychic realm of the mother than in any other of Morrison's works. The disintegration of family, the denial of a mother's right to love her daughter, Morrison reiterates, is perhaps the greatest horror of the black experience under slavery. The final insult, the ultimate cruelty, that causes Sethe to flee Sweet Home is not the beating that results in her choke-cherry tree scars, her own brand that links her to the mothers of Africa, but the act of Schoolteacher's nephews "taking her milk," the milk meant for her "crawling-already baby." Thus the white masters not only violate Sethe in an act comparable to rape, but they also violate the sacred state of motherhood and the African spiritual values which, for Morrison, that state represents. According to Holloway and Demetrakopoulos in *New Dimensions of Spirituality*, much of Morrison's work embodies "a celebration of African archetypes" (160), the most significant of which is the Great Mother, the giver of both life and wisdom, who is *nommo*, the creative potential and the sacred aspect of nature itself. But only in freedom can Sethe celebrate her love for her children, her sense of herself as Great Mother: "It felt good. Good and right. I was big . . . and deep and wide and when I stretched out my arms all my children could get in between" (162).

Sethe and many of the other women in Morrison's novels are, like the Great Mother, metaphorically linked with images of trees and are thus representatives of the powers of nature, no matter how subverted those powers might be by circumstance or the realities of history. Like Sula, who can change the weather and identifies herself with the redwood tree, like Pilate who smells like pine trees and who can defy gravity and teach men to fly, and like the mystical women who hang from the swamp trees in *Tar Baby*, Sethe manifests power that transcends ordinary nature. Baby Suggs, too, is "holy," a magic healer who can salve the chokecherry on Sethe's back and bind the violated breasts. She is able to conjure a feast for ninety people from two buckets of blackberries, thus rivaling the miraculous powers of the mythic Christ, and to summon the spirits that pervade the forest clearing where she calls. Hers is "the heart that pumped out love, the mouth that spoke the Word" (180). Pilate in *Song of Solomon* also manifests a love that mothers the world; her dying words to Milkman testify to a spirit that negates the atrocities of history: "I wish I'd a knowed more people. I would of loved 'em all. If I'd a knowed more, I would a loved more" (340).

Also like nature, the ultimate power of which is greater than that of history, the African Great Mother can kill as well as create; she is Kali as well as Demeter, and, as is evident in every chapter of this study, the image of the "phallic mother" is always problematic for Morrison. While she represents enduring and infinite love, the mother/ancestor is simultaneously what Cixous and Clément have defined as "The Virago, the woman with sperm," who "has a tongue that foams" (106). The Great Mother resolves polarities of creativity and destruction. As Eva Peace embraces her son before she sets him on fire in *Sula*, as Pilate Dead almost literally loves her granddaughter Hagar to death in *Song of Solomon*, so Sethe in *Beloved* takes a saw to her daughter's throat because "The best thing she was, was her children. Whites might dirty *her* all right, but not her best thing, her beautiful, magical best thing—that part of her that was clean" (151).

Sethe's mother-love is so strong that, like Demeter, she can also reverse history, resurrect that daughter, bring her back from dark water as tall and "thunderblack and glistening" (261), an image of Africa itself. According to Wilfred Cartey in "Africa of My Grandmother's Singing," within the African view of nature, "nothing is dead, no voice is still. An essential continuity is preserved between earth-mother and child" (quoted by Holloway and Demetrakopoulos, 118). And, as was discussed in Chapter 2, Beloved is an aspect of Sethe's self and of her lost heritage, but she is also the incarnation of the "Sixty Million and more" of the novel's dedication, victims of the effectively genocidal campaign that was slavery.

But the African Great Mother is muted through slavery and the political realities of history, her powers relegated to the natural rather than the political; and, for Morrison, this is an ambiguous qualification. Sethe is surely the victim, the image of woman as token of economic exchange rather than as a figure of glory, as she buys the engraving on Beloved's gravestone with her body, "rutting among the headstones with the engraver. . . . That should certainly be enough. Enough to answer one more preacher, one more abolitionist and a town full of disgust" (5). Pilate, too, commits a similar act of prostitution in *Song of Solomon*, not the sale of her body but the exchange of her integrity for Milkman's freedom, as she transforms herself, witchlike, into Aunt Jemima in the police station: "Now, is that voluntary slavery or not?" Guitar asks, and we agree, for a moment, that "She slipped into those Jemima shoes cause they fit" (226). Helen Wright's smile at the white train conductor in *Sula*, and her resultant transformation into "custard pudding" (24), is further evidence of the political victimization of women. Through her very mythological status, the stereotype reflected in her image, woman in all of Morrison's texts is rendered a victim, a study in powerlessness within the context of a history that does not value her kind of wisdom.

In spite of the fact that Sethe's language is that of the mother, the tale-telling woman, she has no way to speak with political effectiveness, no power to change her own condition, let alone that of the world. Perhaps, as was also discussed in Chapter 1, this is partly Morrison's motivation to have Sethe act/speak with her body, to commit that one politically significant act—the murder of her own child—which translates the body into the word, establishes her place in history, and serves to document the nature of the most brutal of realities, to indict slavery as an institution, for, as Paul D knows, "there was no way in hell a black face could appear in a newspaper if the story was about something anybody wanted to hear" (155).

Along with other critics, Marilyn Sanders Mobley has noted, in "A Different Remembering: Memory, History, and Meaning in Toni Morrison's *Beloved*," that Sethe has her origin in "real" history (193), that she is Morrison's reinscription of Margaret Garner, a runaway slave from Kentucky whose act of infanticide was a subject for abolitionist publications at the time and is still a reminder of the atrocity that was slavery. Mobley also relates that Morrison published *The Black Book* in 1974, a collection of documents including news clippings, bills of sale, and other evidence pertaining to African American history, a historical record which Morrison felt necessary to correct what Mobley calls "a romanticization of both the African past and the American past that threatened to devalue 300 years of black life . . . as 'lived' experience" (190). But, of course, Morrison herself romanticizes the African past in *Beloved* as in other novels, inscribing it as myth and reclaiming it as part of African American identity, although her ethical position in regard to a lost Africa is always one of ironic qualification; the myth of the African Great Mother, for example, is used, not as an ideal of redemption, but as a reminder that history is the antagonist which has silenced myth, subverted nature, and dispossessed the African American of the crucial link with Africa.

Nor were Africans the only victims of dispossession and the genocidal inclinations apparently peculiar to white men in American history. Native Americans, too, are deeply symbolic for Morrison, and they haunt the pages of *Beloved* as their mythic presence does the streets of Cincinnati, where their ancient burying places are "as old as sky, rife with the agitation of dead Miami no longer content to rest in the mounds that covered them . . . they growled on the banks of Licking River, sighed in the trees on Catherine Street and rode the wind above the pigyards" (155). In his desperate escape from the inhumanities of the chain gang in Alfred, Georgia, Paul D happens upon a camp of sick and renegade Cherokee "for whom a rose was named":

> Decimated but stubborn, they were among those who chose a
> fugitive life rather than Oklahoma. The illness that swept them
> now was reminiscent of the one that had killed half their num-

ber two hundred years earlier. In between that calamity and this, they had led Oglethorpe through forests, helped Andrew Jackson fight Creek, cooked maize, drawn up a constitution, petitioned the King of Spain, been experimented on by Dartmouth, established asylums, wrote their language, resisted settlers, shot bear and translated scripture. All to no avail. The forced move to the Arkansas River, insisted upon by the same president they fought for against the Creek, destroyed another quarter of their already shattered number.

That was it, they thought, and removed themselves from those Cherokee who signed the treaty, in order to retire into the forest and await the end of the world. (111)

Only Sixo, himself soon to experience "the end of the world," respects their sacred suffering, asking their deserted structure for permission to enter and showing reverence for "the Redmen's Presence" (24).

Native Americans as the victims of history and the ghosts of myth are also a presence in *Song of Solomon*, and it is a part of Milkman's moral regeneration that he realizes the myth they represent. The immediate connection is with his grandmother, Sing Byrd, whose original identity may well have been Native American and her actual name Singing Bird. But the more important association is not personal but racial, the recognition that African Americans share with Native Americans a heritage of dispossession: "Ohio, Indiana, Michigan were dressed up like the Indian warriors from whom their names came. Blood red and yellow, ocher and ice blue. . . . The Algonquins had named the territory he lived in Great Water, *michi gami*. How many dead lives and fading memories were buried in and beneath the names of the places in this country?" (333).

Most of Morrison's characters, including Sixo, who mocks his white lynchers with the only laughter of his life, hold the white race as a whole responsible for the historic subjugation of people of color, whether it is the white farmer who perpetrates the "Nigger joke" in *Sula*, the social workers and church ladies who are so patronizing in *The Bluest Eye*, the businessmen whom Macon Dead strives so urgently to imitate to his own psychic destruction in *Song of Solomon*, the pseudoliberals and self-appointed white fathers like Valerian Street in *Tar Baby*, and—perhaps most of all—the slave owners, like Mr. Garner in *Beloved*, who see themselves as benevolent patrons, permitting manhood but denying the expression of it. According to Guitar in *Song of Solomon*, the actions of the Seven Days, exacting revenge on whites in retaliation for the crimes perpetrated on blacks, are totally justifiable. He does not kill "people," he explains, but "white people," Hitler being "the most natural white man in the world" (156).

The possible exception to this general indictment is Amy Denver, she of "the good hands," who delivers Sethe's baby and saves her life in *Beloved*. She, too, is an escapee in flight from indentured servitude and has endured her own share of oppression; that fact and her apparent limitation of intelligence act to absolve her of responsibility for what her race has perpetrated. But Sethe knows, in general, "That anybody white could take your whole self for anything that came to mind. Not just work, kill, or maim you, but dirty you. Dirty you so bad you couldn't like yourself anymore" (151). Beloved, for another, has good reason to dread "the men without skin," for their arrival is the moment of her death. Baby Suggs, too, repeatedly comments: "There is no bad luck in the world but whitefolks" (89). The Ku Klux Klan infects even the free world that Sethe believes for a time she has found: "Desperately thirsty for black blood, without which it could not live, the dragon swam the Ohio at will" (66). And Stamp Paid, who carries with him a red ribbon found on the banks of the Ohio, a red ribbon "knotted around a curl of wet wooly hair, clinging still to its bits of scalp" (180), can reflect:

> Eighteen seventy-four and whitefolks were still on the loose. Whole towns wiped clean of Negroes; eighty-seven lynchings in one year alone in Kentucky; four colored schools burned to the ground; grown men whipped like children; children whipped like adults; black women raped by the crew; property taken, necks broken. He smelled skin, skin and hot blood. The skin was one thing, but human blood cooked in a lynch fire was a whole other thing. . . . What *are* these people? You tell me, Jesus. What *are* they? (180)

Morrison fragments black history into symbols the color of blood: the choke-cherry scars on Sethe's back, Stamp Paid's piece of red ribbon, Paul D's loss of "a red, red heart," in order to tell the story of "the people of the broken necks, of fire-cooked blood and black girls who had lost their ribbons" (181). Thus does Morrison bear historical witness and redeem her muted African mothers.

Because of what she has endured from history, and because

of what it has cost her, Sethe spends her present "beating back the past" (73), her eyes "two open wells that did not reflect firelight" (9), their "iron" extinguished by unimaginable sights and the inescapable reality of "rememories." The rememories are surely intended to denote a form of racial memory, a knowledge which even future generations cannot escape or forget. Morrison has written that there is "no time" in *Beloved*, "especially no time because memory, pre-historic memory, has no time" (1990, 229). Sethe tells her daughter about the nature of time, the psychic law, not that history repeats itself, but that it exists as a place, a dimension, in the collective unconscious:

> Some things you forget. Other things you never do. . . . Places, places are still there. If a house burns down, it's gone, but the place—the picture of it—stays, and not just in my rememory, but out there, in the world. What I remember is a picture floating around out there outside my head. I mean, even if I don't think it, even if I die, the picture of what I did, or knew, or saw is still out there. Right in the place where it happened. . . . Someday you be walking down the road and you hear something or see something going on. So clear. And you think it's you thinking it up. A thought picture. But no. It's when you bump into a rememory that belongs to somebody else. Where I was before I came here, that place is real. It's never going away. Even if the whole farm—every tree and every grass blade of it dies. The picture is still there and what's more, if you go there—you who never was there—if you go there and stand in the place where it was, it will happen again; it will be there for you, waiting for you. So, Denver, you can't never go there. Never. (36)

Beloved, who, thanks to her mother, has never been a slave and who, murdered at the age of two, has no personal memory, nevertheless retains a psychic racial memory of capture and transport, of slave ships and the Middle Passage. It is Morrison's novelistic genius which dictates that these memories be thought or spoken by Beloved herself in concert with Sethe, as their identities and their racial memories become one, in an elliptical, fragmented, and purely poetic sequence of images. That which is too raw, too cruel, must be rendered sparingly, imagistically, and "how can I say things that are pictures" (210). The pictures themselves are unbearable, a series of almost cinematic clips which document that human beings were packed in layers in the hold of a ship: "I am always crouching the man on my face is dead . . . someone is thrashing but there is no room to do it in"; that extreme hunger and thirst led to the necessity to consume human excrement: "some who eat nasty themselves I do not eat the men without skin bring us their morning water to drink we have none . . . if we had more to drink we could make tears we cannot make sweat or morning water so the men without skin bring us theirs one time they bring us sweet rocks to suck . . . in the beginning we could vomit now we do not now we cannot" (210). Rape and death, rats and starvation—the memories are so traumatic and so graphic that we accept with Morrison that they must persist to become universally shared, cosmically experienced.

Sethe says that it is hard for her to "believe" in time (35), and for her, as well as other of Morrison's characters, time is not linear; history is only "recovered time," stratified, circular, like language, as was discussed in Chapter 1. Sixo, for example, exists outside time in the same way that many of Morrison's women do: "Time never worked the way Sixo thought, so of course he never got it right" (21). Whether it is cooking potatoes or planning his night visits to the Thirty-Mile Woman, Sixo's time-lapse mentality provides some of the only humor in the novel. For Sethe, however, "tomorrow" is a concept too painful to consider: "Today is always here," she tells Denver. "Tomorrow, never" (60). It is deeply significant, for example, that when Sethe is recounting her past in an attempt to justify to Paul D the murder of her child, she moves about the room in circles, knowing that "the circle she was making around the room, him, the subject, would remain one. That she could never close in, pin it down for anybody who had to ask. If they didn't get it right off—she could never explain" (163).

Particularly when women live communally without men, as is the case in all five of Morrison's novels, they operate outside of history and outside of the dominant culture, even outside of black culture. Perhaps because history as a progression has been so antagonistic, they live also on a different time scheme, without schedules, without clocks, eating and sleeping according to whim or to nature rather than sanctioned custom, thus collapsing conventional temporal coherence. The three whores in *The Bluest Eye*, despite their historically significant names—China, Poland, and the Maginot Line—live outside of history and distort time itself, turning night into day; Pilate in *Song of Solomon*, and her daughter and granddaughter, live "pretty much as though progress was a word that meant walking a little farther on down the road" (27); Nel in *Sula* prefers the timelessness in Sula's "wooly house, where a pot of something was always cooking on the stove; where the mother, Hannah, never scolded or gave directions; where all sorts of people dropped in; where the newspapers were stacked in the hallway, and dirty dishes left for hours at a time in the sink, and where a one-legged grandmother named Eva handed you goobers from deep inside her pockets or read you a dream" (25). Morrison's women seem always to operate on what Kristeva has called "women's time," that arrangement of existence which refutes the value of "production" in the interest of "*reproduction*, survival of the species, life and death, the body, sex and symbol" (1981, 22).

If time and philosophy are thus inverted, then the concept of history as a linear projection is also inverted, and subverted as well. In Morrison's works, history exists as it is recalled, in fragments and pieces. Morrison's technique, thus, is to render history through the aesthetic image, to accomplish what Kristeva, in *Desire in Language*, has described as a process of the "desubstantification" of "mythic idealities, reconstructed like crystals from the practice of subjects in history" (103). This, for Kristeva, and I think for Morrison as well, is a political act, a technique that challenges the primacy of Western philosophy. Morrison provides us with the untold story, the other side of history, the reinscription of both myth and fact. Hortense Spiller sees the importance of rewriting and changing concepts of history: "Women must seek to become their own historical subject in pursuit of its proper object, its proper and specific expression in time. . . . Through the discipline and decorum exacted by form, the woman's reality is no longer a negation, but a positive and dynamic expressiveness—a figure against a field—shaped by her own insistence" (1979, 105).

Morrison's purpose in both the style and the subject of her histories is not only to invert time and disrupt chronology, but also to shock her reader into a political awareness, to challenge not only attitudes about African Americans and women but about patterns of thinking and systems of belief in general: "If my work is to confront a reality unlike that received reality of the West, it must centralize and animate information discredited by the West—discredited not because it is not true or useful or even of some racial value, but because it is information described as 'lore' or 'magic' or 'sentiment'" (Evans, 388).

Certainly there is no "sentiment" in Morrison's subjects themselves, which are often violent, always disquieting, and sometimes almost unbearable to consider. Partly because her subjects are based on historical fact and have their origins in "reality," hers is a voice of political conscience, making poverty, slavery, oppression immediate even to those readers who have never experienced them, even to those readers who would choose to forget. Morrison thus challenges what psychiatrist Robert Jay Lifton has defined, in his work with survivors of the Jewish holocaust, Hiroshima, and Vietnam, as a modern cultural "psychic numbness." According to Lifton,

> The problem is less repression of death than an impairment in the general capacity to create viable forms around it, [to bring] imagination to bear upon the unpalatable existential-historical truths, to expand the limits of that imagination on behalf of species survival . . . to overcome psychic numbing and . . . , in Martin Buber's words, to "imagine the real." (129–30)

For Lifton, it is only through art that the apocalyptic realities and the global hysteria which characterize history can be rendered bearable, and those few artists who attempt thus to reinscribe history touch the "mythic or formative zone of the psyche" (70). Morrison does this; "imagining the real," she brings us to an awareness of truth beyond "reality" and to an experience beyond "history."

And, as in many other postmodern texts, when history and the concept of reality become so brutal, so horrific and unnatural, the only "natural" element becomes the supernatural. Morrison does not permit us to escape into magic realism; instead, we confront the fact that evil as it is manifested in history has cosmic reverberations. "Quiet as it's kept," writes Morrison at the opening of *The Bluest Eye*, "there were no marigolds in the fall of 1941" (9). And that fact is attributable, not to seeds having been planted too deeply or to the quality of the soil (as Claudia and her sister later rationalize), but to a supernatural reaction to the unnatural fact that "Pecola was having her father's baby" and, even worse, that not a single person in Lorain, Ohio, was able to love or help her. The blight is universal, a cosmically ordained punishment for a community's sin of omission: "the land of the entire country was hostile to marigolds that year. This soil is bad for certain kinds of flowers. Certain seeds it will not nurture, certain fruit it will not bear, and when the land kills of its own volition, we acquiesce and say the victim had no right to live. We are wrong, of course . . . " (160).

The plague of robins that accompanies Sula's return to Medallion in 1937 after an absence of ten years is a similarly unexplainable and supernatural phenomenon, as is the sudden January thaw that follows her death and leads to the deaths of others of the community who, in a mood of mass hysteria, enter the abandoned tunnel—itself a historical artifact and testament to the inevitable failure of the white man's promises—where they are drowned and crushed, entombed. Nature itself, in Morrison's worlds, can manifest evil, an evil deliberate as that of history, construed to punish and chastise:

> They did not believe death was accidental—life might be, but death was deliberate. They did not believe Nature was ever askew—only inconvenient. Plague and drought were as "natural" as springtime. If milk could curdle, God knows robins could fall. The purpose of evil was to survive it and they determined (without ever knowing they had made up their minds to do it) to survive floods, white people, tuberculosis, famine and ignorance. They knew anger well but not despair, and they didn't stone sinners for the same reason they didn't commit suicide—it was beneath them. (*Sula*, 78)

Morrison has said that she writes about "good and evil," but not in "Western terms," that the ways in which a black community responds to evil differ from the ways another community would respond:

> they thought evil had a natural place in the universe; they did not wish to eradicate it. They just wished to protect themselves from it, maybe even to manipulate it, but they never wanted to kill it. They thought evil was just another aspect of life. The ways black people dealt with evil accounted in my mind for how they responded to a lot of other things. It's like a double-

edged sword. . . . It's because they're not terrified by evil, by difference. Evil is not an alien force; it's just a different force. That's the evil I was describing in *Sula*. (Tate 1989, 129)

Evil and its manifestations in the realm of the supernatural are thus an integral part of Morrison's world in which the oxymoron of "magic realism" is perfectly resolved. As Morrison has written about *Song of Solomon*, the novel focuses on "the acceptance of the supernatural and a profound rootedness in the real world at the same time with neither taking precedence over the other. It is indicative of the cosmology, the way in which Black people looked at the world . . . superstition and magic [are] another way of knowing things" (Evans, 339). Toward the end of *Song of Solomon*, Milkman rationalizes, "Jesus! Here he was walking around in the middle of the twentieth century trying to explain what a ghost had done. But why not? he thought. One fact was certain: Pilate did not have a navel. Since that was true, anything could be, and why not ghosts as well?" (298).

Just as she blends distinctions and denies polarities in ideology and identity as well as in language, so Morrison incorporates magic and lore into the realm of reality, revising both in the process. In *Tar Baby*, black folklore as an antidote to "received" history and as an alternative mode of transferring information is invoked by the title and by fictional incorporation of the familiar story of the trickster Rabbit, who is himself tricked by the tar baby from which he cannot separate himself. Son, of course, is the rabbit, and Jadine, product of the white world, is the tar baby (although these roles might conceivably be reversed, depending upon with whom the reader's sympathies lie). But Son is also a kind of frog prince to Jadine's princess, as well as a Black Orpheus to her Eurydice,[1] and, like all characters in love stories, they comprise, finally, an archetype that transcends the story itself. In "The Briar Patch as Modernist Myth: Morrison, Barthes, and Tar Baby As-Is," Craig H. Werner refers to *Tar Baby* as "postmodern metamythology" in which Barthes's theory of myth is linked to the African American folk tradition which "precedes, echoes, and revises it" (151). Samuels and Hudson-Weems state that "Morrison has used folklore and mysticism throughout this novel as a matrix for articulating the interlocking nature of the past and the present as well as the spiritual and the physical worlds" (92). For Son, the blind horsemen of Isle des Chevaliers exist as both history and that revision of history which is legend. His final flight into the swamp to join the horsemen is a flight into a mythic past, into the conjure world, which paradoxically both liberates and annihilates him. Jadine, however, excluded from myth and folklore by her white-world connections, is equally trapped in a present constituted of false realities, and she is surely wrong when she tells Son that "There is nothing any of us can do about the past but make our own lives better" (234).

As Son accepts without question the validity of myth, so that same acceptance of manifestations beyond nature is also intrinsic in *Beloved*: "Not a house in the country ain't packed to its rafters with some dead Negro's grief" (5), says Baby Suggs, who knows that the spirit world is everywhere—in the houses, in the trees, in the rivers, manifested in hellish light or in hands that reach out to caress or to strangle. It is no cause for surprise that Sethe's murdered daughter, "Rebuked. Lonely and rebuked" (13), returns "out of blue water" (213) to plague her family and fill the house at 124 Bluestone Road with "baby's venom" (3). The women in that house "understood the source of the outrage as well as they knew the source of light" (4); they accept that "If it's still there waiting, that must mean that nothing ever dies" (36).

Writing itself, for Morrison, is a process of undoing the work of death, of conjuring ghosts, of accounting for "the disremembered and unaccounted for" (*Beloved*, 274). It is true that she writes a history and a literature that, as Otten quotes her as saying, is "irrevocably, indisputably Black" (1989, 2). She has also told Claudia Tate, "When I view the world, perceive it and write about it, it's the world of black people. It's not that I won't write about white people. I just know that when I'm trying to develop the various themes I write about, the people who best manifest those themes for me are the black people whom I invent" (1989, 118).[2] But Morrison's racial consciousness might well provide a model for all women writers to conceive of history in terms that are different, revolutionary, in a way that, as Cixous writes, "unthinks the unifying, regulating history that homogenizes and channels forces, herding contradictions into a single battlefield. In woman, personal history blends together with the history of all women, as well as national and world history" (1986, 313).

It seems an understatement to summarize that Morrison reinscribes history just as she inverts both time and Western ontology. In every generation, women writers have struggled to find themselves *within* history, to force or cajole a recognition of their historical existence and their value. Perhaps that has been an error. To re*define* history, as Morrison does, is surely the greater accomplishment—to, as Kristeva says, "set history to rhythm, let us introduce history's rhythm into our discourses, so that we might become the infinitized subject of all histories—be they individual, national, or class histories—which henceforth nothing can totalize" (1980, 203).

City and Islington Sixth Form College
283-309 Goswell Road
London
EC1
020 7520 0601

CITY AND ISLINGTON COLLEGE

This book is due for return on or before the date last stamped below.
You may renew by telephone. Please quote the Barcode No.
May not be renewed if required by another reader.

4

Rainbows and Brown Sugar: Desire and the Erotic

To Love is to survive paternal meaning.

—Kristeva, *Desire in Language*

Morrison has said that "Love, in the Western notion, is full of possession, distortion, and corruption. It's slaughter without the blood" (Tate 1989, 123). Morrison's novels are always about love and its distortions, and also about slaughter, often *with* the blood; but rarely do they reflect a purely traditional "Western notion" in which desire is repressed, compartmentalized, set apart from the rest of experience, defined, and psychoanalyzed. Outside of the dominant signifying order, writers of the feminine discourse seem to communicate desire differently than men do, and their language to describe pleasure is often untranslatable, indistinguishable from other kinds of experience. For Morrison, the entire world is erotic, and all language is always the expression, the proclamation, of desire.

Eating, for example, is not merely a euphemism for sexual intercourse or an image of sensuality, as occurs in the works of male writers since *Tom Jones*. Rather, in Morrison's texts, food, like everything else in her worlds, is metaphoric, diffusely erotic, expressive of *jouissance*. Meanings radiate, textures permeate, color illuminates—all of which is present, not only in the image, but in the writing itself. The watermelon in *The Bluest Eye* that Cholly Breedlove remembers for the rest of his life appeals not only to the sense of taste; it becomes, in fact, a metaphor for love, an emblem for female sexuality: "Blood red, its planes dull and

83

blunted with sweetness, its edges rigid with juice. Too obvious, almost obscene, in the joy it promised." The seedless, deep red heart, as Cholly places it in his mouth, becomes "The nasty-sweet guts of the earth" (107). This watermelon and the female sexuality it represents have cosmic signification; the great sphere of the fruit, raised high above the head to be split against a rock, becomes "the world," and the man holding it "the strong, black devil . . . blotting out the sun and getting ready to split open the world" (107).

Or: the round, unbearably bright orange that Pilate is eating in *Song of Solomon* the first time Milkman comes to visit signifies a very great deal more than Pilate's own navel-less stomach; Milkman is fascinated by how sensuously she peels the orange and separates the sections, holding each so precisely to her "berry-black" lips: "She held the peelings precisely as they had fallen in her lap, and as she walked up the steps she looked as though she were holding her crotch" (38).[1] If the orange were not sufficient enticement for the dazzled Milkman, who is confronting the female essence for the first time in his life, Pilate also offers that perfect soft-boiled egg: "The yolk I want soft, but not runny. Want it like wet velvet. How come you don't just try one?" (39).

But nowhere in Morrison's work (or perhaps in all of literature) is food more explicitly sexual than is the ice-cream imagery in *Sula*. Preadolescent, "wishbone thin and easy-assed" (45), knowing that "It was too cool for ice cream" (42), Nel and Sula approach "Edna Finch's Mellow House, an ice-cream parlor catering to nice folks—where even children would feel comfortable, you know" (42). The approach to the ice-cream parlor is lined with men, young and old, who "open and close their thighs" as women walk by:

> It was not really Edna Finch's ice cream that made them brave the stretch of those panther eyes. . . . The cream-colored trousers marking with a mere seam the place where the mystery curled. Those smooth vanilla crotches invited them; those lemon-yellow gabardines beckoned to them.
>
> They moved toward the ice-cream parlor like tightrope walkers, as thrilled by the possibility of a slip as by the maintenance of tension and balance. The least sideways glance, the merest toe stub, could pitch them into those creamy haunches spread wide with welcome. Somewhere beneath all of that

daintiness, chambered in all that neatness, lay the thing that clotted their dreams. (43)

Houston A. Baker, Jr., having almost as much fun with this section as Morrison obviously did, comments, "Surely, Edna's mellow confections appear more like the male equivalent of the blues' 'jellyroll' than Baskin-Robbins' twenty-one flavors" (95).[2]

Even in *Beloved*, a much bleaker novel in which joy is the exception, food and sex are metaphorically entwined. Sethe is making biscuits, "fat white circles of dough" (17) lining the pan, as Paul D cups her breasts with his hands for the first time. Also the songs Paul D sings are deeply suggestive: "Little rice, little bean, / No meat in between. / Hard work ain't easy, / Dry bread ain't greasy" (40). And Sethe, who is wise in any number of ways, including the ways of love, knows just what will translate into eroticism:

> On her mind was the supper she wanted to fix for Paul D— something difficult to do, something she would do just so—to launch her newer, stronger life with a tender man. Those litty bitty potatoes browned on all sides, heavy on the pepper; snap beans seasoned with rind; yellow squash sprinkled with vinegar and sugar. Maybe corn cut from the cob and fried with green onions and butter. Raised bread, even. (99–100)

Whether or not Sethe ever actually cooks this dinner ("soul food" indeed) is left to the reader's imagination, for just reciting the menu to Paul D is sufficiently appetizing to drive them both upstairs to bed. Years earlier, Sethe remembers, she and Halle had consummated their marriage in the cornfields of Sweet Home, imagining they had privacy, while in reality the other men, denied expression of their own sexuality, sat, "erect as dogs," watching "corn stalks dance at noon." The following feast on the corn plucked from the broken stalks becomes a signification for virgin sex:

> The pulling down of the tight sheath, the ripping sound always convinced her it hurt.
> As soon as one strip of husk was down, the rest obeyed and the ear yielded up to him its shy rows, exposed at last. How loose the silk. How quick the jailed-up flavor ran free.
> No matter what all your teeth and wet fingers anticipated,

there was no accounting for the way that simple joy could
shake you.

How loose the silk. How fine and loose and free. (27)

But food, even candy, is not always so erotic, linked though
it inevitably is with sexuality and, most frequently, with humor.
In *Tar Baby*, the "Valerians," manufactured by Valerian Street's
father and named for Valerian, are "red and white gumdrops in a
red and white box (mint-flavored, the white ones; strawberry-
flavored, the red)." The fake flavors and the sickeningly sweet Val-
entine sentiments they symbolize are metaphors for Valerian's
own questionable masculinity and, presumably, for that of all
white men. Black children will not buy them because the candies
are "faggoty. . . . Can you see a kid sitting on a curb tossing those
fairy candies in his mouth? . . . Give us something with nuts, why
don't you? . . . Nobody can make a dollar selling faggot candy to
jigs" (42–43). Significantly, Valerian's wife is also "all red and
white, like the Valerians" (43). Son, on the other hand, is called
"the chocolate eater," and the racial reference is obvious.

Candy in *The Bluest Eye*, particularly the Mary Janes that Pecola sacrifices so much of her pride to buy, becomes an emblem
of shame in its association with white privilege and of envy for
the blue eyes of the little blonde girl depicted on the package. To
eat the candy, however, is also orgasmic, sexual, an act of possession, even of violence; surely Pecola is practicing some secular
communion, or perhaps she enacts a primitive rite of passage, a
cannibal feast, as she gorges herself on the body of the enemy in
order to assume its power: "To eat the candy is somehow to eat
the eyes, eat Mary Jane. Love Mary Jane. Be Mary Jane. Three
pennies had bought her nine lovely orgasms with Mary Jane.
Lovely Mary Jane, for whom a candy is named" (43).

Even more sombre is the image of candy in *Song of Solomon*;
Guitar grows ill even at the smell of sweets, which make him
"think of dead people. And white people. And I start to puke"
(61). But it is not only the memory of sweet white divinity given
by the white boss to Guitar in compensation for the death of his
father that makes him sick, but the recollection of his mother's
sweet acquiescence, her utter victimization; and his fury is directed at her and at all women who are similarly accessible. The
peppermint stick his mother buys for him on the day of his
father's funeral is surely a surrogate penis, but one that only
serves to emphasize his own impotence to protect his mother, or

any woman; therefore, he discards the candy as he discards the women: "he could not eat it or throw it away, until finally, in the outhouse, he let it fall into the earth's stinking hole" (227). As an adult, Guitar is incapable of relationships with women, preferring the male camaraderie of the Seven Days and his vaguely homoerotic friendship with Milkman, "My man. . . . My main man" (341).

Similarly, Milkman associates the "faintly sweet" taste of his mother's milk with both shame and impotence, recalling the darkened and secret room in which she daily reenacted the ritual of a grotesque and carnivalesque *pietà*, the perversity with which she nursed him until his feet reached the floor, the sexuality with which she unbuttoned her blouse, closed her eyes, and smiled (13). Milkman shares more than a little in Macon Dead's opinion of his son's nickname: "It sounded dirty, intimate, and hot" (15). In fact, all food prepared by the mother in this family is unacceptable: "She did not try to make her meals nauseating; she simply didn't know how not to" (11). Interestingly, for this particular meal, Ruth substitutes a rennet dessert for the impossibly difficult sunshine cake. It cannot be surprising, then, given the food symbolism in this novel and the association of the mother and all women, except Pilate, with a sensation of nausea, that Milkman has such difficulty committing himself to sexual relationships with women.

Milk and the image of motherhood are most particularly associated with male impotence in *Beloved*, as Halle watches helplessly from the loft above while Schoolteacher's nephews violate Sethe so brutally by taking her milk. Halle's response to his inability to protect his wife from such perversity, such outrageous violence, is to go mad, to smear butter and clabber over his own face almost in imitation of the act he has witnessed, to disintegrate completely. Up to this point, Halle has been a noble figure, a good husband and son, the best of the Sweet Home men, all of whom are respectful to each other and to Sethe. But here the outrage is unbearable, and he loses his manhood with his sanity. Finally, he is less strong than Sethe, who is condemned to her sanity by the necessity to survive for her children's sake: "Other people went crazy, why couldn't she? . . . And how sweet that would have been: the two of them back by the milk shed, squatting by the churn, smashing cold, lumpy butter into their faces with not a care in the world" (70).

A similar event to that Halle cannot endure, the inability to protect the woman for whom one perceives responsibility, occurs also in *The Bluest Eye*. The reader's sympathy for Cholly Breedlove, despite his later unforgivable action of raping his daughter, is assured by that scene in which, having been discovered by white hunters just as he is about to make love for the first time in his life, he is unable to protect either himself or Darlene from the obscenities that follow. Not milk, but the taste of unripe muscadine grapes, their bloodlike stains covering Darlene's white dress, are associated with sex and its failure in this instance, and "the sweet taste of muscadine" turns to "rotten fetid bile" (117), as Cholly transfers his hatred for the hunters into hatred for Darlene, holding her responsible for his impotence. As Davis explains in "Self, Society, and Myth in Toni Morrison's Fiction":

> The desire to "protect" her was the desire to create himself as her protector. All he can do to restore his selfhood is to deny hers further. In the recurring scene of black male resentment at black women's submission to oppression (the soldiers' stony stares at Helene and the conductor, Guitar's hatred of his mother's smile and of Pilate's "Aunt Jemima act"), Morrison shows the displacement of male humiliation onto the only person left that a black man can "own"—the black woman. . . . The black woman—doubly Other—is the perfect scapegoat. (330)

Male impotence and images of castration, whether created by female submission or female power, are certainly problematic for a great many readers and critics of Morrison's work as well as that of other black American women writers. Richard K. Barksdale, one example among many, links Morrison with Alice Walker and Paule Marshall, holding all guilty of producing "within the context of the feminist movement a fictional whirlwind of protest over what history has wrought": "Their message is clear and direct: because of the wanton abuse of his assumed superior sexual status, the black male of the twentieth century has become a psychological and economic disaster who should be promptly castrated and cast aside on history's junkpile. And the prototypical male castaway can be found in abundant numbers on the pages of their fiction" (407). While a full discussion of this controversy is beyond the scope and interest of this study,[3] one must agree that a great many of Morrison's male characters are, in fact, psychological and economic disasters, symbolically castrated and rendered infantile and ineffectual. In her novels, however, such depictions are most often justified by historical conditions (see Chapter 3) and explicable by at least the partial responsibility of her female characters, most obviously those archaic and phallic mothers, those strong and dominant food-givers and man-eaters who bond together in twos and threes, and who dictate the terms of their own metafictions. That Morrison herself trembles before their power should be obvious from discussions in previous chapters.

Least complex because least developed of these figures are the three prostitutes in *The Bluest Eye*. So castrating are these women that it is a wonder they have customers at all, for

> these women hated men, all men, without shame, apology, or discrimination. They abused their visitors with a scorn grown mechanical from use. Black men, white men, Puerto Ricans, Mexicans, Jews, Poles, whatever—all were inadequate and weak, all came under their jaundiced eyes and were the recipients of their disinterested wrath. They took delight in cheating them. On one occasion the town well knew, they lured a Jew up the stairs, pounced on him, all three, held him up by the heels, shook everything out of his pants pockets, and threw him out of the window. (47–48)

This is broad, even slapstick comedy, but the three whores are also a prototype for their more sinister sisters in later novels, in which Morrison is not laughing but extending a cautionary example, a warning to women readers and feminist critics that, if women participate in the castration of men, whether through love or malice (both and either of which is effective toward this end), they will end up with no men at all, only children.

As almost every critic of *Sula* has noted, most males in this novel are infantilized, even by their very names: BoyBoy, Tar Baby, Sweet Plum, Chicken Little. And, they behave accordingly: abandoning families, going insane, becoming alcoholic or drug-addicted. Only the women in this novel have "real" names, and they are the agents of power, even of castration—at least symbolically. Sula and Nel are formidable adversaries of men even when they are preadolescent. Certainly the threat is of castration in that incident in which Sula and Nel, coming home from school, are bullied by a group of white boys. In parody of a circumcision rite, Sula takes a knife and cuts off the tip of her own finger: "If I can do that to myself, what you suppose I'll do to you?" (47). Even white boys understand how dangerous she is: "The shifting dirt was the only way Nel knew that they were moving away" (47).

More threatening is the following series of events, which takes place shortly after the ice-cream parlor episode. It is the summer, "limp with the weight of blossomed things" and of "The beautiful, beautiful boys who dotted the landscape like jewels. . . . Even their footprints left a smell of smoke behind" (48). Nature itself and the corresponding blossoming maturity of Nel and Sula seem to demand some ritual, what Baker terms a "three-fold enactment of Phallic rites" (97). But this might also be a defloration ritual, like those performed in connection with some historical matriarchal cultures. Nel and Sula sit beside a river, playing with two thick twigs which they have "undressed," "stripped to a smooth, creamy innocence" (49–50):

> But soon [Nel] grew impatient and poked her twig rhythmically and intensely into the earth, making a small neat hole that grew deeper and wider with the least manipulation of her twig. Sula copied her, and soon each had a hole the size of a cup. Nel began a more strenuous digging and, rising to her knees, was careful to scoop out the dirt as she made her hole deeper. Together they worked until the two holes were one and the same. When the depression was the size of a small dishpan, Nel's twig broke. With a gesture of disgust she threw the pieces into the hole they had made. Sula threw hers in too. Nel saw a bottle cap and tossed it in as well. Each then looked around for more debris to throw into the hole: paper, bits of glass, butts of cigarettes, until all the small defiling things they could find were collected there. Carefully they replaced the soil and covered the entire grave with uprooted grass.
> Neither one had spoken a word. (50)

Immediately following these ceremonies and this significant silence (see Chapter 1 for a discussion of similar symbolic silences) is the ritualized sacrifice of the male-child; Chicken Little happens by, innocently picking his nose: "You scared we gone take your bugger away?" Sula teases. His name, according to Baker, is "Morrison's own mocking designation of the Phallus, in all of its mystery, as a false harbinger of apocalypse" (98). The apocalypse, however, is Chicken Little's own; Sula swings him out over the water—and lets go.

The butterflies that fly among the flowers on Chicken Little's grave presage the butterflies Ajax brings as courtship offering to Sula, just as the stick ceremony has presaged the sexual relationships of both Nel and Sula. While Nel's adolescent dreams of "lying on a flowered bed, tangled in her own hair, waiting for some fiery prince" (44) prefigure her passivity in her marriage to Jude, Sula's dreams indicate the active sexual power she will assume as she gallops "through her own mind on a gray-and-white horse tasting sugar and smelling roses in full view of a someone who shared both the taste and the speed" (44).

"It was manlove that Eva bequeathed to her daughters" (35), Morrison's narrator tells us, and like Hannah, who required "some touching every day" (38), Sula enjoys sex for its own sake and for the reflection of her own power that it provides:

> During the lovemaking she found and needed to find the cutting edge. When she left off cooperating with her body and began to assert herself in the act, particles of strength gathered in her like steel shavings drawn to a spacious magnetic center, forming a tight cluster that nothing, it seemed, could break. And there was utmost irony and outrage in lying under someone in a position of surrender, feeling her own abiding strength and limitless power. But the cluster did break, fall apart, and in her panic to hold it together she leaped from the edge into soundlessness and went down howling, howling in a stinging awareness of the endings of things, an eye of sorrow in the midst of all that hurricane rage of joy. (106)

Thus does Morrison give a voice to female desire by providing what is possibly the best description in American literature of the feminine orgasm; it is *jouissance*, in fact—a transcendent experience that reclaims the female body from the male inscription—but it is also an expression of pain, a complex howl of sorrow that is both birth and death, political and even cosmic in its implications.

With Ajax, who loves the female power in Sula as he has loved it in his own mother, Sula assumes the upper position, swaying "like a Georgia pine on its knees, high above the slipping, falling smile, high above the golden eyes," drifting toward "the high silence of orgasm. . . . He swallowed her mouth just as her thighs had swallowed his genitals, and the house was very, very quiet" (112–13). Baker writes that this is a rewriting, perhaps even a

retraction, of the phallic ceremony of childhood: "The swallow-
ing of the actual penis, rather than the burial of the Phallus, might
produce a resounding quiet and a genuine Peace" (102). But perhaps Sula's aims are less redemptive than Baker indicates, for
surely there is ambiguity, if not actual violence, in her fantasy that
accompanies the sexual act: "If I take a chamois and rub real hard
on the bone, right on the ledge of your cheek bone, some of the
black will disappear. . . . And if I take a nail file or even Eva's old
paring knife—that will do—and scrape away at the gold. . . .
Then I can take a chisel and small tap hammer . . . " (112). According to Patricia Yaeger, similar literary renditions of the "female sublime" constitute a "liberating structure of female violence
and aggression" (1989, 209).

Baker also argues that this sexual relationship between Sula
and Ajax redeems the heterosexuality which suffers as an ideal so
frequently in Morrison's novels and serves to invalidate Barbara
Smith's argument in "Toward a Black Feminist Criticism" for *Sula*
as a lesbian novel.[4] Morrison herself has unequivocally stated that
"there is no homosexuality in *Sula*" (Tate 1989, 118). But Smith
is certainly correct in her appraisal of the consistent failure of heterosexual relationships in Morrison's fiction. Even Ajax, that phe-
nomenal lover, cannot cope with Sula's possessive demands, and
he leaves for a Dayton air show. Sula, like Nel, like Eva and Hannah, is finally abandoned. For Morrison, *jouissance* always depends upon escape from patriarchally sanctified sexuality, upon
freedom from romantic ideals like love and possession. Sula's tem-
porary surrender of her own life-giving eroticism in her attempt
to possess Ajax, her lapse into domesticity signified by the green
hair ribbon and the sparkling bathroom, not only alienate Ajax
but represent her own death knell, her descent into a sleep of
"cobalt blue" where "she tasted the acridness of gold, left the chill
of alabaster and smelled the dark, sweet stench of loam" (118).

Ajax, like so many of Morrison's men, is effectively though
symbolically castrated, not by Sula, despite her nail file and
knives fantasy, but by his own mother, "an evil conjure woman,
blessed with seven adoring children whose joy it was to bring her
the plants, hair, underclothing, fingernail parings, white hens,
blood, camphor, pictures, kerosene, and footstep dust that she
needed. . . . She knew about weather, omens, the living, the dead,
dreams and all illnesses" (109). Sula herself is witchlike by this

point in the novel; but she cannot replace the mother, although a surrogate for his mother is what Ajax really wants; he brings Sula a bottle of milk on his first visit, which he drinks himself. But Sula has not named him, and, in fact, has incorrectly called him Ajax when his name was Albert Jacks: "so how could he help but leave me since he was making love to a woman who didn't even know his name" (117).

To name is to have power over the individual named, as was discussed in Chapter 2, and the namer in *Sula* is Eva, whose power is symbolic of her function as the phallic mother to destroy as well as to create life. There is no question that she loves her children; she has sacrificed even her leg (which is no castration symbol in this case) to provide for them; to relieve the baby Plum's life-threatening constipation, as Eva recites ritualistically and repeatedly, she has taken a lump of lard and "shoved the last bit of food she had in the world (besides three beets) up his ass" (29). But Plum returns from war to his mother's house a drug addict, helpless as an infant again. She murders him, burns him alive in his bed, because he "wanted to crawl back in my womb:"

> I ain't got the room no more even if he could do it. There wasn't space for him in my womb. And he was crawlin' back. Being helpless and thinking baby thoughts and dreaming baby dreams and messing up his pants again and smiling all the time. I had room enough in my heart, but not in my womb, got no more. I birthed him once. I couldn't do it again. He was growed, a big old thing. Godhavemercy, I couldn't birth him twice . . . so I just thought of a way he could die like a man not all crunched up inside my womb, but like a man. . . . But I held him close first. Real close. Sweet Plum. My baby boy. (62)

As Eva pours the kerosene over her son, before she lights the match, he feels the sensation of "an eagle pouring a wet lightness over him. Some kind of baptism, some kind of blessing" (40). The fire Eva lights is as paradoxical as her love; it purifies as it destroys. As Clément and Cixous define the "sorceress" who haunts our dreams, "She is innocent, mad, full of badly remembered memories, guilty of unknown wrongs; she is the seductress, the heiress of all generic Eves" (6).

Also, as Rubenstein has suggested in *Boundaries of the Self: Gender, Culture, Fiction*, Morrison's novels are replete with images of incest, desired or enacted. Like that of Ajax, Plum's desire to return to the mother is unconscious, but, more perversely, Eva is perfectly aware of her own desire to permit that return:

> I'd be laying here at night and he be downstairs in that room, but when I closed my eyes I'd see him . . . six feet tall smilin' and crawlin' up the stairs quietlike so I wouldn't hear and opening the door soft so I wouldn't hear and he'd be creepin' to the bed trying to spread my legs. . . . One night it wouldn't be no dream. It'd be true and I would have done it, would have let him. . . . (62)

The return to the mother, erotic as this return always is in all of Morrison's novels, is also always associated with castration, death, oblivion, but also—paradoxically—with enlightenment, revelation, transcendence. For the women assembled at Chicken Little's funeral, all the dead sons become "Sweet Jesus" himself, who is both "son and lover in whose downy face they could see the sugar-and-butter sandwiches and feel the oldest and most devastating pain there is: not the pain of childhood, but the remembrance of it" (56). In *Desire in Language*, Kristeva refers to a "non-Oedipal incest" that "opens the eyes of a subject who is nourished by the mother . . . neither animal, god, nor man, he is Dionysus, born a second time for having had the mother" (192). The artist of a culture, says Kristeva, is one who seeks maternal *jouissance*, who is a "servant to the maternal phallus" (246).

"Artist" or not, Milkman in *Song of Solomon* also seeks the maternal phallus, not in his own ineffectual and powerless mother, but in his aunt, Pilate, who, as discussed earlier, is a mother surrogate and as powerful as Eva or any other of Morrison's archaic mothers. Pilate is also a seductress in her offering of food and her telling of tales, and Milkman is unconsciously drawn to her in ways that are often sexual. In Shalimar, Milkman considers the beautiful women he sees all around him, and he is reminded of Pilate: "They sat on porches, and walked in the road swaying their hips under cotton dresses, bare-legged, their unstraightened hair braided or pulled straight back into a ball. He wanted one of them bad. To curl up in a cot in that one's arms, or that one, or that. That's the way Pilate must have looked as a girl, looked even now . . . " (266). Both Pilate and Circe represent for Milkman the forbidden part of himself, that zone of the erotic that subverts reason and patriarchal inscriptions; he is quite literally bewitched by them:

> He had had dreams as a child, dreams every child had, of the witch who chased him down dark alleys, between lawn trees, and finally into rooms from which he could not escape. Witches in black dresses and red underskirts; witches with pink eyes and green lips, tiny witches, long rangy witches, frowning witches, smiling witches, screaming witches and laughing witches, witches that flew, witches that ran, and some that merely glided on the ground . . . but he knew that always, always at the very instant of the pounce or the gummy embrace he would wake with a scream and an erection. Now he had only the erection. (241–42)

Pilate is an Eve figure, as was mentioned earlier, but she is also the snake of Macon Dead's imagination (54), and the crawling, flying witch of Milkman's dreams. Finally, she is the "Sugargirl" of Milkman's death song on the last page: "There must be another one like you. . . . There's got to be at least one more woman like you" (340).

Just as Hagar cannot hope to compete with Pilate for Milkman's affection or Sula to replace Ajax's powerful mother, so Jadine in *Tar Baby* cannot succeed in her attempts to rescue Son from the "diaspora mothers," the ancestor figures, the witches with the magic breasts: "She thought she was rescuing him from the night women who wanted him for themselves, wanted him feeling superior in a cradle, deferring to him. . . . Mama-spoiled black man, will you mature with me? Culture-bearing black woman, whose culture are you bearing?" (231–32). But Son, as his name indicates, has always belonged to the mothers and the night women, to the wild zone.

Son's very inaccessibility and his wildness are what attract Jadine in the first place, along with his potential for violence, which fits perfectly into her unconscious rape fantasies. His skin is very black in contrast to her diluted coloring, and he wears his hair in dreadlocks: "his hair looked overpowering—physically overpowering, like bundles of long whips or lashes that could grab her and beat her to jelly. And would. Wild, aggressive, vicious hair that needed to be put in jail. Uncivilized, reform-school hair. Mau Mau, Attica, chain-gang hair" (97). Part of Jadine's fascination is a perversion of racial stereotypes, her own aspiration to "white-

ness" depending on a rejection of what she defines in herself as
"black" and what she interprets as animal sexuality: "Like an animal. Treating her like another animal and both of them must have
looked just like it in that room. One dog sniffing at the hindquar-
ters of another" (105–6). Jadine revels in such fantasies, debased
not so much by Son as by her own imagination. Her "animal" self
is in reality masturbatorially manifested by the baby sealskin coat,
gift of a white male admirer, on which she lies naked and "spread-
eagled . . . nestling herself into it. It made her tremble. She
opened her lips and licked the fur" (96). Jadine's perversity is no
less than that of Margaret Street, who is also titillated by the potential violence Son represents in her neurotic white woman's
fantasy of the black rapist who has hidden himself in her closet,
"Actually in her things. Probably jerking off. Black sperm was
sticking in clots to her French jeans or down in the toe of her
Anne Klein shoes. Didn't men sometimes jerk off in women's
shoes?" (73).

And there is much basis in such fantasies, for Son's sexual
philosophy includes the viability of violence and the conviction of
male superiority, as he indicates in his first conversation with Valerian in the greenhouse: women, he says, are like plants; "you
have to jack them up every once in a while. Make em act nice, like
they're supposed to" (127). Son has murdered one wife, and he
does beat Jadine, for all of which the night women forgive him,
although, one hopes, Morrison does not. Even though Son is
metaphorically the male soldier ant of Jadine's jungle fantasy, fer-
tilizing the queen ant and doing "the single thing he was born
for," which the queen remembers until the fortieth generation,
and even though he is "the man who fucked like a star" (250–
51)—"Star throbs. Over and over and over. Like this. Stars just
throb and throb and throb and sometimes, when they can't throb
anymore, when they can't hold it anymore, they fall out of the
sky" (184)—his destiny is finally the mother space of the swamp,
the reentry into the womb. "Small boy," Thérèse addresses him,
as she directs him into oblivion.

Many women in Morrison's fictions, and most particularly
the mother-women, are often servile and indulgent, if only with
their sons, and thus they are guilty of destroying the very sons
about whom they are so passionate, rendering them into chronic
infancy, usurping their masculinity, and effectively ensuring that

they are unfit for adult sexual relationships with other women. But Morrison's men, too, are often responsible for their own condition; they have surrendered masculinity deliberately and of their own free will, preferring the role of pampered infant. Milkman, for example, has accepted the homage and deference of women whom he has, in turn, mistreated all his life, so locked is he in the prison of his male ego. His very walk is characterized, not by a limp as he imagines, but by a strut. He himself is so like the male peacock with the jeweled tail that he and Guitar admire, and he so richly deserves his sisters' scorn:

> Our girlhood was spent like a found nickel on you. When you slept, we were quiet; when you were hungry, we cooked; when you wanted to play, we entertained you; and when you got grown enough to know the difference between a woman and a two-toned Ford, everything in this house stopped for you. You have yet to wash your underwear, spread a bed, wipe the ring from your tub, or move a fleck of your dirt from one place to another. . . . You are a sad, pitiful, stupid, selfish, hateful man. I hope your little hog's gut stands you in good stead, and that you take good care of it, because you don't have anything else . . . you have pissed your last in this house. (216–18)

Although there is some regeneration for Milkman by the end of the novel in his recognition that "From the beginning, his mother and Pilate had fought for his life, and he had never so much as made either of them a cup of tea" (335), and in his compensatory action of repaying Sweet's kindnesses by rubbing her back and cleaning her tub, it is all ironically too late and too little.

Nel's husband, Jude, in *Sula* is similarly and deservingly castigated by Sula, who answers his plea for feminine sympathy and comfort with the statement that "everything in the world loves you. . . . And if that ain't enough, you love yourselves. Nothing in this world loves a black man more than another black man" (89). Morrison herself is surely outraged at male behavior, and the feminist reader cheers her on, feels vindicated and grateful. And we are grateful, too, when she finally redeems the male sex and provides us with the closest thing to a "fiery prince" that she can conjure.

One of the few male characters in Morrison's novels who survives as a hero, who is able to withstand maternal aggression at least for a time, and who preserves his life, his manhood, and his dignity, is Paul D in *Beloved*. Perhaps because his suffering under slavery has been equal to Sethe's, or perhaps because he has retained the ancient African worship for womanhood in general as well as for the Great Mother, Paul D has "the thing in him, the blessedness, that has made him the kind of man who can walk in a house and make the women cry. Because with him, in his presence, they could. Cry and tell him things they only told each other" (272). He is "a singing man," "a tender man," and he understands the female language:

> Trust and rememory, yes, the way she believed it could be when he cradled her before the cooking stove. The weight and angle of him; the true-to-life beard hair on him; arched back, educated hands. His waiting eyes and awful human power. The mind of him that knew her own. Her story was bearable because it was his as well—to tell, to refine and tell again. The things that neither knew about the other—the things neither had word-shapes for—well, it would come in time. . . . (99)

As I discussed in Chapter 1, the body and the word become synonymous, and both are erotic; Paul D "wants to put his story next to hers" (273). Or perhaps the eroticism so inherent in this relationship comes from the context of history itself, the continuing presence of danger or death, the necessity to seize the erotic moment from a hostile world, the need to affirm a life that is not a gift but that is stolen from history. Paul D meets Sethe on the street one winter afternoon, and they share such a moment:

> She let her head touch his chest, and since the moment was valuable to both of them, they stopped and stood that way— not breathing, not even caring if a passerby passed them by. The winter light was low. Sethe closed her eyes. Paul D looked at the black trees lining the roadside, their defending arms raised against attack. Softly, suddenly, it began to snow, like a present come down from the sky. Sethe opened her eyes to it and said, "Mercy." And it seemed to Paul D that it was—a little mercy—something given to them on purpose to mark what they were feeling so they would remember it later on when they needed to.
>   Down came the dry flakes, fat enough and heavy enough to crash like nickels on stone. It always surprised him, how quiet it was. Not like rain, but like a secret. (129)

But even the love of Paul D cannot totally compensate for the reality of the atrocities that are history; no purely edenic return is possible in Morrison's world. The reader cannot help but interpret Paul D's almost incestuous sexual surrender to Beloved's supernatural powers as a betrayal. Nor can he, being merely human, easily confront the face of female murder; even he wavers before that which Sethe represents—the phallic mother, the Medusa.

However, like Paul D and like Milkman and Son, all of Morrison's male characters are helpless with desire for the Great Mother—terrifying though she always is, representing as she always does the violation of the law of the father. The desire for the mother is itself a form of incest, and incest in all its guises, according to Freud, is an expression of the human desire for disorder, counterorder. And this is true for Morrison as well, although she makes no moral judgments about the nature of disorder, recognizing it as dangerous but also as a valid aspect of human experience. Those of Morrison's characters who have not encountered their own jungles, never been enmeshed within the preoedipal bond, never explored the foreign territory of their own sexuality, are condemned to innocence in which they suffer the extreme deprivation of their humanity.[5]

There are also those characters, however, who lose humanity through an excess of freedom, whose drive to disorder is so unfettered that it becomes destructive to self as well as to others. Cholly Breedlove in *The Bluest Eye* is one such character, guilty of what Morrison terms "illicit, traumatic, incomprehensible sex coming to its dreaded fruition" (1990, 219), which is the rape of his daughter. But even this dreadful event, within Morrison's ethical system, punished as it is with disgrace and death, is nonetheless at least partially understandable, a "hatred mixed with tenderness" (129). As Morrison has explained in an interview, "I want you to *look* at him and see his love for his daughter and his powerlessness to help her pain. By that time his embrace, the rape, is all the gift he has left" (Tate 1989, 125).

For Morrison, however, extreme repression is even more destructive than unfettered freedom. Cholly's wife, Pauline, has lost her sexual self in her rage for order and her fascination with the cleanliness (sterility) of the white woman's kitchen, in which she could "arrange things, clean things, line things up in neat rows" (101). Religion replaces sexuality as a far more destructive drive, entailing an idea, not of morality, but of revenge: "Mrs. Breedlove was not interested in Christ the Redeemer, but rather Christ the Judge" (37). And her battles with Cholly involving both psychological abuse and physical violence are of epic scope; these take place, not in order for her to save his soul or he hers, for each needs the excesses of the other to exist, but to forget that there was once another kind of existence, another place in which sex was erotic rather than merely violent and where rainbows could be both seen and felt: "those little bits of color floating up into me—deep in me. That streak of green from the june-bug light, the purple from the berries trickling along my thighs. . . . Then I feel like I'm laughing between my legs, and the laughing gets all mixed up with the colors, and I'm afraid I'll come, and afraid I won't. But I know I will. And I do. And it be rainbow all inside . . . " (103–4).

Pauline's life is ugly and violent, but it is some compensation that she has such memories, the preservation of which is surely her intention when she refuses her white woman employer's well-meaning but culturally obtuse advice to leave Cholly, to deny her own sexual reality. Pauline is thus fortunate in comparison to that amorphous group of "sugar-brown Mobile girls" who have lost their sugar, who spend their lives fighting "the dreadful funkiness of passion," and who build their nests, "stick by stick" (68–69), even to the destruction of husbands and sons. One such woman who does not "sweat in her armpits nor between her thighs" (70) is Geraldine, who never kisses her baby boy and thus turns him into the monster who so tortures Pecola with his mother's only erotic object, that pathetic remnant of lost witchcraft and female power, her cat:

> The cat will settle quietly on the windowsill and caress her with his eyes. She can hold him in her arms, letting his back paws struggle for footing on her breast and his forepaws cling to her shoulder. She can rub the smooth fur and feel the unresisting flesh underneath. . . . When she stands cooking at the table, he will circle about her shanks, and the trill of his fur spirals up her legs to her thighs, to make her fingers tremble a little in the pie dough. (70)

Nel of *Sula* has no comparable familiar, but she is more than a bit like Geraldine, particularly after she is married to Jude and thus estranged from the wild side of herself, which is Sula. Nel's adolescent dreams of passive sexuality are manifest in her indulgence of a husband who only seeks another mother; his desire is for a woman who will sympathize with the pain he suffers at the hands of the white man, who will be the "the hem—the tuck and fold that hid his raveling edges; a someone sweet, industrious and loyal to shore him up. . . . Without that someone he was a waiter hanging around a kitchen like a woman. With her he was head of a household pinned to an unsatisfactory job out of necessity. The two of them together would make one Jude" (71). In her willing assumption of the role Jude requires, Nel effectively depletes his integrity and his masculinity along with her own female power, thereby assuring his eventual desertion of her, her own sexual deprivation, and her own misery. Ajax is right about some women: "all they want, man, is they own misery. Ax em to die for you and they yours for life" (71).

Guitar, himself psychologically fit only for celibacy in the priesthood of the Seven Days, says to Hagar in *Song of Solomon*: "You're turning over your whole life to him. Your whole life, girl. And if it means so little to you that you can just give it away, hand it to him, then why should it mean any more to him? . . . Pretty little black-skinned woman. Who wanted to kill for love, die for love" (310). Dying for love, in fact, is a part of African American folklore, the subject of music and stories, and Hagar is no aberration in this respect: "The lengths to which lost love drove men and women never surprised them. They had seen women pull their dresses over their heads and howl like dogs for lost love" (128). But, in the case of Hagar, there is truly something "askew," as even Ruth Foster can detect: not a "wilderness where there was system, or the logic of lions, trees, toads, and birds, but wild wilderness where there was none" (138).

Perhaps Hagar's "wilderness" comes from her life experience in the mother space, the preoedipal condition of Pilate's house, where she is the pampered daughter, the only one with sheets on her bed, the loved and spoiled darling. Pilate introduces her to Milkman as "your brother" (43), and the forbidden, incestuous nature of their long relationship is characterized by the image of wilderness, violence, and ultimately by Milkman's reenactment of his great grandfather's flight from responsibility and Hagar's death from sorrow, which imitates Ryna's destruction. "My baby girl," Pilate mourns at Hagar's funeral, and her words are tossed "like stones into a silent canyon" (323), that same canyon that is

Ryna's Gulch in which the cries of abandoned women echo throughout the centuries.

But dying for love, Morrison implies, is better than dying for the lack of it, and, particularly in *Song of Solomon*, there are a great many women who do just that. Ruth Foster, for example, has a husband named "Dead," which indicates more than his personality, for he has punished her for years by denying her (although not thereby himself as well, it is hinted) sexual gratification. In Morrison's terms, Ruth is like "a lighthouse keeper," "a prisoner automatically searching out the sun" (11), and her perversions—nursing her half-grown son and, according to her husband's account, sucking the fingers of her dead father—shrink in comparison to that most perverse behavior of Macon Dead's. And Macon has terrorized his daughters as well, seeking to doom them to perpetual virginity, the velvet rose petals they spend their time in manufacturing being emblematic of their enforced and artificial condition. Lena tells Milkman about the significance of making the roses: "I loved to do it. It kept me . . . quiet. That's why they make those people in the asylum weave baskets and make rag rugs. It keeps them quiet. If they didn't have the baskets they might find out what's really wrong and . . . do something. Something terrible" (215). Rather than relive her mother's madness, Corinthians, Milkman's other sister, will in fact do "something terrible," which is to prostrate herself on the hood of Porter's old car, begging for his love, his sex, anything but the roses: "This is for you, girl. Oh, yes. This is for you" (201).[6]

Deprivation of sexual love is catastrophic for almost all characters in Morrison's novels, and perversity, even madness and brutality, is more likely to coincide with sexual abstinence than with sexual excess. Chastity is the key to Soaphead Church's perverse love for "clean little girls" in *The Bluest Eye*, and his confusion of lovemaking with "communion and the Holy Grail" loses him his wife who "had not lived by the sea all those years, listened to the wharfman's songs all that time, to spend her life in the soundless cave of Elihue's mind" (134). Prudently, Velma refuses to play the role of Beatrice, refuses to be robbed of her own sexuality and subsumed into the stereotype of a diseased male fantasy that cannot cope with life or with the living woman.

Male discomfort with and denial of female sexuality is a pattern in Morrison's fiction, just as it is in Cixous's ironically humorous analyses: "Conquering her, they've made haste to depart from her borders, to get out of sight, out of body. . . . One can understand how man, confusing himself with his penis and rushing in for the attack, might feel resentment and fear of being 'taken' by the woman, of being lost in her, absorbed or alone" (310). Sexual deprivation, apparently, is the price for female power, but also paradoxically, for the surrender of power. For Nel in *Sula*, the loss of, not Jude himself, but Jude's sexuality is so debilitating that death seems preferable:

> And what am I supposed to do with these old thighs now, just walk up and down these rooms? What good are they, Jesus? They will never give me the peace I need to get from sunup to sundown. . . . O Jesus, I could be a mule or plow the furrows with my hands if need be or hold these rickety walls up with my back if need be if I knew that somewhere in this world in the pocket of some night I could open my legs to some cowboy lean hips but you are trying to tell me no and O my sweet Jesus what kind of cross is that? (95–96)

Sexual deprivation, too, is the source of Margaret's rape fantasies about Son in *Tar Baby*, but even more significantly, it is the ostensible reason behind her abuse of her own son as well as the conscious process of self-annihilation that occupies her life. The "dark continent" of feminine sensibility and eroticism, according to Cixous and Clément, is in reality "neither dark nor unexplorable" (68), at least not for women, and most particularly not for Morrison.

"To *love*," says Kristeva in *Desire in Language*, "is to survive paternal meaning" (150). But sex and even love are finally not separable from paternal meaning; they do not save the world or even the individual in Morrison's fictions, where the edenic return remains firmly in the realm of the imagination rather than in the area of possibility. Morrison does not offer redemption through her portrayal of sexuality but only reminders: "Not love, but a willingness to love" (*Song of Solomon*, 226).

And yet always in Morrison's texts there *is* a possible kind of redemption through that which is erotic: it lies in her language, resonates in her imagery, provides meaning and texture to structure. Another kind of *jouissance* apparently exists in the pleasures of the writerly text. At the close of Chapter 1 it was suggested that Morrison writes the female body, that her texts imitate and recreate the feminine orgasm, that they constitute what Cixous calls "the flesh of language," the "feminine" style, "the savage tongue" (1981, 52). Morrison's language itself is erotic, an erogenous zone, so full of color and rainbows and summer smoke: "Jesus, there were some beautiful boys in 1921. . . . The sun heated them and the moon slid down their backs. God, the world was *full* of beautiful boys in 1921" (*Sula*, 140). Finally, her rendering of the erotic and the feminine is so euphoric and so life-giving that we hardly recognize the failure of love or its absence within the context of history and political realities. "And that will have to do until someone else comes in a burst of song, color, and laughter to conquer the last refuge of the sacred, still inaccessibly hidden" (Kristeva 1980, 158).

Afterword

> When "The Repressed" of their culture and their society come back, it is an explosive return, which is *absolutely* shattering, staggering, overturning, with a force never let loose before.
> —Cixous and Clément, *The Newly Born Woman*

Finally, Morrison's texts represent this kind of "shattering" and "explosive" return, for through her language (most particularly through her language), she speaks what is unspeakable for mainstream discourse: the juxtaposition of woman and collective history, the dissolution of boundaries between sign and historical event, the unification of myth and cultural codes, the reinscription of meaning itself through a rendering of identification and desire. She *does* write the feminine text; she *does* compose a literature that is distinctly African American; her works *do* constitute a contribution to postmodernism; she *is* a deconstructionist. Or, she is none of these things because she is *all* of them—and more. She writes in the *difference*, in the spaces and the margins, from the vantage of otherness which then becomes the familiar.

The foregoing study has stressed this difference, a difference by which Morrison also defines her own text: "I am not *like* James Joyce; I am not *like* Thomas Hardy; I am not *like* Faulkner. I am not *like* in that sense" (McKay 1988, 1). As we have also seen, Morrison's novels defy those critical straitjackets which seek to analyze and define strictly within the contexts of either Freud or Marx, psychoanalysis or politics, although her works are always political, always concerned with class distinctions, and always profoundly psychoanalytic. Morrison is clearly outside of traditional dominant cultural inscriptions, but she does not create in a vacuum. She is, of course, not the first writer to stress the diffusion of the text as well as of identity, nor the first to articulate female desire, nor the first to reinscribe history. Nor is she exempt from the context of contemporary critical theory, particularly French feminist theory, which also seeks to break down oppositions and hierarchies, to diffuse modalities, and reinscribe identity

105

and desire. However, Morrison is greater than the terms em-
ployed to define her. She represents the *extreme* of that which
critical theory has conceptualized, taking theory itself to the edge
of the abyss, to a point beyond meaning, to signification that is
truly "unspeakable."

Thus Morrison's texts are prophetic in many ways, another
of which is that they give voice to a cultural rupture which has
already occurred and is now being documented by a great deal of
critical attention and literary analysis. In light of the tremendous
impact of Morrison's fictions and those of other contemporary
women writers (and particularly African American women writers), arguments about canonicity that have preoccupied scholars
in the recent past seem already anachronistic, for the sanctity of
the canon is already threatened, demasculinized if not actually
feminized.

Appropriately, Morrison has spoken on revolutionizing the
Western literary canon and defined it in its political context:

> Canon building is Empire building. Canon defense is national
> defense. Canon debate, whatever the terrain, nature, and range
> (of criticism, of history, or the history of knowledge, of the
> definition of language, the universality of aesthetic principles,
> the sociology of art, the humanistic imagination), is the clash
> of cultures. And *all* of the interests are vested. (1990, 207)

Changes in the humanistic status quo, Morrison indicates, are not
so much historical events, temporal and physical processes, as
mental structures, new ways of seeing even the history that has
informed and dictated culture. She would not wish, she has said,
the destruction or the elimination of that which comprises the
canon: "And, I, at least, do not intend to live without Aeschylus
or William Shakespeare, or James or Twain or Hawthorne, or
Melville, etc., etc., etc." Rather, it is canonicity itself, the sanctity
and the political conservatism that sanctity represents, which
Morrison would eliminate: "There must be some way to enhance
canon readings without enshrining them" (1990, 204–5).

Morrison's fictions are foremost among those which challenge the institutions that are indifferent to difference and intent
on preserving a myth of a homogeneous tradition for its own sake
and for its political ramifications. Canon-building has been ac-
complished by scholars who universalized texts by ignoring the

cultural specificities that differentiated them and who insisted on totalizing concepts of gender, race, and subjectivity. The very concept of canonicity is subverted by writers like Morrison who represent language as difference rather than as unified or cohesive discourse, and who also represent more accurately the plurality of the American heritage, including that of the African American woman writer. Morrison's work both poses and represents the intellectual crisis that will surely engage readers and critics for the next generation.

Notes

Introduction

1. For an analysis of the specific relevance of the term "conjure" in African American discourse, see Marjorie Pryse and Hortense Spillers, eds., *Conjuring: Black Women, Fiction, and Literary Tradition*.
2. According to Showalter: "We can think of the "wild zone" of women's culture spatially, experientially, or metaphysically. Spatially it stands for an area which is literally no-man's land, a place forbidden to men. . . . Experientially it stands for the aspects of the female life-style which are outside of or unlike those of men; again, there is no corresponding zone of male experience alien to women. But, if we think of the wild zone metaphysically, or in terms of consciousness, it has no corresponding male space since all of male consciousness is within the circle of the dominant structure and is thus accessible to or structured by language. In this sense, the "wild" is always imaginary; from the male point of view, it may simply be the projection of the unconscious. In terms of cultural anthropology, women know what the male crescent is like, even if they have never seen it, because it becomes the subject of legend (like the wilderness). But men do not know what is in the wild" (1985, 262).

Chapter 1

1. Morrison writes, in "Unspeakable Things Unspoken: The Afro-American Presence in American Literature," that what most concerns her in *The Bluest Eye* is "the silence at its center. The void that is Pecola's 'unbeing'" (220).
2. Keith E. Byerman argues that Son's destiny is more heroic: "He does not go back to the womb, as Jadine thought, but into the domain of the true black man" (84).
3. Freud's analogy of the preoedipal phase with archaeology might well

109

link with Milkman's archaeological quest in *Song of Solomon* and with Pilate's directions to the cave. Both the cave and the field of archaeology, in essence, are areas of privileged femininity.

4. Showalter writes, in "Feminist Criticism in the Wilderness": "For some feminist critics, the wild zone, or "female space," must be the address of a genuinely women-centered criticism, theory, and art, whose shared project is to bring into being the symbolic weight of female consciousness, to make the invisible visible, to make the silent speak" (263).

5. Mae Gwendolyn Henderson defines "speaking in tongues" as the "ability to speak in and through the spirit. Associated with glossolalia—speech in unknown tongues—it is ecstatic, rapturous, inspired speech based on a relation of intimacy and identification between the individual and God" (23).

6. According to Marianne Hirsch, silence is a form of discourse between all mothers and daughters, and, particularly in *Sula*, there is much that "remains unspeakable and indeed unspoken. A focus on this mother/daughter plot may suggest a particular form of the postmodern, deeply rooted in racial history, feminist consciousness, and political engagement."

7. Susan Gubar, in "The Blank Page," sees absence, blankness, as "a mysterious but potent act of resistance" (305) and as "a sacred space consecrated to female creativity" (307).

8. In a public lecture in Columbus, Ohio, in 1988, Morrison responded to a question about the stylistic shifts in *Beloved* by stating that they represented "writer's block," that the world she had created was so painful to her that at times she found that world impossible to reenter.

9. We shall also see in Chapter 3 that history itself partakes of a dreamscape or a nightmare, and that, again, boundaries between reality and fantasy are confused.

Chapter 2

1. Susan Willis writes in "I Shop Therefore I Am" that Hagar has destroyed herself through her own and Milkman's rejection of blackness: Hagar "decides that in order to hold on to her boyfriend she must make herself into a less-black woman. What Hagar does not grasp is that Milkman's uncaring regard for her is an expression of his primary sexism as well as his internalized acceptance of the larger society's racist measure of blacks in terms of how closely an individual's skin and hair approximate the white model" (1989, 178).

2. In an interview with Claudia Tate, for example, Morrison stated, "I don't use much autobiography in my writing. My life is uneventful. Writing has to do with the imagination. It's being able to open a door or think the unthinkable, no matter how silly it may appear" (1989, 127).

3. Nellie Y. McKay quotes Morrison as saying, "No author tells these stories. They are just told—meanderingly—as though they are going in several directions at the same time" (1983, 417).

4. See the discussion in Chapter 1 of blackness as invisibility and absence in *The Bluest Eye*.

5. In *Beloved*, whiteness rather than blackness becomes the signifier for absence, as Beloved recalls the slavers in the Middle Passage as "men without skin" (212).

6. Henderson argues that Sula's mark indicates as much about the sexism inherent in the black community as it does about her own identity: "Sula is marked from birth. Hers is a mark of nativity—a biological rather than a cultural inscription, appropriate in this instance because it functions to mark her as a 'naturally' inferior female within the black community" (27).

7. Roberta Rubenstein interprets the significance of marking quite differently. She writes, in *Boundaries of the Self*, "Whether self-created, imposed by others, or dictated by accident, each of the representations of physical or psychic mutilations or incompleteness expresses the characters' inner distress and social or cultural plight" (233).

8. As Trudier Harris has written in "Reconnecting Fragments: Afro-American Folk Tradition in *The Bluest Eye*," "To be called 'out of one's name' . . . can be just as negatively powerful as a nickname can be positive" (1988, 72).

9. It is interesting that Margaret Street enjoys romanticizing Jadine's blackness, at one point insisting on a comparison with Eurydice of the film *Black Orpheus*. Jadine resists: "She was uncomfortable with the way Margaret stirred her into blackening up or universaling out, always alluding to or ferreting out what she believed were racial characteristics" (54). Morrison implies, however, that Jadine's resistance indicates a problem with her own self-image as well as with Margaret's patronizing perceptions.

10. In an interview with Sandi Russell, Morrison commented on the strong ties among the women of her family: "I remember my grandmother and my great-grandmother. I had to answer to those women, had to know that whatever I did was easy in comparison with what they had to go through. . . . They taught me how to dream" (45).

11. Marianne Hirsch also explores ideas of subjectivity in *Beloved*:

"When Sethe tentatively says, at the end of the novel, 'Me? Me?', she begins for the first time to speak *for herself.* However, she can do so only in the context of another human bond; she can do so only because Paul D is holding her hand." Hirsch concludes that this represents "an affirmation of subjectivity which, even when it is maternal, can only emerge in and through human interconnection" (198).

12. Morrison's recurring image in this novel of the single eye—recall the reference quoted earlier in this chapter to women without men as "sour-tipped needles featuring one constant empty eye" (105)— may be associated with the fairy tale about the three sisters, One-Eye, Two-Eye, and Three-Eye.

13. According to Reddy in "The Tripled Plot and Center of *Sula*," Sula's "wish to be Nel is what drives Sula into her sexual experimentation with Jude" (37).

14. The single exception to this rule in Morrison's novels is the relationships that exist among the men at Sweet Home in *Beloved* and among the convicts in Alfred, Georgia, who are literally chained together and mutually dependent for survival itself. Perhaps the element of common victimization is the basis of the respect, even brotherhood, which characterizes these relationships.

15. Morrison states, in "The Afro-American Presence in American Literature," that she perceives the Tar Baby folktale to which her novel refers as being about masks: "Not masks as covering what is to be hidden, but how masks come to life, take life over, exercise the tensions between itself and what it covers. For Son, the most effective mask is none. For the others the construction is careful and delicately borne, but the masks they make have a life of their own and collide with those they come in contact with" (1990, 227).

Chapter 3

1. Morrison suggests a comparison of Jadine's and Son's relationship to the classic myth of Orpheus and Eurydice in that conversation early in the novel when Margaret and Jadine discuss the film *Black Orpheus*. Margaret comments on the beauty of Eurydice's hair, but Jadine subverts the implied romantic notion of race by interpreting the reference as being to the hair in Eurydice's armpits (54). Nevertheless, the allusion is relevant: Son unsuccessfully attempts to rescue his Eurydice from the hell that is her white-world identification.

2. Morrison has also commented: "There's a notion out in the land that there are human beings one writes about, and then there are black people or Indians or some other marginal group. If you write

about the world from that point of view, somehow it is considered lesser. It's racist, of course. The fact that I chose to write about black people means I've been stimulated to write about black people. We are people, not aliens. We live, we love, and we die. . . . Insensitive white people cannot deal with black writing, but then they cannot deal with their own literature either" (Tate 1989, 121).

Chapter 4

1. Hélène Cixous describes the orange as a symbol of female sexuality and also as an image of the perfect zero in *Vivre l'orange*.
2. As Deborah E. McDowell notes in her excellent article on "'The Self and Other': Reading Toni Morrison's *Sula* and the Black Female Text," "Jelly and pudding are metaphors of sexuality characteristic in classic blues lyrics" (1988, 82).
3. McDowell, for one, disagrees with such an assessment of any such agenda as castration in the works of black women writers: "What lies behind this smoke screen is an unacknowledged jostling for space in the literary marketplace . . ." (1989, 83).
4. Smith writes: "Despite the apparent heterosexuality of the female characters I discovered in re-reading *Sula* that it works as a lesbian novel not only because of the passionate friendship between Sula and Nel, but because of Morrison's consistently critical stance toward the heterosexual institutions of male/female relationships, marriage, and the family. Consciously or not, Morrison's work poses both lesbian and feminist questions about Black women's autonomy and their impact upon each other's lives" (165).
5. Theodore O. Mason, Jr., comments on the number of critics who object to just such patterns in Morrison's fictions and claim that she "unnecessarily problematizes Afro-American cultural patterns by representing them as anarchic and frequently violent" (173). Valerie Smith's concern, one that I feel sure is shared by Morrison, is that the symbolic and imagistic "return to earth" is a dangerous precedent for women: "This association of black women with reembodiment resembles rather closely the association, in classic Western philosophy and in nineteenth-century cultural constructions of womanhood, of women of color with the body and therefore with animal passions and slave labor" (45).
6. Jane Bakerman, in "Failures of Love: Female Initiation in the Novels of Toni Morrison," argues that First Corinthians is the only woman in *Song of Solomon* who has "a chance for even modified happiness" (563).

Bibliography

Primary Sources

Beloved. New York: Knopf, 1987.
The Black Book. Comp. Middleton Harris, ed. Toni Morrison. New York: Random House, 1974.
The Bluest Eye. New York: Pocket Books, 1970.
Song of Solomon. New York: Signet, 1978.
Sula. New York: Bantam, 1975.
Tar Baby. New York: Signet, 1981.
"Unspeakable Things Unspoken: The Afro-American Presence in American Literature." In *Modern Critical Views: Toni Morrison,* ed. Harold Bloom, 201–30. New York: Chelsea House, 1990.

Secondary Sources

Adams, Hazard, and Leroy Searle, eds. *Critical Theory since 1965.* Tallahassee: Florida State University Press, 1986.
Awkward, Michael. "'Appropriative Gestures: Theory and Afro-American Literary Criticism." In *Gender and Theory: Dialogues on Feminist Criticism,* ed. Linda Kauffman, 238–45. New York: Basil Blackwell, 1989.
———. "Roadblocks and Relatives: Critical Revision in Toni Morrison's *The Bluest Eye.*" In *Critical Essays on Toni Morrison,* ed. Nellie Y. McKay, 57–67. Boston: G. K. Hall, 1988.
Baker, Houston A., Jr. "When Lindbergh Sleeps with Bessie Smith: The Writing of Place in Toni Morrison's *Sula.*" In *The Difference Within: Feminism and Critical Theory,* ed. Elizabeth Meese and Alice Parker, 85–113. Philadelphia: John Benjamin's Publishing Company, 1989.
Bakerman, Jane S. "Failures of Love: Female Initiation in the Novels of Toni Morrison." *American Literature* 52 (1981): 541–63.
Banyiwa-Horne, Naana. "The Scary Face of the Self: An Analysis of

the Character of Sula in Toni Morrison's *Sula*." *Sage* 2 (1985): 28–31.

Barksdale, Richard K. "Castration Symbolism in Recent Black American Fiction." *College Language Association Journal* 29, no. 4 (June 1986): 400–413.

Bell, Roseann, Bettye Parker, and Beverly Guy-Shiftall, eds. *Sturdy Black Bridges: Visions of Black Women in Literature.* New York: Doubleday, 1979.

Berg, Temma F., Anna Shannon Elfenbein, Jeanne Larsen, and Eliza Kay Spacks, eds. *Engendering The Word: Feminist Essays in Psychosexual Poetics.* Urbana: University of Illinois Press, 1989.

———. "Suppressing the Language of Wo(man): The Dream as a Common Language." In *Engendering The Word*, ed. Berg et al., 3–28. Urbana: University of Illinois Press, 1989.

Blau du Plessis, Rachael. *Writing Beyond the Ending: Narrative Strategies of Twentieth-Century Women Writers.* Bloomington: Indiana University Press, 1986.

Bloom, Harold, ed. *Modern Critical Views: Toni Morrison.* New York: Chelsea House, 1990.

Brenner, Gerry. "*Song of Solomon*: Morrison's Rejection of Rank's Monomyth and Feminism." In *Critical Essays on Toni Morrison*, ed. Nellie Y. McKay, 114–24. Boston: G. K. Hall, 1988.

Butler, Judith. *Gender Trouble: Feminism and the Subversion of Identity.* New York: Routledge, 1990.

Byerman, Keith E. "Beyond Realism: The Fictions of Toni Morrison." In *Modern Critical Views: Toni Morrison*, ed. Bloom, 55–84. New York: Chelsea House, 1990.

———. *Fingering the Jagged Edge: Tradition and Form in Recent Black Fiction.* Athens: University of Georgia Press, 1985.

Campbell, Jane. *Mythic Black Fiction: The Transformation of History.* Knoxville: University of Tennessee Press, 1986.

Chodorow, Nancy J. *Feminism and Psychoanalytic Theory.* New Haven: Yale University Press, 1989.

———. *The Reproduction of Mothering: Psychoanalysis and the Sociology of Gender.* Berkeley: University of California Press, 1978.

Christian, Barbara. *Black Feminist Criticism: Perspectives on Black Women Writers.* New York: Pergamon Press, 1985.

———. *Black Women Novelists: The Development of a Tradition, 1892–1976.* Westport, Ct.: Greenwood Press, 1980.

———. "But What Do We Think We're Doing Anyway: The State of Black Feminist Criticism(s), or My Version of a Little Bit of History." In *Changing Our Own Words: Essays on Criticism, Theory, and Writing by Black Women*, Cheryl A. Wall, ed., 58–74. New Brunswick: Rutgers University Press, 1989.

————. "Community and Nature in the Novels of Toni Morrison." *Journal of Ethnic Studies* 7 (Winter 1980): 64–78.

————. "The Race for Theory." *Feminist Studies* 14, no. 1 (Spring 1988): 67–79.

Cixous, Hélène. "Castration or Decapitation?" trans. Annette Kuhn. *Signs* 7, no. 11 (Autumn 1981): 41–55.

————. "The Laugh of the Medusa." In *Critical Theory since 1965*, ed. Adams and Searle, 309–20. Tallahassee: Florida State University Press, 1986.

————. *Vivre l'orange*. Paris: Editions des femmes, 1980.

————, and Catherine Clément. *The Newly Born Woman*, trans. Betsy Wing. Minneapolis: University of Minnesota Press, 1986.

Davis, Cynthia A. "Self, Society, and Myth in Toni Morrison's Fiction." In *Modern Critical Views: Toni Morrison*, ed. Bloom, 7–26. New York: Chelsea House, 1990.

de Lauretis, Teresa, ed. *Feminist Studies/Critical Studies*. Bloomington: Indiana University Press, 1986.

Denard, Carolyn. "The Convergence of Feminism and Ethnicity in the Fiction of Toni Morrison." In *Critical Essays on Toni Morrison*, ed. McKay, 171–78. Boston: G. K. Hall, 1988.

de Weever, Jacqueline. "Toni Morrison's Use of Fairy Tale, Folk Tale, and Myth in *Song of Solomon*." *Southern Folklore Quarterly* 44 (1980): 131–44.

Dixon, Melvin. "Like an Eagle in the Air: Toni Morrison." In *Modern Critical Views: Toni Morrison*, ed. Bloom, 115–42. New York: Chelsea House, 1990.

Donovan, Josephine. *Feminist Literary Criticism: Explorations in Theory*. Louisville: University of Kentucky Press, 1989.

Epstein, Grace. "An Interview with Toni Morrison." *Ohio Journal* 9, no. 3 (Spring 1986): 3–8.

————. "Fluid Bodies: Female Narrative Desire and Layering in the Novels of Morrison, Lessing, and Atwood." PhD. diss., The Ohio State University, 1991.

Evans, Mari, ed. *Black Women Writers: 1950–1980, A Critical Evaluation*. New York: Doubleday, 1984.

Fabre, Genevieve. "Genealogical Archaeology or the Quest for Legacy in Toni Morrison's *Song of Solomon*." In *Critical Essays on Toni Morrison*, ed. McKay, 105–13. Boston: G .K. Hall, 1988.

Fisher, Dexter, ed. *The Third Woman: Minority Women Writers of the United States*. Boston: Houghton Mifflin, 1980.

Gallop, Jane. *The Daughter's Seduction*. Ithaca, N.Y.: Cornell University Press, 1982.

Gates, Henry Louis, Jr., ed. *Black Literature and Literary Theory*. New York: Metheun, 1984.

————. *Figures in Black: Words, Signs, and the "Racial" Self.* New York: Oxford University Press, 1987.

————, ed. *"Race," Writing, and Difference.* Chicago: University of Chicago Press, 1986.

————. *The Signifying Monkey: A Theory of Afro-American Literary Criticism.* New York: Oxford University Press, 1988.

Gelfand, Elissa D., and Virginia Thorndike Hulls. *French Feminist Criticism: Women, Language and Literature.* New York: Garland, 1984.

Giddings, Paula. *When and Where I Enter: The Impact of Black Women on Race and Sex in America.* New York: Bantam, 1984.

Grant, Robert. "Absence into Presence: The Semantics of Memory and 'Missing' Subjects in Toni Morrison's *Sula*." In *Critical Essays on Toni Morrison*, ed. McKay, 90–104. Boston: G. K. Hall, 1988.

Grosz, Elisabeth. *Sexual Subversions: Three French Feminists.* Sydney: Allen and Unwin, 1989.

Gubar, Susan. "The Blank Page." In *The New Feminist Criticism*, ed. Elaine Showalter, 243–70. New York: Pantheon, 1985.

Harris, Trudier. *Exorcising Blackness: Historical and Literary Lynching and Burning Rituals.* Bloomington: Indiana University Press, 1984.

————. "Reconnecting Fragments: Afro-American Folk Tradition in *The Bluest Eye*." In *Critical Essays on Toni Morrison*, ed. McKay, 68–76. Boston: G. K. Hall, 1988.

Henderson, Mae Gwendolyn. "Speaking in Tongues: Dialogics, Dialectics, and the Black Woman Writer's Literary Tradition." In *Changing Our Own Words: Essays on Criticism, Theory, and Writing by Black Women*, ed. Wall, 16–37. New Brunswick: Rutgers University Press, 1989.

Hernton, Calvin C. *The Sexual Mountain and Black Women Writers.* New York: Doubleday, 1987.

Hirsch, Marianne. *The Mother/Daughter Plot: Narrative, Psychoanalysis, Feminism.* Bloomington: Indiana University Press, 1989.

Holloway, Karla F. C., and Stephane Demetrakopoulos. *New Dimensions of Spirituality: A Biracial and Bicultural Reading of the Novels of Toni Morrison.* New York: Greenwood Press, 1987.

House, Elizabeth B. "Artists and the Art of Living: Order and Disorder in Toni Morrison's Fiction." *Modern Fiction Studies* 34 (1988): 27–44.

Hull, Gloria T., Patricia Bell Scott, and Barbara Smith, eds. *All the Women Are White, All the Blacks Are Men, But Some of Us Are Brave: Black Women's Studies.* Old Westbury, N.Y.: Feminist Press, 1982.

Irigaray, Luce. *This Sex Which Is Not One*, trans. Catherine Porter. Ithaca, N.Y.: Cornell University Press, 1985.

————. *The Speculum of the Other Woman*, trans. Gillian C. Gill. Ithaca, N.Y.: Cornell University Press, 1985.

Jardine, Alice, and Hester Eisenstein, eds. *The Future of Difference: The Scholar and the Feminist*. Boston: G. K. Hall, 1980.

———. "Gynesis." In *Critical Theory since 1965*, ed. Adams and Searle, 559–70. Tallahassee: Florida State University Press, 1986.

———. *Gynesis*. Ithaca, N.Y.: Cornell University Press, 1985.

Jones, Ann Rosalind. "Writing the Body: Toward an Understanding of *l'Ecriture feminine*." In *The New Feminist Criticism*, ed. Showalter, 361–78. New York: Pantheon, 1985.

Jones, Bessie W., and Audrey L. Vinson. *The World of Toni Morrison*. Dubuque: Kendall/Hunt, 1985.

Joseph, Gloria I., and Jill Lewis. *Common Differences: Conflicts in Black and White Feminist Perspectives*. New York: Doubleday, 1981.

Joyce, Joyce A. "The Black Canon: Reconstructing Black American Literary Criticism." *New Literary History* 18, no. 2 (1987): 335–44.

Kauffman, Linda, ed. *Gender and Theory: Dialogues on Feminist Criticism*. New York: Basil Blackwell, 1989.

Keohane, Nannerl O., Michelle Z. Rosaldo, and Barbara C. Gelpi, eds. *Feminist Theory: A Critique of Ideology*. Chicago: University of Chicago Press, 1982.

Kessler-Harris, Alice, and William McBrien. *Faith of a (Woman) Writer*. Westport, Conn.: Greenwood Press, 1988.

Kristeva, Julia. *About Chinese Women*, trans. Anita Barrows. London: M. Eoyers, 1977.

———. *Desire in Language: A Semiotic Approach to Literature and Art*, ed. Leon S. Roudiez, trans. Thomas Goza, Alice Jardine, and Leon Roudiez. New York: Columbia University Press, 1980.

———. *Polylogue*. Paris: Editions du Seuil, 1977.

———. "Women's Time," trans. Alice Jardine. *Signs* 7, no. 1 (Autumn 1981): 13–35.

Le Clair, Thomas. "'The Language Must Not Sweat': A Conversation with Toni Morrison." *New Republic* (March 1981): 21–29.

Lester, Rosemarie K. "An Interview with Toni Morrison: Hessian Radio Network, Frankfurt, W. Germany." In *Critical Essays on Toni Morrison*, ed. McKay, 47–54. Boston: G. K. Hall, 1988.

Lifton, Robert Jay. *The Life of the Self: Toward a New Psychology*. New York: Simon and Schuster, 1976.

Marks, Elaine, and Isabelle de Courtivron, eds. *New French Feminisms: An Anthology*. Amherst: University of Massachusetts Press, 1980.

Mason, Theodore O., Jr. "The Novelist as Conservator: Stories and Comprehension in Toni Morrison's *Song of Solomon*." In *Modern Critical Views: Toni Morrison*, ed. Bloom, 171–88. New York: Chelsea House, 1990.

McConnell-Ginet, Sally, Ruth Borker, and Nelly Furman, eds. *Women and Language in Literature and Society*. New York: Praeger, 1980.

McDowell, Deborah E. "New Directions for Black Feminist Criticism." In *The New Feminist Criticism*, ed. Showalter, 186–99. New York: Pantheon, 1985.

———. "Reading Family Matters." In *Changing Our Own Words: Essays on Critical Theory and Writing by Black Women*, ed. Wall, 75–97. New Brunswick, N.J.: Rutgers University Press, 1989.

———. "'The Self and the Other': Reading Toni Morrison's *Sula* and the Black Female Text." In *Critical Essays on Toni Morrison*, ed. McKay, 77–89. Boston: G. K. Hall, 1988.

McKay, Nellie Y., ed. *Critical Essays on Toni Morrison*. Boston: G. K. Hall, 1988.

Meese, Elizabeth, and Alice Parker, eds. *The Difference Within: Feminism and Critical Theory*. Philadelphia: John Benjamin's Publishing Company, 1989.

Middleton, David L. *Toni Morrison: An Annotated Bibliography*. New York: Garland, 1987.

Miner, Madonne M. "Lady No Longer Sings the Blues: Rape, Madness, and Silence in *The Bluest Eye*." In *Modern Critical Views: Toni Morrison*, ed. Bloom, 85–100. New York: Chelsea House, 1990.

Mobley, Marilyn Sanders. "A Different Remembering: Memory, History and Meaning in Toni Morrison's *Beloved*." In *Modern Critical Views: Toni Morrison*, ed. Bloom, 85–100. New York: Chelsea House, 1990.

Moi, Toril, ed. *The Kristeva Reader*. New York: Columbia University Press, 1986.

———. *Sexual/Textual Politics: Feminist Literary Theory*. New York: Methuen, 1985.

Newton, Judith, and Deborah Rosenfelt, eds. *Feminist Criticism and Social Change: Sex, Class and Race in Literature and Culture*. New York: Methuen, 1985.

Nicholson, Linda J., ed. *Feminism/Postmodernism*. New York: Routledge, 1990.

O'Shaughnessy, Kathleen. "'Life life life life': The Community as Chorus in *Song of Solomon*." In *Critical Essays on Toni Morrison*, ed. McKay, 125–34. Boston: G. K. Hall, 1988.

Otten, Terry. *The Crime of Innocence in the Fiction of Toni Morrison*. Columbia: University of Missouri Press, 1989.

———. "The Crime of Innocence in Toni Morrison's *Tar Baby*." In *Modern Critical Views: Toni Morrison*, ed. Bloom, 101–14. New York: Chelsea House, 1990.

Pateman, Carol, and Elizabeth Gross. *Feminist Challenges: Social and Political Theory*. Boston: Northeastern University Press, 1986.

Pryse, Marjorie, and Hortense J. Spillers, eds. *Conjuring: Black Women,*

Fiction, and Literary Tradition. Bloomington: Indiana University Press, 1985.

Rainwater, Catherine, and William J. Scheick, eds. *Contemporary American Women Writers: Narrative Strategies.* Lexington: University Press of Kentucky, 1985.

Reddy, Maurine T. "The Tripled Plot and Center of Sula." *Black American Literature Forum* 22, no. 1 (Spring 1988): 29–45.

Rich, Adrienne. *On Lies, Secrets, and Silence: Selected Prose 1966–1978.* New York: Norton, 1979.

———. "Compulsory Heterosexuality and Lesbian Existence." *Signs* 5, no. 4 (1980): 212–41.

Rigney, Barbara Hill. *Lilith's Daughters: Women and Religion in Contemporary Fiction.* Madison: University of Wisconsin Press, 1982.

Rubenstein, Roberta. *Boundaries of the Self: Gender, Culture, Fiction.* Urbana: University of Illinois Press, 1987.

Russel, Sandi. "Conversation from Abroad." In *Critical Essays on Toni Morrison,* ed. McKay, 45–47. Boston: G. K. Hall, 1988.

Samuels, Wilfred D., and Clenora Hudson-Weems. *Toni Morrison.* Boston: Twayne Publishers, 1990.

Sargent, Robert. "A Way of Ordering Experience: A Study of Toni Morrison's *The Bluest Eye* and *Sula.*" In *Faith of a (Woman) Writer,* ed. Alice Kessler-Harris and William McBrien. Westport, Conn.: Greenwood Press, 1988.

Scruggs, Charles. "The Nature of Desire in Toni Morrison's *Song of Solomon.*" *Arizona Quarterly* 38 (1982): 311–35.

Shannon, Anna. "'We Was Girls Together': A Study of Toni Morrison's *Sula.*" *Midwestern Miscellany* 10 (1982): 9–22.

Showalter, Elaine. "Feminist Criticism in the Wilderness." In *The New Feminist Criticism,* ed. Showalter, 243–70. New York: Pantheon, 1985.

———, ed. *The New Feminist Criticism: Essays on Women, Literature, and Society.* New York: Pantheon, 1985.

Smith, Barbara, ed. *Home Girls: A Black Feminist Anthology.* Watertown, Mass.: Persephone Press, 1983.

———. "Toward a Black Feminist Criticism." In *The New Feminist Criticism,* ed. Showalter, 168–85. New York: Pantheon, 1985.

Smith, Valerie. "Black Feminist Theory and the Representation of the 'Other.'" In *Changing Our Own Words: Essays on Criticism, Theory, and Writing by Black Women,* ed. Wall, 38–57. New Brunswick, N.J.: Rutgers University Press, 1989.

Spiller, Hortense J. "A Hateful Passion, A Lost Love." In *Modern Critical Views: Toni Morrison,* ed. Bloom, 27–54. New York: Chelsea House, 1990.

Spivak, Gayatri Chakravorty. "A Response to *The Difference Within*." In *The Difference Within: Feminism and Critical Theory*, ed. Meese and Parker, 207–18. Philadelphia: John Benjamin's Publishing Company, 1989.

Stein, Karen F. "Toni Morrison's *Sula*: A Black Woman's Epic." *Black American Literature Forum* 18, no. 4 (Winter 1984): 146–50.

Stepto, Robert B., and Michael S. Harper, eds. *Chant of Saints: A Gathering of Afro-American Literature, Art, and Scholarship*. Urbana: University of Illinois Press, 1979.

————. *From Behind the Veil: A Study of Afro-American Narrative*. Urbana: University of Illinois Press, 1979.

————. "'Intimate Things in Place': A Conversation with Toni Morrison." In *Chant of Saints*, ed. Stepto and Harper, 213–29. Urbana: University of Illinois Press, 1979.

Tate, Claudia. "On Black Literary Women and the Evolution of Critical Discourse." *Tulsa Studies in Women's Literature* 5 (1986): 111–23.

————. *Black Women Writers at Work*. New York: Continuum, 1989.

Todd, Janet, ed. *Gender and Literary Voice*. New York: Holmes and Meier, 1988.

Traylor, Eleanor W. "The Fabulous World of Toni Morrison: *Tar Baby*." In *Critical Essays on Toni Morrison*, ed. McKay, 135–49. Boston: G. K. Hall, 1988.

Wagner, Linda J. "Toni Morrison: Mastery of Narrative." In *Contemporary American Women Writers: Narrative Strategies*, ed. Rainwater and Scheick, 191–205. Lexington: University of Kentucky Press, 1985.

Wall, Cheryl A., ed. *Changing Our Own Words: Essays on Criticism, Theory, and Writing by Black Women*. New Brunswick, N.J.: Rutgers University Press, 1989.

Washington, Mary Helen. *Invented Lives: Narratives of Black Women, 1860–1960*. New York: Doubleday, 1987.

Waugh, Patricia. *Feminine Fictions: Revising the Postmodern*. New York: Routledge, 1989.

Weixlmann, Joe, and Houston A. Baker, Jr., eds. *Black Feminist Criticism and Critical Theory*. Greenwood, Fla.: Fenkevill, 1988.

Werner, Craig H. "The Briar Patch as Modernist Myth: Morrison, Barthes, and Tar Baby As-Is." In *Critical Essays on Toni Morrison*, ed. McKay, 150–70. Boston: G. K. Hall, 1988.

Willis, Susan. "Eruptions of Funk: Historicizing Toni Morrison." *Black American Literature Forum* 16 (1982): 34–42.

————. "I Shop Therefore I Am: Is There a Place for Afro-American Culture in Commodity Culture?" In *Changing Our Own Words*, ed. Wall, 173–95. New Brunswick, N.J.: Rutgers University Press, 1989.

————. *Specifying: Black Women Writing the American Experience*. Madison: University of Wisconsin Press, 1987.

Wittig, Monique. *Les Guérillères*, trans. Peter Owen. New York: Avon, 1971.

Winnett, Susan. "Coming Unstrung: Women, Men, Narrative, and Principles of Pleasure." *PMLA* 105, no. 3 (May 1990): 505–18.

Yaeger, Patricia. *Honey-Mad Women: Emancipatory Strategies in Women's Fiction*. New York: Columbia University Press, 1988.

————. "Toward a Female Sublime." In *Gender and Theory: Dialogues on Feminist Criticism*, ed. Kaufman. New York: Basil Blackwell, 1989.

Index

Baker, Houston A., Jr., 24, 28, 85,
  90, 91–92
Bakerman, Jane, 114
Bambara, Toni Cade, 2
Barksdale, Richard K., 88
Barthe, Roland, 79
Beloved, 5, 8–10, 15, 16–18, 21, 25–
  26, 33, 39–41, 46, 48–49,
  52, 57, 59–60, 63, 66, 67–75,
  80, 85–86, 87, 98–99, 112
Berg, Temma, 12, 16
The Black Book, 71
Black Orpheus, 112, 113
"The Blank Page," 111
The Bluest Eye, 5, 8, 11, 13, 21–23,
  27–28, 32, 39, 44, 51, 53–54,
  56, 59, 62, 63–64, 66, 72,
  75–76, 77–78, 83–84, 86,
  88–89, 99–100, 102, 110,
  112
*Boundaries of the Self: Gender, Culture,
  Fiction*, 93, 112
Brenner, Gerry, 30
"The Briar Patch as Modernist Myth:
  Morrison, Barthes, and Tar
  Baby As-Is," 79
Buber, Martin, 77
Byerman, Keith E., 52, 110

Cartey, Wilfred, 70
"Castration or Decapitation?," 20–21
Chodorow, Nancy J., 17, 46–47
Christian, Barbara, 4
Cixous, Hélène, 1, 3, 4, 9, 11, 12, 18,
  20–21, 27, 31–32, 35–36,
  37, 46, 61, 69, 80, 93, 102–3,
  104, 105, 114

Clément, Catherine, 1, 3, 4, 18, 35–
  36, 61, 69, 93, 103, 105
*Conjuring: Black Women, Fiction, and
  Literary Tradition*, 110

Davis, Cynthia A., 30, 47, 53, 88
Demetrokopoulos, Stephanie, 10, 68,
  70
Desire in Language, 12, 76, 83, 94,
  103
"A Different Remembering: Memory,
  History, and Meaning in Toni
  Morrison's *Beloved*," 71
Duras, Marguerite, 3

*Engendering the Word: Feminist Essays
  in Psychosexual Politics*, 12
Epstein, Grace, 27
Evans, Mari, 52, 77

Fabre, Genevieve, 65–66
"Failures of Love: Female Initiation in
  the Novels of Toni Morrison,"
  114
"Female Sexuality," 17
*Feminine Fictions: Revisiting the Post-
  modern*, 36
Feminism and Psychoanalytic Theory, 17
"Feminist Criticism in the Wilder-
  ness," 111
Freud, Sigmund, 17, 62, 99, 110

Garner, Margaret, 71
Gates, Henry Louis, Jr., 22, 37–38

Gubar, Susan, 111
Gynesis, 61

Harris, Trudier, 112
Henderson, Mae Gwendolyn, 19–20, 111
Hirsch, Marianne, 24, 111, 112–13
Holloway, Karla, 10, 68, 70
Hudson-Weems, Clenora, 26, 79

Irigaray, Luce, 1, 3, 27, 36–37
"I Shop Therefore I Am," 111

Jardine, Alice, 20, 37, 61–62
Jones, Ann Rosalind, 4
Jung, Karl, 55

Kristeva, Julia, 3, 11, 12, 15, 20, 45, 46, 76, 81, 83, 94, 103, 104
Ku Klux Klan, 73

"The Laugh of the Medusa," 9, 46
Le Clair, Thomas, 40
Les Guérillères, 44, 61
Lester, Rosemarie K., 2
Lifton, Robert Jay, 77

McDowell, Deborah E., 39, 114
McKay, Nellie Y., 7, 30, 45, 112
Magic realism, 27
Marks, Elaine, 4
Marshall, Paule, 4
Mason, Theodore O., Jr., 114
Mobley, Marilyn Sanders, 71
Moi, Toril, 37
The Mother / Daughter Plot, 24

Native Americans, 71–72
Native Son, 28
Naylor, Gloria, 2
New Dimensions of Spirituality, 10, 68
The Newly Born Woman, 1, 4, 36, 61, 105

Otten, Terry, 52, 56

Parker, Bettye J., 45
Polylogue, 11
Pryse, Marjorie, 110

"The Race for Theory," 4
"Reconnecting Fragments: Afro-American Folk Tradition in *The Bluest Eye*," 112
Reddy, Maureen T., 64, 113
The Reproduction of Mothering, 17, 46–47
"Rootedness: The Ancestor as Foundation," 52
The Rose Tattoo, 55
Rubenstein, Roberta, 56, 93, 112
Russell, Sandi, 112

Samuels, Wilfred D., 26, 79
Scruggs, Charles, 13
"Self, Society, and Myth in Toni Morrison's Fiction," 88
Semiotic, 7, 11, 12, 15, 19
Showalter, Elaine, 3, 110, 111
Smith, Barbara, 5, 92, 114
Smith, Valerie, 114
Song of Solomon, 8, 9, 10, 13–14, 15, 17, 20, 24–25, 28–31, 33–34, 35–36, 39, 41–42, 47–48, 50–51, 59, 63, 65–66, 67, 69, 70, 72–73, 76, 79, 84, 86–87, 94–95, 97, 101–2, 103, 111, 114
Spiller, Hortense, 76, 110
Sula, 4, 14, 15, 16, 17, 19–20, 23–24, 25–26, 27, 28, 32, 38–39, 43–44, 45, 47, 50, 51–52, 54–56, 58, 59, 64–65, 69, 70, 76, 78–79, 84–85, 89–94, 95, 97, 100–101, 103, 104, 111

Tar Baby, 14, 17, 18–19, 32–33, 39, 42–43, 52, 56–57, 58–59, 63, 66–67, 72, 79–80, 86, 95–96
Tate, Claudia, 2, 25, 32, 51, 54, 63, 78–79, 80, 83, 99, 112, 114
"'The Self and Other': Reading Toni Morrison's *Sula* and the Black Female Text," 39, 114

This Sex Which Is Not One, 1
"Toward a Black Feminist Criticism,"
    5, 92
"The Tripled Plot and Center of *Sula*,"
    113

"Unspeakable Things Unspoken: The
    Afro-American Presence in
    American Literature," 7, 24,
    55, 110, 113

Walker, Alice, 2, 88

Washington, Mary Helen, 11–12
Waugh, Patricia, 36
Werner, Craig H., 79
"When Lindbergh Sleeps with Bessie
    Smith," 28
Williams, Tennessee, 55
Willis, Susan, 111
Wittig, Monique, 3, 44, 61
"Women's Time," 46
Wright, Richard, 28

Yaeger, Patricia, 92